"Should Obama Be Impeached?"

—— "TAKING BACK AMERICA - II" ——

Thomas R. Meinders

iUniverse, Inc.
Bloomington

iUniverse books may be ordered through booksellers or by contacting:

iUniverse
1663 Liberty Drive
Bloomington, IN 47403
www.iuniverse.com
1-800-Authors (1-800-288-4677)

ISBN: 978-1-4620-1436-1 (pbk)
ISBN: 978-1-4620-1437-8 (cloth)
ISBN: 978-1-4620-1438-5 (ebk)

Printed in the United States of America

iUniverse rev. date: 5/3/2011

Introduction

"Should Obama Be Impeached" will attempt to point out some of the problems that are currently happening with the President of the United States and our government.

I was going to title the book "Taking Back America -II" but realized that America needed to consider impeaching Obama. The information that I am going to present and the comments from the American citizens indicate that in reality the President should be impeached for more than one action that he has taken.

I am going to get a little off the Obama programs and look at the situation in Wisconsin that the unions are fighting so hard to stop. They even have a local judge in their pockets.

Americans are frustrated with the direction our country is taking. The sad fact is we are all tired of working harder and not being able to improve our standard of living. Politicians tell you that you are all going to have to sacrifice more for the state. You will either pay higher taxes, or many services will be cut in order to balance the budget. Like it is somehow the average Americans fault that the economy is in trouble. It was the will of the people! The truth is the politicians not the average American got us in this mess. As Americans we can no longer remain complacent, we must hold our leaders accountable for their decisions. Participate in the political process, attend town hall meetings, write letters make calls to your representatives and if necessary exercise your right to peaceful protest. That is what democracy is all about.

This is all a result of the financial crisis, which was caused by decades of irresponsible policies and lax financial regulation in Washington. It is going to get worse as the magnitude of the nation's losses becomes clear;

current monetary and fiscal attempts to paper over the losses will fail. Madison is just the tip of the iceberg. It is understandable that people get upset over givebacks, but it won't change anything - massive amounts of money were simply lost, gone. National and state governments have been setting people up for this for years, and it is a shame. We are all in this together, except for the majority in Washington, because they just don't get it, or don't care.

What I do not understand with the Wisconsin passing legislation that the voters desired. How can one old lady that is a local judge in Madison say that the law can not be implemented? How does this judge Maryann Sumi believe that her one opinion is more important that what the voters wanted? It would seem that the legislative process is more important that one persons union biased opinion. If anyone needs to be impeached it is Maryann Sumi. "That is what I now want to make crystal clear." Looks like Obama's speech writers wrote her comments.

The United States of America is currently in three wars. What the American people would like to know is why we engaged in any of them since the President of the United States doesn't make a commitment to winning any of them. The President has stated that we would start withdrawing troops from Afghanistan within a few months. If we are going to withdraw the troops in a few months without any hope of winning the war it makes more sense to withdraw the troops immediately. The Taliban is just waiting for the troops to withdraw. The Taliban already knows that they have won the war. The President needs to make the commitment to win the war or get out now. This is a huge waste of the resources of the United States with no hope for a positive outcome. If the President is going to have a plan to win the war then he needs to discuss it with the Generals in charge. The President does not know who we are fighting or why. When Obama was asked who the rebels are in Libya there was complete silence. Why are we there when no one knows who we are supporting? Then the President has made comments that Gadhafi must go. Then in the next sentence Obama states that we will not target Gadhafi with the air strikes. The President can not have it both ways. Either eliminate Gadhafi and his leaders or forget about winning this war. When you cut off the head of the dog, the rest of the dog is going to stop functioning. This does not seem like a very hard decision to make. Get serious about winning or get out of the game. Another thing that is disturbing is that instead of being the leading military power in the world we have been reduced to following orders from another organization. Then the decision to attack the Libyan's was made by an appointed Secretary of State instead of the President. America did not elect a President to sit on the sidelines until someone has made decisions for him. Stop the rhetoric and make the decisions. Bring the troops back from Iraq, Libya and Afghanistan since they do not have a leader that is committed to winning any of these wars. Save the billions of taxpayer's money and use these troops to secure the borders of the United States. America needs to wake up and realize that Obama has zero military experience or foreign policy experience and it is showing. It is past time to start "Taking Back America".

"PRIDE IN AMERICA"

I'm proud to be an American
I'm proud of the "Pledge of Allegiance"
I'm proud of the "National Anthem"
I'm proud to display the "American Flag"
I'm proud to defend the "American Freedoms"
I'm proud to communicate in "English"
I'm proud of freedom of "Religion"
I'm proud to be an American
God Bless the United States of America

Thomas R. Meinders

Contents

CHAPTER ONE:

TRYING TO GAIN RESPECT FOR OBAMA

The American Citizens Political Action Committee would like to know if anyone else has noticed that when Obama ends his speeches he usually says thank you very much. What ever happened to the President saying **"God Bless America"?** It is disgusting that the President has to have Teleprompters and speech writers prepare his comments on everything that should be coming from the heart of the President of the United States. It is becoming apparent that the President does not have any opinions of his own and is afraid to make any decisions on his own. All he can do is deliver speeches that are prepared by his lemmings. Just once it would be nice to see the President speak with a true conviction about what the policy of the United States is going to be. The President never takes a stand until after the rest of the world has decided which direction the world is going to take on sticky situations. America is supposed to be the leader of the free world and not a follower. When the world opinion shifts Obama will flip flop on his direction. That is a sign of a very weak president and not the leader of the free world. It is past time for the citizens of this great country to start "Taking Back America".

DES MOINES, Iowa – Former United Nations Ambassador John Bolton says President Barack Obama isn't qualified to lead the country. Bolton was among the featured speakers at a conference of conservative Republicans in Iowa. Bolton was nominated for the ambassadorship in 2005 by President George W. Bush.

Bolton told the crowd that Obama doesn't care enough about national security issues and doesn't view the world as a threatening place. Bolton

1

also says the U.S. could have made a big difference in Libya, but Obama couldn't make up his mind on which steps to take.

I watched the entire speech that President Obama made to the United States people on March 18, 2011. Not once during that speech did Obama look straight ahead like he was actually talking to the people. It was always looking to the left and then to the right. Will there ever be a time when Obama speaks from his own heart? The American people are tired of Obama reading from Teleprompters on both sides of the room. Then to insult the American people even more, Obama closes with thank you very much. Any real president closes with "God Bless America". It was very difficult to sense any feeling of sincerity in what the President said to the American people.

Then where was the leadership from President Obama? He did not make any comments regarding Libya until the United Nations made it impossible for him to duck the situation any longer. I would have hoped that the United States of America would have taken a leadership role instead of taking a follower role. America has always been the leader of the free world. What has happened to the respect that America used to demand and receive? I am going to watch and see how the main stream media spins these actions by President Obama.

Back in 2007, as the race for the White House intensified, the AP asked federal agencies for copies of correspondence between officials there and 16 prospective presidential candidates. On Tuesday, the Homeland Security Department notified the AP to say it was still searching for the records — two years after Barack Obama defeated John McCain.

In its request, AP sought copies of any letters sent to the department by then-prospective candidates Obama, McCain, Joe Biden, Mitt Romney, Mike Huckabee and 11 others. Such correspondence can reveal circumstances when candidates asked the government for help on behalf of a constituent or campaign donor, and provide insights into connections between candidates and government officials.

The AP asked federal agencies to search for any letters quickly because information about the election was newsworthy. The department said AP's request didn't merit special consideration. Now, nearly four years later, it says it is reconsidering.

Now that is real transparency in the operation of the federal government.

World events test 'No Drama Obama'

Glenn Thrush, Josh Gerstein – Wednesday March 16, 2011
A dizzying succession of major world events is bombarding a president who insists on controlling his own time, emotions and political message.

The manner in which this President acts has been evident since his campaign. While running for President he started taking hits politically because of his association with Rev Wright. So Obama calls a prime time news conference and gives a speech on race. Later, McCain started gaining traction by criticizing Obama for not once going to Iraq. So, Obama makes quick trip there. After the BP Gulf Oil Spill Obama took a hit in the polls because he had not visited the Gulf Coast once since the spill. So Obama makes a quick one day trip before his week long vacation. All this President knows how to do is react to polls. These activities are not leadership.

With Japan's nuclear crisis teetering on the verge of catastrophe, with <u>Libya and Bahrain in violent turmoil</u>, and with financial markets crashing in response, President Barack Obama has been adamantly sticking to his own political and policy playbook.

The authors state that Obama is stubbornly sticking to his playbook. With the exception of the obvious fact that his highness is turning our country into his private little socialist fiefdom, I cannot see any playbook at all. He has done nothing since gaining this country's highest office except to take control of our nation's banks, financial institutions, auto makers, etc., and cram the most expensive national healthcare program down our throats in our nation's history. Then he claims he is not a socialist. But he is afraid to actually be a leader. Instead he runs around the planet apologizing to the world and acting subservient to a host of evil little third world nations. He had a chance to be a leader regarding the incident in Libya. He had a chance to be

a leader regarding the hostages held by the Somali pirates. Instead he does nothing while the carnage in Libya continues and the hostages are executed by the pirates. If Bush had been in office acting like Obama, the liberals and Democrats would be asking for his head. They are nothing more than a bunch of two faced hypocrites. The main stream media is so biased that they can not see the forest for the trees. There needs to be objective reporting by the main stream media but that is probably not going to happen. The media has been supporting Obama exclusively and the blacks and Hispanics are buying the biased news hook line and sinker. How else can anyone explain how 95% of the blacks and 67% of the Hispanics voted Democratic? Where is the reporting on the issued instead of the personal lives of the Republicans while the news hides the personal life of Obama and buries all his records?

That has meant muscling past the red-siren headlines to hammer away at the jobs-and-education message that will be the centerpiece of his 2012 campaign, the kind of discipline that is a hallmark of his new senior adviser, David Plouffe.

President Obama's play book doesn't include how to protect our borders either. Let the citizens help themselves then when a state like Arizona finally passes a law to do what the so called federal government is responsible for, they sue the state and take sides with illegals and Mexico. Some President he is. This is a sad day for America.

And it also meant refusing to scrap a five-day trip to Latin America on Friday that will take him to sun-dappled Rio de Janeiro, among other places, rather than staying home to focus on the increasingly disastrous international news confronting his crisis-weary White House.

How does a 5 day trip to Latin America help the economy? It seems like every time there's a crisis, he takes a trip! Wouldn't it be nice to have a President who actually spends time in the Oval Office dealing with United States issues? Filling out his brackets for the March Madness of basketball does not count. I know what I'm doing in 2012 and it's not voting for this worthless wonder.

"The president is taking this trip because he is committed to growing the economy [and] rebalancing our national security posture," White House press secretary Jay Carney shot back on Tuesday when an incredulous reporter asked if he would consider delaying the five-day swing through Brazil, Chile and El Salvador.

Obama is off to Rio, another vacation at our expense, is the old lady going along with the kids? How many planes are we paying for this time with our taxes? I wish I had a job where I could go on vacation all the time! Hell, I'm retired and I can't afford that. I need tax payer money so I can go places too, maybe bring a few friends, my family, I can invite Oprah! What a life! Lets dump this looser who acts like a welfare recipient who's been given the keys to the kingdom so he and his wife can play till the bottom drops out on all of us!

We are wondering if the President is going to spend millions of the tax payer's money to go on this 5 day trip like he did when he went to London on a 3 day trip.

The following information was reported by the Press in England. You may have already read about this in your local newspaper. Oh no, you didn't? OK then, you saw in on CNN or the main stream media. No? I didn't think so. Those outlets are too lame to publish or broadcast real stories about their fair haired leader Obama. You and I may never see health care again the way it used to be, but "Emperor Obama" took six (6) doctors with him on a three (3) day visit to London. Not to mention the other 494 member essential staff.

You have to love this spread the wealth vote for change operation. This is while he says he is going to freeze government employee's salaries for two years. The money Obama wasted on this trip could have paid the majority of these salaries for about a year. Obama just keeps on wasting the taxpayers money like it is his personal bank with no limits on the spending he does for personal reasons.

President Barack Obama proposed a two-year freeze of the salaries of some 2 million federal workers, trying to seize the deficit-cutting initiative from Republicans with a sudden, dramatic stroke. Though signaling White House concern over record deficits, the freeze would

make only a tiny dent in annual deficits or the nation's $14 trillion debt.

Would you like to see what "Big Government" implies? Take a look at the following information that was published by Dale McFeatters, a writer for Scripps Howard News Service concerning Obama's trip to the G-20 summit in London, England.

President Obama arrived at the G-20 summit in London with everything but the kitchen sink. He did however bring the White House chef and the entire kitchen staff.

The heads of government are in London to discuss serious and weighty issues. The news is not focused upon the Obama entourage that landed in London for the summit.

Obama arrived with a staff of 500 including 200 secret service agents and a staff of 6 doctors. Obama had to bring his own water and food. No wonder the rest of the heads of government were laughing. Obama also shipped 35 vehicles to London and brought along a staff of 4 Speech writers and 12 Teleprompters. It appears that Obama is going to have plenty to say at the summit. To bad it will not be what he really believes but what his lackey speech writers prepare.

Then since Obama could not use his Beast, which is Obama's eight ton armored car that just returned from Asia, to get from the Stansted Airport to Central London the government had to ship his private helicopter the Marine One and a fleet of duplicate decoy helicopters to take him from the airport to downtown. You talk about gall. Obama and his ego are the biggest laughing stock of the entire world.

"He remains confident he can fully execute his job when he is on the road."

"He remains confident he can fully execute his job when he is on the Road." I don't know what to do after he said that? Should the American people start to laugh or cry?

But Obama's critics have a different take. They say he's exhibiting a failure of leadership on a whole range of matters, symbolic and substantive, ranging from his lukewarm support for a Libyan no-fly zone to his willingness to let others, especially Republicans, take the lead on entitlement reform.

A compendium of clips sent to reporters by the Republican National Committee on Tuesday was headlined: "Hiding from Reality: Obama's noticeable lack of leadership illustrates a president looking out for himself above all others."

And Obama may have given opponents another talking point by <u>following through</u>, despite the alarming news from overseas, on a promise to appear in a nine-minute ESPN segment to share his NCAA basketball tournament picks.

"Most people when it comes to Obama, you know what they're anticipating? His NCAA brackets," Rush Limbaugh fumed on his syndicated radio show Tuesday. "Every year at this time people wonder what the president's brackets are going to be, who he's gonna pick?

"We got the world on fire. We got Libya and the Middle East on fire and the guy's out playing golf," he added, referring to the round Obama played on Sunday.

Republicans say one compelling reason for Obama to stay home, is to work on an elusive long-term budget deal – with a confrontation looming on April 8 when the just-completed three-week stopgap funding measure expires.

"How can Barack Obama say he is leading when puts his NCAA bracket over the budget & other pressing issues?" new Republican National Committee chairman Reince Priebus tweeted Tuesday

All of this dovetails with a larger GOP argument against Obama that was underscored by a Washington Post/NBC poll released Tuesday that showed Americans giving Republicans higher scores on leadership than him by a margin of 46 to 39 percent.

Some questions about Obama's leadership are the results of his somewhat detached style.

"Some questions about Obama's leadership are the results of his somewhat detached style". What leadership? What detached style? To me, he's demonstrated no leadership and isn't somewhat detached, he is completely detached from the struggles in the United States and worldwide issues. This is painfully evident every time he plans yet another vacation. Really, what has this man done? We're still just as deeply ingrained in the war as when Bush was in...We're just as deeply dependant on foreign oil... foreclosures and jobless rates still unacceptably high...still too many people don't have or can't afford health insurance...and his answer is another trip. He needs to take a permanent trip out of the Oval Office.

On Friday Obama made Japan a centerpiece of his news conference, and he has dispatched a massive deployment of U.S. military and nuclear safety personnel to the region. "I believe I heard him use the phrase today — heartbroken by what he sees unfolding in Japan and the effect on the Japanese people," Carney said at his briefing Tuesday.

But to some, the response has seemed muted.

"It's a gap between the kind of personal reaction that I myself received from my American friends and the somewhat ceremonial, rhetorical statements that Mr. Obama makes... I was taken aback. I have yet to feel any personal feeling coming from Mr. Obama himself," said Yoshi Komuri, editor-at-large of Sankei Shimbun, one of Japan's leading newspapers.

"It seems a bit remote, too official, that's my personal opinion."

Andrew Gordon, director of Harvard's Reischauer Institute of Japanese Studies, said Obama's handling of the Japan crisis so far was appropriate, but it would be wise now for him to make a greater overture to one of his country's most important allies and trading partners.

"Even compared to what people were thinking Friday or Saturday, by Tuesday this is a considerably graver event, so for Obama to do something - in public and visibly - probably wouldn't be a bad idea, whether that's

Obama going to visit the Japanese Embassy or inviting the ambassador to the White House …to sort of lay out some ongoing commitment," he said.

The White House dismisses criticism that the president hasn't been sufficiently engaged, pointing out that Obama has been immersed in back-to-back meetings all week on the emerging crises, culminating with a Tuesday afternoon gathering of his national security team to discuss a dwindling set of options for Libya.

And they argue that the president's take-it-in stride approach reflects his calm temperament, the demands of a modern, multi-tasking presidency and his refusal to lurch from crisis to crisis.

He is headed to Brazil to ensure that their Oil exploration and production are advancing. All the while he has been "keeping his boot on the neck" of the oil companies in our own gulf, all but shutting down offshore drilling. He will go to any extreme to look after his beloved unions or George Soros, but don't EVER expect him to be a leader. He has not so much as managed a lemonade stand on a street corner, much less run the country. I am certain that there is a teleprompter somewhere that will be addressing his shortcomings soon.

They also say that breaking routine could, in itself, constitute a breach in leadership by proving he's too willing to let circumstance derailed from his objectives.

More important than the optics, Obama has also refused to make any major policy shifts in response to events over the last several weeks.

I see people saying Obama is doing the right thing! The President isn't doing anything. That cannot possibly be the right thing. Come on people, take a look at reality. Take off the rose colored glasses and see what the President really stands for. President Obama has a tendency to run from the issues instead of confronting them with positive action that would gain the respect of the world and the citizens of the United States.

Despite criticism from conservatives pressing for aggressive action by the United States, hawks, he's waited for NATO and United Nations to approve a no-fly zone for Libya, a plan that seems less likely than ever given the rout of pro-democracy rebels this week.

Nor has he heeded demands by some fellow Democrats, including Reps. Henry Waxman (D-Calif.) and Ed Markey (D-Mass.), that he embrace a moratorium on the construction of new domestic nuclear plants as a result of the Japanese disaster.

"I think it's very important to make sure that we are doing everything we can to ensure the safety and effectiveness of the nuclear facilities that we have," Obama said in an interview with a local TV station in Pittsburgh on Tuesday.

But he refused to shelve expansion of the plants, which are a key part of his energy strategy, pledging instead to increase efforts to ensure that nuclear power is safe.

"I've already instructed our nuclear regulatory agency to make sure that we take lessons learned from what has happened in Japan and that we are constantly upgrading how we approach our nuclear safety in our country," he said.

Carney told reporters that Obama essentially views events in Japan as a crisis afflicting a foreign country, passing along the views of Nuclear Regulatory Commission officials that even under a worst-case scenario, the Fukishima nuclear plant poses next to no health risks to U.S. citizens on the mainland or in Hawaii.

Given recent events, it's hard to believe that it was barely two months ago that David Axelrod, Plouffe's predecessor, told POLITICO on his way out of the White House that he finally saw a "clear field" for Obama to focus on the sole issue he believed would decide the 2012 election – jobs.

Since that time, Obama has seen a succession of challenges and cataclysms not seen since the financial meltdown he inherited when taking office in January 2009:

A rolling series of bloodless revolutions and bloody civil wars have spread through Egypt, Yemen, Bahrain and Libya; a rebellion by Tea Party Republicans who threaten to scuttle his plans for a big bipartisan budget deal; and then the earthquake, tsunami and nuclear debacle in Japan, a one-of-a-kind chamber of horrors that melds a humanitarian tragedy with a terrifying atomic threat.

In the days ahead, Carney promised, Obama will monitor "all major issues, all the time" wherever he is.

Here are the comments from average American citizens and what they think about President Obama and his travel plans. In some cases the comments are extreme but for the most part they are right on. They have not been altered in any way except for spelling and grammar. I hope you enjoy the comments and can get a clearer picture of what is happening with the President of the United States of America.

We finally have a president more incompetent than Jimmy Carter and that is saying something. He is voting present as he did in the Illinois state house. He has zero, absolutely zero, leadership abilities and it is showing. Libyan rebels are being overrun and what they needed was a no fly zone two weeks ago. He did talk about Bahrain, but why not support the Libyan rebels with a no fly zone. (No fly zone could have been started with a massive cruise missile strike to crater their runways to prevent their jets form taking off) Crisis in Japan is impacting our markets and we have $100 a barrel oil Last time oil took off ($140 per barrel, in 2008, the press blamed Bush and Cheney. I do not see the press blaming Obama. We admit that no president can control it, but why the double standard on blaming Bush in 2008 and not equally blame Obama? We have no budget and the spenders want to spend more. Obama is showing no leadership in this area. Appointing Biden to head it, he has one meeting and leaves the country that is not leadership. It is dodging the issue. Even the Democrats are asking for his leadership (Senator Manchin for one is very vocal) Again Obama is voting present. It shows a clear pattern of total lack of leadership abilities. Sad but he is what he is. Our country needs a strong leader, especially at this time, but we have one who votes present and lets it ride.

In my lifetime (70 years as an independent voter), this country has never had a president that looked this weak on the world stage. America has always led and not stood around waiting for other countries to make the first move. We have always had medium to great presidential leaders to cope with our own problems and international ones. THE WAIT AND SEE POLICY OF OBAMA IS A POOR SUBSTITUTE FOR LEADING THE UNITED STATES AND OUR ALLIES! I can't believe I voted for a person that is so lacking in leadership skills. I guess I was fooled like everyone in the HOPE & CHANGE speeches. I felt the old ways of doing business (country club membership) would go out the door and a new breath of fresh air had arrived, but things have only gotten worse. Can't wait for November 2012!

First it was Healthcare in the midst of the economic meltdown. Now it's Latin America as Japan smokes, the Middle East burns, and we still have no budget from last year or this year.

Living in California and hearing the Surgeon General tell us that buying potassium iodide is a good precaution against any effects of nuclear fallout, and nothing from the president. Then first thing I read about this morning is that he is going to Rio de Janeiro. REALLY PLEASE AMERICA...no more community organizer in 2012! America has had enough of the lack of leadership by this president.

Obama's check list since he started to run for president:

Tell them what they want to hear to win election. Check
Vacation. Check
After winning fly around world wide
apologizing for America. Check
Vacation. Check
Take over auto makers. Check
Vacation. Check
Take over banks and student loans. Check
Vacation. Check
Nationalize healthcare. Check
Vacation. Check
Take over Wall Street. Check
Vacation. Check

Collapse the housing market. Check
Vacation. Check
Man made disaster great for more regulations and photos. Check
Vacation. Check
Sue a sister state trying to protect its real citizens. Check
Vacation. Check
Amnesty for all illegals = million's of votes. Check
Vacation. Check
Come on everyone give Obama a break!
It's hard work destroying a country!!

Folks, I'm part of that FIVE PERCENT of African-Americans who did not vote for Obama. Understand that there is a growing group of us (particularly those in business) who see this brotha for what he is. It isn't about him loading up the tanks and invading Libya (we SHOULDN'T be involved in all these wars), but it is about leadership and diplomacy. His handling of Iran in the last two years, Egypt, and Libya, and now Japan, from a diplomatic perspective is disgraceful.

This slick brotha involves himself in the local dealings of an arrest of a fellow African-American by a white cop, but yet can't bring him self to support freedom in Iran (but instead the "Islamic Republic of Iran" as his press handler noted at the time).

I am a Christian, and I know what's going on here and more of my community does now too. Obama is no more a Christian than "Rev." Wright, who just happens to be friends with Col. Quadaffi (google it). Obama is a Muslim, and he has done NOTHING for our community or America at large. Black unemployment is nearly 15 percent and even higher with young black men. He should resign today, not tomorrow, or in two years. We simply cannot afford any more of this fool. Go ahead and call me a "Tom", nothing we haven't heard before. Join the Black Republicans.

Kagan was representing Obama in all the petitions to prove his citizenship. Now she may help rule on them.

Folks, this is really ugly Chicago Politics; and the beat goes on and on and on. Once again the United States Senate sold us out!

Well, someone figured out why Obama nominated Elena Kagan for the Supreme Court. Pull up the Supreme Courts website and go to the docket and search for Obama.

Kagan was the Solicitor General for all the suits against him filed with the Supreme Court to show proof of natural born citizenship. He owed her big time. All of the requests were denied of course. They were never heard. It just keeps getting deeper and deeper, doesn't it? The American people mean nothing any longer. It's all about payback time for those who compromised themselves to elect someone that really has no true right to even be there. I have information on three cases that were thrown out by the courts. You can see that the one and only Elena Kagan is the attorney representing Obama.

Clearly Obama is in way over his head. The obvious disconnect and reactive vs. proactive posture is probably a result of a few elements: 1. Incompetence 2. Obama's uncertainty of the impact that is caused by his 4 year campaign plan? 3. This clown is nothing more than a mouthpiece for the Democratic Party and his financiers. He will do nothing until he is ordered to by those two entities.

Another opportunity to become a proactive leader - again his level of incompetence and fear of losing his backers trumps the greater good and has him hog tied. Clearly an example of how inexperience in leadership clearly results in an irreversible liability for the United States of America.

Elections do have consequences. When he had the majority everywhere the press talked him up like a superstar and no problems other than paying off the unions and big money folks he was really laying down the law and talking the talk. Now when we have some real problems to deal with, that takes real leadership and some actual character he is lost. He doesn't have the knowledge, experience or strong character to be a good president.

For 8 years you Democrats called Bush every name in the book and then you elect this clueless idiot? He's such a joke and talks so much with out any action that people just tune him out. It's laughable. He can't make a decision on anything. He goes golfing, takes vacations and generally screws off most of the time. If a Republican President did this, the so called "news media" would be reporting it non stop. Instead, they do all they can daily to prop up this empty suit Obama. He has surpassed Carter as the worst President ever.

Disasters are above Obama's pay grade and are affecting his golf scores, so he's leaving until things cool down a bit and maybe he can get his basketball brackets correct.

Barack Hussein Obama is an embarrassment to those who voted ignorantly for his "hope and change" message and an embarrassment to world leaders as a counterpart for a failing America. Remove him because he's an illegitimate elected official in the first place.

President Obama was elected to be a figurehead President. He never intended to put in the actual work of being President. He delegates the work to unelected czars while he struggles to be the USA's first "rock star president". "Hope and change" was just a campaign slogan–just like closing Gitmo, transparency in government, leading by example, etc. It's sad to see a President who is all style and no substance.

Never fear Obama will get his golf game in and to hell with the United States, what a dud and I hope the liberal idiots come to their senses soon. The only support he has is the welfare class and dead beats waiting on another handout from the Government. If the shoe fits wear it

He and that horse he is married to are going to get every free trip out of this administration they can possibly get! He is not a leader; he is a lame duck whose own "people" have turned against him! The man and his horse are ashamed of being black and try to act white. Any President, black or white, that is out playing golf while the world is ablaze should be impeached! He is despicable and a liability to all of us. It doesn't matter if we are black or white.

There are no surprises here whatsoever. The truth is we know nothing about Obama. He is a complete fake and phony person, fabricated by his handlers to look good in front of a microphone. But, he obviously has zero depth, zero experience and zero understanding. What in the world would you expect from a Chicago community organizer? My dog could handle things better than Obama. He's a simpleton, and it's clearly showing today.

He's incompetent. He should resign and let someone competent get in there. Even Sarah Palin could do a much better job.

Can the President of the United States possibly suck any worse? He makes the wrong decision on everything and never leads. He waits for the Congress or one of his czars or his wife to take the lead. We need a real President of the United States.

I sure hope the Japanese people realize that the American people as a whole have the caring heart and compassionate spirit that is so absent from our Presidents present demeanor.

By now we should not be surprised; he has not reacted as a President to anything as yet. He is NOT a President, but a community organizer. He has no idea what he's doing. The world is falling apart around him and he's talking about our food...which is important, but lacks the breadth and depth required of his office. He never had the qualification to be President. So why would you expect any different now...lucky for us, 2012 is next year?

Even Jimmy Carter is rolling his eyes...This guy is a smurf...Complete failure and is clueless...but not to worry folks the American people will vote for the next loser the mainstream media tells them to vote for...... You will not get change until America goes outside that box that everyone talks about...Time to grow up and pay attention America...Wait is this America anymore?

This change the liberals were is such a hurry to get has nearly killed off this nation...he is unable to make a logical decision on anything...he wants to lecture the American people instead of looking for solutions to the growing debt, spending and taxes. His stimulus and bailouts have been a colossal flop along with his death sentence to America with his health care bill. And this new adviser of his calls it "discipline", what kind of rhetoric is that? Obama is unable to lead this country...yet he is already on the campaign trail for 2012...all of his lies, deceptions and failed promises will come back to haunt him...we the American people will see to that. When will the rest of you get tired of this man's rhetoric?

A five-day vacation in the sun, and he claims it is regarding jobs. Please be informed that the last time he said that and went tripping off to India, India got the jobs, and the United States continued with unemployment. The only real jobs Obama has created are the thousands of government jobs that have done absolutely nothing but increase our debt. He's so paranoid about his socialist healthcare program that he has hired more than twenty thousand additional IRS workers to play Gestapo for the purpose of scrutinizing all our insurance data. Japan has an earthquake and tsunami, and he goes to some silly social gathering or pontificating about who's going to play whom in the playoffs.

Palestinians break into the home of Jews and slaughter the parents and three little children, and he busies himself with golfing. Anyway, it's sickening that he is our President.

Is it just me or was there much more of an urgency, disaster aid, and general responsiveness by our President, African Americans and the entertainment industry during the Haiti tragedy? Where are all these selective givers now? Your rules of engagement are so transparent! By the way, has anyone noticed that the only continent that hasn't given to the Japanese cause is Africa? Take, and take, and take the good old liberal agenda.

Obama is the worst president every, this guy is just a politician who doesn't care what is happening as long as he can go and play golf and does his basketball cards for ESPN while Japan is about to explode, at least comment on the crisis that's going on in other parts of the world. I guess it's too hard to play golf and do that at the same time, this guy needs to go.

I hope that all of the Democrats who voted for Obama realize that they were suckered into voting for a shiny package with nothing inside. He is merely the front man for the socialist /communist czars who with the help of union bosses are destroying the American way of life as it used to be. This also seems to be helping his Muslim friends.2012 can't come quick enough to vote out this inexperienced idiot and put someone in office who knows what they are doing.

Mr. Obama, is your administration concerned about the rising price of gas in the United States? Obama: Present

Mr. President, what can the US do to aid our Japanese friends in their time of need? Obama: Ah, present!

President Obama, what is your administration doing to get the American economy back on track? Obama: Present!

Mr. President, is there anything that the US can do to influence the outcome of all the uprising in the Middle East? Obama: Err, ah, present!

President Obama, Are you going to be following the NCAA Basket Ball playoffs? Obama: Yes and I have made my pick for all four No. 1 seeds to go to the Final Four and the Kansas Jay Hawks to cut down the nets in Houston.
Obama voted present 129 times in the Illinois State Senate. Obama voted present 36 times in 150 days in the United States Senate. That's all folks!

"A nation can survive its fools, and even the ambitious. But it cannot survive treason from within. An enemy at the gates is less formidable, for he is known and he carries his banners openly. But the traitor moves among those within the gate freely, his sly whispers rustling through all the alleys, heard in the very halls of government itself. For the traitor appears not traitor, he speaks in the accents familiar to his victims, and he wears their face and their garments, and he appeals to the baseness that lies deep in the hearts of all men. He rots the soul of a nation, he works secretly and unknown in the night to undermine the pillars of a city, he infects the body politic so that it can no longer resist. A murderer is less to be feared." - Cicero, 42 B.C.

Obama's method of operation:

1. Wait a while after something happens, gauge what the consensus is.

2. Announce that you are doing what consensus is (don't acknowledge that you are aware of consensus) just pretend this is your unfettered decision.

3. Wait a while, hoping people forget and the liberal media doesn't bring it up.

4. Enjoy life, golf, basketball, coach your daughter's team, and raise money for next election, make NCAA selections.

5. Bash the Republicans; tell everyone you're tightening the noose on Libya, Iran, and North Korea.

6. Next day: same thing, mix it up a bit, giving a shout-out to Hugo Chavez, Putin and Hu Jintao.

He is so paralyzed by his fear to make a decision and maybe end up on the wrong side of an issue that he would rather make no decisions just like the cup of coffee he had in the Illinois Senate when he voted present most of the time. Spineless. He's got his picks in though. Boo-yaw!

Obama, another failed social idea. I hope America feels better now that we have elected an African American into the White House. After 2012, he can get a job in Ohio. The Attorney General just told Ohio they must let blacks become police officers even with a failing test score.

Hey Obama, maybe you wouldn't be getting criticized so much if you didn't go on a golfing trip the day after Japan had a 9.8 earthquake and was facing a possible nuclear meltdown and then say, "I'm not spending time on the golf course, I'm investing time on the golf course." Gee, and not sounding so tough about Gadhafi anymore now that it's clear he's going to crush the rebellion and stay in power, huh?

Hmm and now jetting off to Rio de Janeiro are we? For business that's funny I didn't know they did any business there during Carnival.

Typical elitist plays and parties while the whole world burns.

Interesting how he is already creating a centerpiece message about jobs and education for the 2012 election, yet he can't get anything done in concerning the 2011 and 2012 budgets.

In other words he is running away. Taking another vacation! Making sure that he is outside of the United States while there is another false

flag attack. Lets let him go and then not let him back in again, ever. We will be better off without him and his regime, here.

The reason Obama hasn't done anything about Libya or Japan is because the unions aren't concerned about what's happening overseas only about union dues and power. That's where Obama gets his orders from the Unions!

It doesn't matter whether he's on the road or at the White House, he can't execute his job properly in either place. Might as well get him out the Country–we're all probably better off for it!

Maybe instead of jaunting off to Rio Obama should have made a visit to Japan to show solidarity and support. Maybe the country will think next time Oprah Winfrey pontificates about who would make a good president.

You can't be serious. This guy doesn't have a playbook unless you're talking about basketball. Since the day he took the oath of office he has been totally dependent on the advice of his lieutenants. What really gals me are the dupes in the national media. They just won't admit their mistake in having supported him in the first place.

It took the American public this long to realize that the liberal media built up a facade image of this man-child and anointed him as some great leader, but he is being exposed like an emperor with no clothes. Basketball takes precedent over dire issues. Nero Fiddled, Obama dribbled.

If you had to define the exact opposite of a leader Obama would be the perfect definition. It's laughable listening to the people still defending him. I guess they can't admit out loud their mistake in voting for him…you know they know the truth inside though.

Obama is not a Leader. He is an affirmative action cop out. All through his political career, he was present, without taking any stand. That is what qualified him to become the President of our Great Nation. Thanks to the Political Correctness Liberal Media, they crowned a person of color. What we have got is a sorry reflection of the state of affairs in our country. Martin Luther King stated in the 60's" do not judge a person by the color of his skin, but by his/her character". The Liberal/socialist/Racist Media built this guy up and it isn't pretty any more.

How's that Obama economy working out for all of you in Nevada? Your state has one of the highest unemployment rates, the largest percentage of mortgages underwater, the most foreclosures and the steepest decline in housing values. Oh yeah, I remember when Obama said: "Don't go to Las Vegas and spend your money there" And you dumb Democrats re-elected Harry Reid, Obama's buddy.

Psychologists would say the President is implementing a simple defense mechanism, 'denial". If you don't want to deal with a situation, just pretend it does not exist. This is what happens when a community organizer is faced with global scenarios that require leadership, courage and the ability to make a decision without checking the most recent polls or reading from a teleprompter. The smoke has cleared and the mirrors are cracked. President Obama is in over his head and America knows it.

Obama would have been fired by now if he was doing a real man's job. He hasn't done anything for this country but split this country in half. Oh, let me not forget letting 5000 Muslims pray on our White House lawn when he came into office. Obama had a Ramadan in the White House. Oh, but he is not a Muslim. Muslims even believe Obama is the man to destroy from within. Out of Obama's mouth: Republicans are his enemy. Out of Obama's mouth: You bring a knife and we will bring a Gun! Just a few of the phrases Obama has used. Sounds like a bully to me.

News reporters are not journalists. They are merely robots that read a teleprompter. The media is a giant propaganda machine of the United States government. Haven't you noticed how all the news channels show the same news? What ever happened to real, independent journalism?

Everyone is making a big deal out of Japan being a "foreign country so why should we care?" How about because the United States has about 90 military installations in mainland Japan and Okinawa? Thousands of Americans are over there. It should be a huge deal for Obama to get that place stabilized. Not to mention that Obama should show some respect for the military stationed there and the people of Japan. He

can visit Rio after the world stabilizes. **What a loser we have for the President of the United States.**

This is the most inept man that could have been chosen of all the candidates, both Democrat and Republican. Barack Obama is an embarrassment to our great country, to those that defend it, and those who helped create it over the years.

I knew this would happen. It's why I didn't vote for him. Go ahead! Speak out and stick up for your mighty Obama! Tell us what he does that is so great and why we are all wrong. I want to hear things of importance not his wives clothes (which I think suck too, but hey! that's just my opinion) or he is smart or any other vague and ambiguous comment you might be inclined to make. Last but not least, I don't think we are paying tax dollars for him to worry about our kids getting bullied in school. I personally can tell you that this is not something a president can control. I worry about my own kids and thanks Obama for acting concerned but I think we can handle these school bullies. Or maybe Obama is not telling us something. Oh my God! Maybe the bullies are really radical Muslim terrorists and that's why this is so important for him to control them.

Exactly!! Messed up priorities! Potential nuclear meltdown, devastating humanitarian crisis, Middle East, not to mention all the flooding in the United States and he is golfing and figuring out his basketball bracket! It's utterly appalling. How many of us would keep our jobs with priorities like that?

Mr. President you listen here. You are not doing your job. You act like you don't care about us and the problems back here at home. Get off your butt and start acting like a man who knows how to run this country. Your first big mistake was the prescription drug plan and meddling with health solutions. We come first, and then other nations last. If you can't solve our problems how do you expect to solve the world's problems? All this money you and your party keep sending overseas should be doled out to us who are getting ripped off by rising costs of living, fuel prices. How can you possible say we do not deserve a cost of living adjustment? Not only the ones on social security but every working man and woman is suffering with today's economy. I

am starting to believe you don't know which way the wind is blowing. You act like you don't know what to do. If this job is too much for you, step down and let someone else take the reins.

There is a photo displaying how President Obama shows respect to the United States of America during the playing of the National Anthem. Here the President is standing with his hands over his groin while Hillary Clinton and another dignitary are holding their right hand over their hearts which is proper. The American people probably will not see the photo since the main stream media will be too ashamed to publish the photo. It might tarnish the main stream medias portrait of their black hero. I have a copy of the photo but do not have the copyrights so that I could include the photo in the book.

One sunny day in January, 2013 an old man approaches the White House from across Pennsylvania Avenue, where he'd been sitting on a park bench. He speaks to the United States Marine standing guard and says, "I would like to go in and meet with President Obama."

The Marine looks at the man and says, "Sir, Mr. Obama is no longer president and no longer resides here."

The old man says, "Okay", and walks away.

The following day, the same man approaches the White House and says to the same Marine, "I would like to go in and meet with President Obama." The Marine again tells the man, "Sir, as I said yesterday, Mr. Obama is no longer president and no longer resides here."

The man thanks him and, again, just walks away.

The third day, the same man approaches the White House and speaks to the very same U.S. Marine, saying "I would like to go in and meet with President Obama."

The Marine (understandably agitated at this point), looks at the man and says, "Sir, this is the third day in a row you have been here asking to speak to Mr. Obama. I've told you already that Mr.

Obama is no longer the president and no longer resides here! Don't you understand?"

The old man looks at the Marine and says, "Oh, I understand. I just love hearing you say it."

The Marine paused for a couple of seconds, then snaps to attention, salutes, and says, "See you tomorrow, Sir!"

The Commander in Chief of the United States military and he does not know how to salute the troops. What a disgrace to all of the brave men and women that are defending the United States of America all over the world. How does Obama ever expect to gain the respect of the American citizens not to mention the military? I have a photo of President Obama standing at a military parade function where he is holding his hands over his groin area instead of saluting the troops. I do not have the copyrights to the photo so I can not include it in the book.

CHAPTER TWO:

MIGRANT FAMILY SUES THE UNITED STATES

The American Citizens Political Action Committee would support the candidate that will finally realize that we are at war with Mexico. They have placed over 20 million illegals in our country. The government does not have a clue about what to do about the problem. The Democrats do not want the problem solved. The Hispanic population voted for the Democrats in 2008 by a margin of 67% to 33% for the Republicans. Harry Reid and other Democrats have pushed for passage of legislation that will provide amnesty to a very large number of illegals. This is nothing more than to shore up the Democratic voting base.

I love how the story headlines the story as a Migrant worker. He was an illegal immigrant who had broken the law for the past 20 years by being in this country. He was a known Meth user and yet they are going to sue the government? Are you kidding me? This guy was a criminal, and when law enforcement (border patrol) tried to arrest him and deport him, he struggled and that is why he was Tasered. I am sorry for any loss of life, but let's call a spade a spade. This guy was an illegal for the past 20 years, he was a meth / drug user, and he was trying to sneak back into the United States after being previously deported. Sorry, but I don't have a lot of sympathy for criminals. This guy is no different than the drug dealers on the corners or the prostitutes on the freeway.

The Associated Press reported on Thursday March 17, 2011 that the family of a dead Mexican migrant sues the United States government.

FAMILY OF MIGRANT SUES THE UNITED STATES

SAN DIEGO – A wrongful death lawsuit against the federal government charges that a Mexican man was beaten by immigration agents before one of them fired a stun gun several times as he lie on the ground.

He wasn't murdered by our law enforcement officers; he killed himself with his meth use. Tasers are in fact NON-LETHAL. In very, very few cases do the people die from Tasers. Almost always when Tasers result in death it is do to drug use. Take Tasers away, you leave our law enforcement with one less non lethal option. This is a bogus suit. I don't condone police abusing their authority, I don't know in this case because I wasn't there. But I'd bet investigations will show they acted appropriately. Cauldron is just a whining president who should never be allowed to speak in the United States again and whose responses should not be printed in our media. In addition, the United States should cancel the $1.4 billion that President Obama has promised to Mexico.

The family of Anastacio Hernandez argues in its suit that agents used excessive force at a San Diego border crossing on May 28, killing the 42-year-old construction worker.

American citizens cannot sue the government but here is a twenty year illegal working construction in our country who died in the border patrols custody and now his family is suing the federal government. What is wrong with this picture? Deport them all now. Enough is enough. We must defend our country. Good job border patrol his time was up anyway.

Family attorney Eugene Iredale said key evidence includes a witness' cell-phone audio of Hernandez crying for help and a witness telling agents to stop.

This Mexican has been crossing illegally for 20 years. Surely he wasn't interested in becoming an American. Surely he had plenty of time to become legal and a taxpaying citizen. He was happy with his drug habit, high blood pressure and the thrill of crossing illegally. Now that lifestyle cost him and his family his life. Why should Americans

pay for his stupidity? Why should we pay for his irresponsibility? Why should we pay for his illegal activity? We shouldn't pay anything period. I hope this attorney doesn't get a penny either. They deserve each other.

The lawsuit, filed Wednesday in federal court in San Diego, seeks unspecified damages.

Folks in the USA need to start suing the Mexican Government for their distress and despair from these "illegal immigrants" stealing away in the night to come here. This guy was in construction…so goes the idea the "illegals" are picking veggies anymore. They are talking good paying jobs from citizens here. And then we have his girlfriend with her anchor babies. That chould have been over $2000 per month for food stamps, housing supplements and health care. This "illegal" population is damaging our entire country and our Government does nothing, in reality. Well, the lawsuit is like the lottery for the girlfriend and she had better not get one penny from the government. The lawyer here should be disbarred.

"This was a man who was frightened and who was really, at the time, pleading for his life," Iredale said at a news conference that was organized by the Mexican consulate in San Diego.

This is why the border patrol should be armed with real weapons and directed to shoot to kill anyone that is attempting to enter the United States illegally. The border patrol would not have to shoot very many and the flow would stop. Better yet, bring the military to the border and secure it with live troops that would know how to stop an infiltrator into this country. God Bless America.

Jackie Wasiluk, a spokeswoman for U.S. Customs and Border Protection, said she would not comment on pending litigation. San Diego police have said an unnamed customs and border officer fired the stun gun. The San Diego County coroner has ruled the death a homicide. The cause was determined to be a heart attack, with methamphetamine abuse and hypertension listed as contributing factors.

Perhaps President Felipe Calderon should make more of an effort to keep these Mexican criminals in Mexico. We all know they are so much safer there. (All illegal immigrants are criminals.) Having the audacity to sue the United States government is typical. The coroners report listed heart attack, methamphetamine, and hypertension as the causes of death. Sounds like his illegal drugs killed his illegal self. I call that suicide by felony. We should eliminate "anchor" baby status for all children of illegal immigrants, deny all social services, including: food stamps, housing, welfare, medical, and all educational benefits. We should bill Mexico for all the costs of incarcerating and deporting their citizens. We should seize all the assets of illegals and their employers, and mandate a 5 year prison sentence for both. No government agency should print anything in Spanish, American English only. Let Mexico, fix Mexico and not send its problems to the United States of America.

Mexican President Felipe Calderon has vigorously denounced the incident, saying a death "with that degree of violence is a truly unacceptable violation." The consulate said in a statement Wednesday that the Mexican government "reiterates its strongest condemnation of the incident that led to the death of one of its citizens."

Mexican President Felipe Calderon why don't you do your job and help keep these illegals in your own country? You openly admit that this was a Mexican citizen. Why was he sneaking over the border? Between this current administration and the current one in Mexico, we might as well put a welcome sign on the border. Yeah come on over and work here, pay no taxes and get all the us taxpayers money for your health, food, and better standard of living than most American citizens. Just make sure you vote for the one doing this for you. Yes they vote with phony names. Don't say they have taxes taken out of their check. They don't! They are exempt from withholding since they aren't American citizens.

"The consulate said in a statement Wednesday that the Mexican government "reiterates its strongest condemnation of the incident that led to the death of one of its citizens." The Mexican government can keep its strongest condemnation and put it where the sun doesn't shin. What about all the Americans that have been killed in Mexico.

Our border patrol agents are not even allowed to arm themselves for protection. What about the tourist killed on the border lake? What about all the other Americans killed in Mexico? Why doesn't the Mexican government try and keep their citizens in Mexico? Why doesn't Calderon realize that he is not the President of the United States? More importantly, why doesn't President Obama stand up for the American people and return some respect to America?

Iredale said the U.S. Justice Department's civil rights division was reviewing a San Diego police investigation.

Can you hear the slimy footsteps of the ACLU running to side with Maria Puga! (They're just about due for another hunk of media time showing off their next worthless cause). To the President of Mexico, shut your mouth and mind your own business. We already have a President that is more supportive of the illegals than he is of the American people. Stop the blood bath occurring in your own country. The Mexican streets are controlled by the drug cartels with total violence and your government does not have enough courage or skill to stop the rampant killing. Try and prosecute the killers of your 35,000 civilians since Calderon took over power in December 2006.

The government denied the family's administrative claim for damages last month a required precursor for a lawsuit. Iredale said he will now gain access to police reports and names of the agents involved.

The man was illegal, the meth was illegal, and they are suing us, What about all the United States citizens they have murdered on the border and in Mexico. Our president is guilty of dereliction of the duty he swore to up hold and protect the citizens of the United States. That is an Impeachable offense. Let's put the blame where it belongs, every president that has turned a blind eye to the illegals including Regan. The United States needs to denounce the citizenship of every anchor baby and send them all packing, This is only the beginning folks, every day they stay here increases their power, they have sucked this country dry, with their entitlements, we can no longer take care of our own and it is the seniors that are being tapped to pay for more welfare for the illegals.

Hernandez had lived in the San Diego area for more than 20 years, according to the lawsuit. He is survived by his partner, Maria Puga, and their five children, ages 4 to 20.

Who was supporting Maria Puga and the 5 kids through the years? 20 years to get legal or too busy being strung out, Looks to me like Mexico lost a Dead beat druggie and America needs to deport these walking baby factories, Anchor babies born to illegal immigrant invaders shouldn't be granted automatic United States citizenship. The Congress of the United States needs to change the 14th Amendment to the Constitution.

Relatives have told the American Friends Service Committee that Hernandez was deported last May after being stopped for a traffic violation in San Diego. He returned to the U.S. through the rugged mountains east of San Diego and was arrested by the Border Patrol. He was being escorted back to Tijuana, Mexico, when he was shot with the stun gun.

He lived in the San Diego area for 20 years with his partner and 5 kids? So he should've known that he was an illegal and tried to find out how to go about becoming an American citizen. Instead of risking his life several times crossing the border through mountains, deserts, using coyotes, etc he could've gone to the local Mexican consulate in San Diego and used the legal process of becoming a United States citizen. But he chose the criminal way of doing things and paid the ultimate price. I hope his family gets nothing in their lawsuit.

Obama needs to take his vacation on the Arizona border instead of Rio. Then maybe Obama would realize that we have a real problem and the government is not doing anything to stop it. I have a picture of the illegals and what damage they have done to Arizona. Unfortunately, I do not have the copyright to the photo so I can not include it in the book. It would not be shown by the main stream media. They don't want all of America to see and understand what the problem is in Arizona. If this was happening in all the states you can bet there would be more demands to stop illegals from entering into the United States.

Here are the comments from average American citizens and what they think about a Mexican illegal being allowed to sue the federal government. The United States is not recommending that illegals cross over the border and the President does not do anything to stop the flow of illegals. Then one of them gets killed and an attorney wants to sue the government. In some cases the comments are extreme but for the most part they are right on. They have not been altered in any way except for spelling and grammar. I hope you enjoy the comments and can get a clearer picture of what is happening in the United States government.

Deborah Schurman-Kauflin of the Violent Crimes Institute of Atlanta estimates there are about 240,000 illegal immigrant sex offenders in the United States who have had an average of four victims each. She analyzed 1,500 cases from January 1999 through April 2006 that included serial rapes, serial murders, sexual homicides and child molestation

When he was deported his family should have been sent scooting with him. Of course, he wanted to be reunited with his family, that's why they all should have left. They are here illegally, too, no doubt.

You have to love the Associated Press use of ``migrant`` headline. They should have stated as an "Illegal immigrant returning after being deported". He leaves 5 children with his partner. AHH the old no father in the house act to cash in those bennies.

He was already deported once, and came back again, it's his own fault. Maybe we should do the same thing to all illegals that ignore deportation. Tell the Mexican government to keep their citizens at home and these things wouldn't happen. As for the lawsuit, screw it! Then go after the American lawyer who dares to file the suit for some illegal.

The Mexican President Calderon seems to easily overlook the violence among his own citizenry. Maybe that is the way that the Mexican's behave with one another. Head choppers and mass murderers are everywhere in Mexico. But, Calderon has issues about illegals getting fixed real good by the Gringos. Easy loving, and easy money…it is what their folk songs are all about. The fact is the man died because

he was in the wrong place at the right time, using meth. The Mexicans will soon learn to really believe it is wrong to enter illegally. The flow of illegals over our border can no longer be tolerated. Bring on the United States military and secure our border.

Just another slime ball attorney wanting his cut of the pie! Lawyers are such scum of the earth, who else has a job freeing guilty people for money?

He came back illegally, probably fighting to get away from the border patrol, got tazed and died. Now the wife and children need to go back to Mexico. Lawsuit, give me a break! He brought this on himself, no one else told him to come back to the United States. I bet his girlfriend and 5 kids have been living on welfare. Using both of their hyphenated names and fake social security cards to get more money. Anchor babies make me sick.

You people who kow tow to the illegal alien's whims need to be put to sleep as well. Mexicans have little to now regard for our laws in the United States. Look at the crooked law enforcement they have there. Really, law enforcement does not exist there… bunch of 3rd world maggots…we don't need these people in the United States. Long gone are the days when we opened our arms and hearts to immigrants. Look how the "melting pot" has become a knife in our backs. Take Miami for instance… You can hardly exist down there because of the language barrier. Better yet, go to Tampa and you have the Puerto Ricans and the Cubans, and Haitians as well that are turning the area into their own scummy reminder of their slum ridden birthplace. Go back to Puerto Rico, Cuba, Haiti, etc, etc,… and take all of your stinking flags with you, we don't bomb around Diego Garcia any more.. Go back to that slum ridden nasty place that you came from.

ILLEGAL ALIENS SHOULD HAVE NO RIGHTS TO SUE THE US. STAY IN YOUR OWN COUNTRY AND TRY TO MAKE IT A BETTER PLACE. BUT JUST STAY THERE.

The following information is compiled from Federal Bureau of Investigation and Department of Homeland Security reports:

80% plus of warrants for murder in Phoenix and Albuquerque are for illegal aliens.

75% of those on the most wanted list in Los Angeles, Phoenix and Albuquerque are illegal aliens.

24.9% of all inmates in California detention centers are Mexican nationals.

40% plus of all inmates in New Mexico and Arizona detention centers are Mexican nationals.

29% (630k) convicted illegal aliens fill our State and Federal prisons at a cost of $1.6 billion annually.

53% plus of all investigated burglaries reported in California, New Mexico, Nevada, Arizona and Texas are perpetrated by illegal aliens.

50% plus of all gang members in Los Angeles are illegal aliens.

71% plus of all apprehended cars stolen in 2005 in Texas, New Mexico, Arizona, Nevada and California were stolen by Illegal aliens or "transport coyotes".

47% of cited/stopped drivers in California have no license, no insurance and no registration for the vehicle. Of that 47%, 92% are illegal aliens.

380,000 plus "anchor babies" were born in the US to illegal alien parents last year alone. (Cost $3 billion)

Additional Facts about Illegal immigration:

There are approx 15 to 20 million illegal aliens in America.

That's 12-15 million jobs desperate Americans could have.

NO AMNESTY, I do not mind paying more for products and services to hire Americans.

Some other countries immigration laws:

If you cross the North Korean border illegally you get 12 years hard labor.

If you cross the Iranian border illegally you are detained indefinitely.

If you cross the Afghan border illegally, you get shot.

If you cross the Saudi Arabian border illegally you will be jailed.

If you cross the Chinese border illegally you may never be heard from again.

If you cross the Venezuelan border illegally you will be branded a spy and your fate will be sealed.

If you cross the Mexican border illegally you will jailed for two years.

If you cross the Cuban border illegally you will be thrown into political prison to rot.

If you cross the United States border illegally you get: a job, a driver's license, a social security card, welfare, food stamps, credit cards, subsidized rent or a loan to buy a house, free education, a lobbyist in Washington, billions of dollars worth of public documents printed in your language, the right to carry your country's flag while you protest that you don't get enough respect. . . and, in many instances, you can vote! Is this not attractive enough to risk your life?

This is getting so old, stale and disgusting. Seal the borders already and fix this illegal immigration mess. All these liberal armchair quarterbacks who weren't present vilifying the BP while these same liberal pro-illegal zealots never mention the atrocities perpetrated by Mexico's Federals upon "illegals" they bust crossing their southern border illegally. Of course, this administration will continue to insist that our border is more secure now than ever before, and will continue to do what previous administrations have done: Absolutely nothing. Actually, that's not entirely true: This current administration DID do what all others never did: Sued the State of Arizona for their efforts in controlling illegal immigration and its negative impact on their state.

Oh, and Obama also reported Arizona to the U.N. for "possible human rights violations". Our government is more responsive to Mexican citizens than its own. Obama is the best President Mexico ever had.

STAY HOME YOU ARE NOT WELCOME HERE! This should happen to all illegal Mexicans! He was a drug abusing criminal who broke the law again! You turned your country into filth and now you are turning my country into filth!!! Where are you going to go next you parasites?

U.S. soldiers who have served their country honorably only to have that government lie and cover up facts that are detrimental to their health have no legal recourse, but the family of a strung out, illegal junkie does? This is FUBAR!

Maybe we can sue Mexico for the boarder patrol costs, drug enforcement costs, medical costs, education costs of illegals and cost of property damage and theft. Shoot them at sight at the border...and leave the dead for the vultures. The problem is that the vultures would not consider them for their meal.

HOPE this lawsuit is drawn out until AFTER the 2012 elections. With our IDIOT in CHIEF and his WATER BOY, Eric Holder in charge, not only would HOLDER and the INCOMPETENT apology to him, but probably give him a position in the White House as Chief Party Organizer. If those two could now lower the scores to 58 for a passing grade for minority law enforcement - they can do anything. Americans are sick of this administration's actions.

When you watch the news, what do you see? I see that almost everyone that commits a crime is not an American. Send there asses home and seal our borders. We need to start taking our country back. It may

be the land of opportunity for illegals and foreigners but not for Americans.

I don't care. He shouldn't have been where he was at. If a United States Court hears the suit and finds in the plaintiffs favor, the judge need's to be lynched.

The headline is typical for our esteemed liberal press; it's "illegal" not migrant you dope! Do you think you could sue the Mexican government over the same in reverse? They would just rightfully laugh at you and call you stupid. The fact that a suit can even be initiated boggles the mind. The world is upside-down.

Gee, an aging illegal alien with heart damage from all the meth he was doing croaks after being legally stunned by an agent after he illegally entered the country a second time. Throw out the frivolous lawsuit, sanction the lawyer who brought it, and go after all the other illegal aliens. They are not immigrants, they are illegal aliens.

He was illegal too bad he made the wrong choice in coming here. He got what all illegals deserve. I want to sue the Mexican government for allowing illegals to come here. Will this get me in the news? I don't think so because it doesn't fit the main stream media and the position that President Obama and the Democrats have on their illegal amnesty agenda.

This story is a bunch of rot. This guy had been sent back where he belonged and his bunch of anchor babies along with his shack up should have been sent back as well. If America pays them anything then Mexico needs to pay for all the murdered Americans as of last count 68 just last year!

The family wants to sue our government! Let's send them to the pot hole in Mexico where they can be killed by the drug cartels. I'm betting his wife and kids are illegals too.

Deported, re entered, meth contributed to death…used illegal drugs, so what all are they not telling us? If he had not broken any of those laws, he would not have been in the position to be there, where he did get killed. Sounds like an outstanding member of the community. His "partner", who is probably illegal too, and 5 kids (anchor babies?) are receiving how much money every month from the United States taxpayers, for nothing?

Of course our U.S. courts are more beneficial to the ILLEGALS than they are to our own citizens and legal immigrants. The 9th District Court of Appeals fined a U.S. border rancher $78,000 for stopping and holding a group of illegals trespassing on his property - and that money went to the illegals. He didn't harm them, just held them at gunpoint until law enforcement came to pick them up.

So much for property rights! Guess if an illegal enters your home without permission, you have no right to hold him for law enforcement. Just welcome the illegal, feed him, give him anything he wants and then you will be okay with our courts. After all, you don't want to deprive the illegals of their "rights" to take, say and do anything they please.

The president of Mexico was "upset"? Then give your people a reason to stay home. We should counter sue and pack up all his illegal family and walk them back. My grand mother use to say…"Just because a kitten is born in the oven, doesn't make it a biscuit,"

Change the laws. No citizenship for anchor babies who are born of illegals. They're all illegal. Why do we not have this problem with Canada? They don't have drug wars, etc. They are north of us with worse weather than Mexico has. Why are they not crossing the border illegally in droves and having their anchor babies. Obviously Mexicans have no respect for American laws, but Canadians do. Different culture obviously. Get the illegals out and kick out their babies too. If they want to come here legally, so be it. If he wasn't on meth it might be better. What is their problem? Fix your own country. Don't keep messing up ours.

If we had a President and administration that cared about the people in this country as much as it does about the illegal immigrants then they would tell the Mexican government to keep these people out of here. As for the lawyer representing this case, he should lose his license to practice and maybe go live in Mexico and see how well he is treated there. This lawyer was probably haired by the ACLU. A government with no backbone is not doing our citizens any good. Stand up for the American citizens and deport all the illegals.

President Obama, Eric Holder and Janet Napolitano need to read and understand the existing laws of the United States concerning illegals entering the United States. Cancel the lawsuit against Arizona and defend our country. Obama you were elected to uphold the law and secure our borders. The other two you appointed without any concern for the American people. I guess it really is the blind leading the blind. Or is the stupid doing as the stupid orders? The Americans citizens and the President need to read the following:

1. There will be no special bilingual programs in the schools.

2. All ballots will be in this nation's language.

3. All government business will be conducted in our language.

4. Non-residents will NOT have the right to vote no matter how long they are here.

5. Non-citizens will NEVER be able to hold political office.

6. Foreigners will not be a burden to the taxpayers. No welfare, no food stamps, no health care, or other government assistance programs. Any burden will be deported.

7. Foreigners can invest in this country, but it must be an amount at least equal to 40,000 times the daily minimum wage.

8. If foreigners come here and buy land... options will be restricted. Certain parcels including waterfront property are reserved for citizens naturally born into this country.

9. Foreigners may have no protests; no demonstrations, no waving of a foreign flag, no political organizing, no bad mouthing our president or his policies. These will lead to deportation.

10. If you do come to this country illegally, you will be actively hunted and, when caught, sent to jail until your deportation can be arranged. All assets will be taken from you.

Are these laws too strict? They are the current immigration laws of Mexico.

An illegal alien and the family are going to sue the United States? You have to be kidding! This shouldn't be allowed. He was being deported. His death was complicated methamphetamine use and an illegal substance.

What about the United States citizens that have been killed in Mexico through the failure of the Mexican government to stop the violence of the drug cartels and the illegal aliens crossing into the United States? The American boater that was killed on the Texas border lake? The American missionary driving home? The ICE agent just doing his job. Those families need to sue the Mexican government for their failure to prevent violence against innocent United States citizens. All of those people were there legally. We need to sue the Mexican government for every United States citizen that is killed by an illegal alien from Mexico.

Felipe Calderon needs to keep quiet about the level of violence. He needs to stop the violence in his country before he worries about the level of violence in this country. He needs to keep his Mexicans at home in Mexico.

He was being escorted back to the border when suddenly the border patrol had to use force? I wonder why. That's the part of the story the leftist main stream media doesn't tell us about. That's because our 21st century main stream media is anti-American and anti-white man.

Jobs Americans Won't Do? Said one woman with a Masters degree willing to take the $8/hour jobs at Phoenix' Pei Wei joints after Sheriff Joe Arpaio liberated them with raids arresting dozens for identity theft crimes. What on earth does Obama and Holder not understands about this? For every illegal with a job, there's an American without one. Thanks Sheriff Joe!

A former Kansas social services case worker urged passage of an Arizona SB1070 style law, citing overwhelming levels of fraud and corruption by a system overrun by illegals. Activists always tell us

illegals contribute to the states they live in. But the ugly truth is they devastate legal workers and drain far more out of the system than they ever put in. They cost the United States taxpayers over $350 billion every single year. This madness must end. The government needs to get its head out of the sand.

Let me get this right. The Mexican was crossing the border illegally. The officers had to restrain him during the arrest. The Mexican had a heart attack because of methamphetamine abuse and high blood pressure. So now the family wants to sue the taxpayer for the relative that was breaking the law. That is special.

Did they consider that he was stealing from the taxpayer? Did they consider he was taking a United States citizen's job? How many anchor babies has he fathered that live off the taxpayer? We know of 5. How many more?

Yet the liberals will say oh that poor man and his family. The same liberals that are crying about unions protect the middle class will be the same ones crying on behalf of the job stealing Mexican. Amazing how stupid some are. Hope the family doesn't get one dime more. When are you going to protect our borders President Obama?

Wait just one minute partners, "The San Diego County coroner has ruled the death a homicide. The cause was determined to be a heart attack, with methamphetamine abuse and hypertension listed as contributing factors." A methamphetamine user had a heart attack and the coroner ruled the death a homicide? Some out of shape Mexican running meth for some drug cartel dies of a heart attack in the United States and we get sued by the criminal's partner? Who herself is here illegally! Bill them for the autopsy and fire that coroner he's on the take!

Let's see…we have an illegal that has been kicked out once trying to break back in. He has a history of methamphetamine abuse and is not in good health…they just happen to be escorting him to Tijuana and decide to beat him and use a stun gun on him…I think there is a missing piece to this story…and the President of Mexico says this degree of violence is unacceptable…has this scumbag opened his eyes lately in his own country?

Close the border…arm the guards well…and do what is necessary to keep people from illegally entering our country.

We need a class action suit on Mexico, from every citizen along the border that has been harmed by the illegals entering the United States. Let's see if we can recoup some of the welfare and entitlement money we have paid out to support the illegals and anchors. Maybe Calderon will have to dig into his own pocket to pay up when we prevail. That is just the tip of the iceberg. Mexico needs to pay support for every illegal in prison. It is time for them to pay up. They have plenty United States dollars they have been receiving from "the illegals" sending it back home instead of taking care of their own here! While we pay their entitlements

These illegals claim to only take the jobs Americans do not want. I worked construction for many years and saw the jobs they were taking with their "government supported lower wages", and I know for a fact there are millions of jobs they have that unemployed Americans would gladly have back. Go after the contractors and others who hire these illegally and you will stop this. In other words, UPHOLD THE LAWS THAT ARE ALREADY IN PLACE LIKE YOU SWORE TO DO! Otherwise you are a law breaker just like the illegals, even if you are the government. They say "nobody is above the law", well it is time for politicians to prove it and quit breaking the laws they made themselves that they punish the true American citizens for breaking, then allow illegals to break them over and over. It was very evident this man had repeatedly broken the law. What happens to a legal citizen who fights with law enforcement officers to keep from getting arrested? Send Calderon a bill for all the Americans who have been killed by his Mexican people who illegally crossed our borders.

Now that's what we call a 'job stimulus' program: Arpaio-Style! Sheriff Joe raided 4 Pei Wei Chinese restaurants and caught over 100 illegals who committed ID theft. Now the chain is putting out ads to hire new workers, and Phoenix citizens will have a chance at those jobs. Too bad Obama won't do a stimulus program like this nationwide. Think how many jobs would be created for LEGAL workers. These workers needed to be deported. I wonder if the immigration people have deported them. Then why doesn't the government have a law that

places severe fines on the Pei Wei Chinese restaurants and seize their business for operating in violation of the laws?

An illegal with no respect for our laws! Throw his lawsuit out. Illegals cannot sue the United States. We should sue the government for letting him stay here for 20 years and have 5 kids. He was stuffed with meth; that's why they had to stun him. Get out and take your illegal kids and common-law wife with you. And I'm sure we American taxpayers paid for the five kids to be born.

Local law enforcement is on alert. They tell CHANNEL 5 NEWS the number of human smugglers transporting illegals is on the rise. Officers we spoke to say in the past week they've captured more than 50 illegals. They say that number is going to continue to increase. La Jolla police Lt. Julian Gutierrez says his officer noticed something suspicious and made traffic stop Monday morning. Fifteen illegals, including women and children, have all been taken into custody. Thirteen of them were Mexican nationals; two were from Guatemala.

I am totally against illegals having jobs in this country. I am not all that thrilled with people with green cards getting jobs that Americans need. I am also totally against mistreatment of any man, woman, or child simply because they are here illegally or of another race, etc. We have allowed illegals here way too long and now the problem needs to be solved. We can't make them legal because that is a slap in the face to those who did come here properly. We can find them all and deport them. We can come down hard on those who hire these undocumented workers. That is where we should be looking and not at the Mexican who has come here to provide for his family - having had to live in terrible conditions in Mexico and being treated like a subhuman to do it. If they do not find a job, they will quit coming here

The American People Stand with Arizona! 67% support the core objective of Arizona's SB1070: the automatic checking of immigration status by police during routine stops. 66% also support strong employer sanctions for hiring illegals. Politicians who plan to cave in to La Raza or the Chamber of Commerce better plan for their retirement instead. The citizens of the United States are going to vote all of them out of office.

So let me get this straight… He is ILLEGAL, got beaten, and his family can sue for when he is in the wrong to begin with? What about all those United States people who get beaten or murdered on the boarder by Mexicans? Can we then sue their government? I say we just tell them to go pound sand the court system should only apply to United States citizens or green card holders. Not Illegals… if so they should be arrested on the spot of them entering the courthouse then given the choice of dropping the case, and going and staying in Mexico or going to prison the rest of their days hard labor… guess what they would pick?

If he hadn't been breaking the law and sneaking into the country he might be alive today. So it should be lesson learned and any video should be posted for all those illegals to see what might happen should they try the same thing. Sort of like the ones who sued a few years ago because one of them died from no water in the desert. They sued because they said the government should provide water along the way. Well the border patrol provided "stimulants" along the way for this guy.

Mexican President Felipe Calderon has vigorously denounced the incident, saying a death "with that degree of violence is a truly unacceptable violation".

Wow! Calderon so what are beatings and decapitations, casual rituals? Are these actions incidental social mores? No, flower, none of this is right and civilized, but you need to check out your own backyard and clean up your own house before you cast dispersions on mine.

Felipe Calderon comes to the United States with his begging bowl every time saying …"don't enforce your laws … let my people in illegally, they are poor … blah, blah, blah" Why doesn't he fix the system so that the criminals and illegals (well if you are illegal you are a criminal) don't come here and suck on my tax dollars. Aren't the Mexican officials ashamed? When you are begging don't think you can start dictating the terms of the United States of America. That is why we have a constitution and immigration laws. It is just too bad that we do not have a President that enforces the laws.

With this situation of the illegals family suing our government when we cannot is absurd. We should sue our government for sending good paying jobs overseas and melting away our retirements and stealing our children's and grandchildren's futures from them. With this guy in the story it's pitiful that Mexico can't do a better job for their people. In Mexico an illegal gets the crud beat out of them, interrogated and a year in a Mexican prison before they are set free. Maybe our government will allow all illegals to become citizens and give them two choices. Stay here and work and pay three times income tax and three times the social security to catch up from where they were allowed not have to pay anything. Also they should no longer have free health care. The other choice is send them to Afghanistan and give them a gun.

Returning a deported Illegal alien for the second time after being in this country illegally for the last 20 years! Has a history of drug use that goes with /or is the cause of the hypertension and a live in partner who probably also doesn't work and lives off our Welfare system with their 5 anchor babies. What a great story to describe their problems. They are the reason our Welfare and other Social systems are overloaded. They are also the reason for our Drug problems, understaffed and over worked Police departments, and continued Gang violence in this country. Not to mention all the jobs being taken by illegals. The answer is to file a wrongful death lawsuit against an officer who was undoubtedly provoked to start with. When are people going to understand that these illegals, the gangs they create and the prisoners shouldn't have any rights in this country? This is just an open door policy for lawyers to pick up cases and the American Public will end up compensating them. Get Rid of all these Illegals and we can enjoy our country again!

Migrant? He was an illegal tell the truth for a change Associated Press. HE WAS NOT SUPPOSED TO BE HERE! To sue someone after you have broken the law and put yourself in his situation is beyond laughable. These illegals are killing Americans everyday somewhere in this country. The Associated Press should be required to carry insurance to cover their journalistic malpractice. Pitiful reporting and hardly qualifies as journalism.

What about the murdered border patrol agent just the other day, hope his family sues the Mexican government? Although I do not support excessive force the bottom line is he was here illegally to start with and was also on drugs and probably was violent himself. The solution seal our borders send the rest of his family back and give them a month free rent along with some grocery money that their suit should award them. Along with some free advice do not come back to the United States of America. And to the Mexican president do something with your own country to make your citizens want to stay.

"The cause was determined to be a heart attack, with methamphetamine abuse and hypertension listed as contributing factors". Really methamphetamine and hypertension (sometimes called high blood pressure or the beginnings of it at the very least) and the family wants to blame the death on border agents? If the guy was taking uppers and blood pressure problems he was a ticking time bomb for a heart attack like the one that killed him. Add to it the fact that if he would have listened to the border agents before all of this started there would have been no problems. The families don't sue the police when it's "suicide by cop" and that's exactly what this appears to be. The guy knew that he was going to die soon and decided to commit suicide by the border agent and hope that his family could get money out of it.

As you can see by reading the comments of the American citizens there is a feeling that the United States is not doing enough to protect the citizens from the flow of illegals that are crossing the southern border of the United States on a daily basis. The people believe that our President should be enforcing the laws and standing up to the Mexican President instead of catering to him. Obama was elected to be the leader of the free world and needs to start doing his job. The American people deserve better than we are receiving.

FEDERAL AGENS TOLD TO REDUCE BORDER ARRESTS

During an exclusive interview with an Arizona sheriff it was reported that United States Border Patrol officials have repeatedly told him they have been ordered to reduce – at times even stop – arrests of illegals caught trying to cross the United States border.

Cochise County Sheriff Larry Dever told Fox News that a supervisor with the United States Border Patrol told him as recently as this month that the federal agency's office on Arizona's southern border was under orders to keep apprehension numbers down during specific reporting time periods.

Dever's charges were vigorously denied by a commander with the United States Customs and Border Protection. "The claim that Border Patrol supervisors have been instructed to under report or manipulate our statistics is unequivocally false." Jeffery Self, commander of the United States Customs and Border Protection Joint Field Command in Arizona, said in a written statement.

National Security Secretary Janet Napolitano has said the United States – Mexican is more secure than ever, and Homeland Security officials have used recent statistics to support these claims.

That would explain why Napolitano wants the arrest numbers to be reduced so that it makes it look like the Department of Homeland Security is doing a better job than they actually are. Just more crooked politics to try and justify their incompetence and the disrespect for the laws of the United States.

The Democratic Party does not want the border secure so they will manipulate the numbers to suit their desires. It is a disgrace to the American citizens. It is very dangerous for the Secretary of Homeland Security to be using incomplete date concerning illegals.

CHAPTER THREE:

TECHNOLOGY SLOW TO BE DEPLOYED

When is the federal government going to do something about the border security of the United States? It has been ten years since the attack on the World Trade Center, the Pentagon and the field in Pennsylvania. All this time there has been very little to protect the United States from terrorists and illegals entering the country at will. Is there some underlying conspiracy that is being conducted to allow all these illegals to enter into the United States?

The policies of the current administration indicate that they are not concerned about the number of illegals that are entering each year or how many of the illegals could be terrorists. The government wasted $1 billion on a high tech virtual fence that they abandoned because it did not work. Now they are planning to do the same thing and are asking the American citizens to wait for about 10 years for the technology to be completed. President Obama, Janet Napolitano, Eric Holder, Harry Reid, Nancy Pelosi, Barbara Boxer and the rest of the Democrats are deliberately trying to build a huge voting block of Hispanics that are hoping to receive their amnesty before the Democrats lose complete control of the Congress and the White House.

Stalled Virtual Border Fence

The Department of Homeland Security Janet Napolitano has already frozen work on the controversial virtual fence that was supposed to secure roughly 1,900 miles along the United States border between

the United States and Mexico. Reports are out that the Department of Homeland Security is going to cancel the entire program sometime in November 2010.

That is probably the only intelligent thing that Janet Napolitano has proposed during her entire time in that office. Now the Department of Homeland Security needs to understand that the Mexicans have invaded the United States and station our military on the southern border.

The questions that most of the American citizens are asking is why in the world the Department of Homeland Security would hire Boeing to be responsible for securing our borders in the first place. Boeing has enough trouble getting their aircraft produced on schedule. Just how lame brained was this selection anyway? Put the United States Corps of Engineers on the job and build a real fence.

The Department of Homeland Security is proposing to increase the number of drones flying along the border. Just look at how effective they have been in Afghanistan after about 10 years of use. Another option would be to increase the number of border patrol agents or rely on the National Guard. The government is hedging on increasing the number of agents due to the 1900 miles of unprotected border. The Department of Homeland Security states that manpower solutions are not cost effective. That is after they have wasted over $1 billion on the program that they intend to scrap. Can anyone figure out these cost effective actions are benefiting our country? Complete the construction of the fence and the America's Highway along the fence which are one time costs. Then the border can be patrolled more efficiently and effectively.

Then if you can believe just how stupid the Department of Homeland Security is they are considering a different type of program that is similar to the one just scrapped. Again with a civilian contractor that is not in the construction business. Starting over with new bids gives the illegals another 24 months of free entry into the United States. How many of the 2 million or more illegals will be terrorists?

The virtual fence should be written off as a very stupid move and move forward with what will be completed in the shortest period of time. The United States is incurring costs because of the illegals at approximately $300 billion per year. How can anyone in government think the cost of the fence is too expensive? Look at the alternative. It is like comparing the problem of getting old compared to dying young.

That brings us to the point. President Bush started the construction of a physical border fence. The Democratic Congress stalled the completion and blamed it on reported legal challenges. It is doubtful that the President would sign any legislation commencing construction of a border fence. The attitude of Janet Napolitano is that is you build a 50 foot fence they will use a 51 foot ladder. What she doesn't understand is that we would have several minutes to use high powered rifles and shoot the illegals while they are climbing the ladder. We would not have to shoot very many and they will take their ladder back to Mexico. That is just another lame excuse by the Department of Homeland Security and Janet Napolitano with the support of President Obama. The Democrats do not want to stop the illegals from entering the United States. There is a hidden agenda to grant amnesty to the 20 plus million illegals that are in the country.

Based on the opinions of President Obama and Janet Napolitano and the rest of the administration we can't stop them so lets just move the border northward about 20 miles per year until they have what they want. Why doesn't someone in the current administration understand that we have military personnel that have the training to defend our borders? We can go all over the world and interfere with other governments and defend their borders. What is the matter with this situation?

People just don't realize how easy it is to cross the border into the United States from Mexico. If you lived in these areas you would realize how sinfully easy it is to make these movements. It is not just an illegal alien issue anymore, national security should be the main goal, so what will it take for people of other countries like Yemen based al-Qaida, terrorist from Iran and others. The United States government is responsible for the nation's borders, instead they're suing the state of Arizona, and other states that are doing what the government is suppose to be doing. It doesn't matter where you live in the United States you should be angry that they're spending taxpayer dollars to go after states that are fighting a border war they should be doing. The only way the citizens are ever going to solve the problem is to send emails and letters every day to the representatives of your local district. Let them know the will of the people and that we will not stand for anything else.

An article from Monterrey, Mexico and reported by Reuters indicated that the Mexican Marines had killed one of the drug lords that was terrorizing the area. The report indicated that this was a victory for President Calderon. The Mexican report indicated that 3 marines and 4 gunmen were killed. It also claimed that a civilian reporter was killed.

This article fails to mention some import information. According to the Valley Morning Star, which is in Harlingen, Texas, not far from Matamoras, stated that there were 47 people killed in this little gun battle? It is suspicious to me that this Reuters report makes is sound like only 8 were killed. Forty seven people being killed in Matamoras is about the same as 47 being killed in Washington, D.C., a city about the same population. Don't you think if 47 were killed in Washington, D.C. that it wouldn't be plastered all over the news? Come on folks, we have a war raging right next door to us and a mainstream news media is failing to report the real news because of their love for President Obama and his administration who finds it more convenient to look the other way.

Every American needs to question ourselves about why President Obama, Senator Reid and the other Democrats refuse to send troops to the borders? Could it be that Reid won Nevada because of the votes in Las Vegas and Reno was funded by money from the drug cartels and unions through the casino industry to support and attract the Hispanic votes?

The border situation has been an ongoing problem for years. The only President in recent history that cracked down on illegal immigration was President Eisenhower. Everyone else has ignored it or has been too enamored with Hispanic votes or cheap labor to close the border. Calderon would have you believe that most of the drug cartels weapons came form United States. Try buying a full automatic weapon, grenade, or grenade launcher, and it is evident that these are military grade weapons from other places. Our federal government has proven to be totally useless and will continue to dance around the issue until a real massacre or ambush occurs in the United States. Then they will want to disarm the law-abiding citizens so we are defenseless. Note how robust the European economies are, and how successful they are in dealing with the illegal Muslim immigrants there. Nothing will change until Americans quit doping themselves for fun and recreation, and we quit voting the same party hacks in that kowtow to the same cheap vote and union labor interests. The best part is that the United States is still one of the best places on earth to live. I wonder how long this will last if we continue to allow millions of illegals to enter our wonderful country every year?

New border technology slow to be deployed

WASHINGTON – March 15, 2011 - As reported by the Associated Press the technology to replace a now defunct virtual fence project at the Mexican border likely won't be fully in place for at least another decade, maybe longer, according to the Government Accountability Office.

Richard Stana, director of homeland security and justice issues at the GAO, said Tuesday that the mix of cameras, radar and other sophisticated technology will first be deployed to the border in Arizona over the next two years. The technology mix is expected to be fully deployed in that state by 2015 or 2016.

The border could be secured with concerned citizens in a heartbeat. It could also be secured by troops that are sitting on their thumbs in Germany and other countries (South Korea). This administration wants the illegal flow of people and drugs into this country and that is outright treason. It's disgusting and will destroy whatever is left of our country when Obama and his tribe of liberal, socialist geeks gets done doing whatever they can to destroy it.

Stana, who testified Tuesday before a House subcommittee on border and maritime security, said the security project would next expand to California, New Mexico and Texas but isn't likely to be fully in place until at least 2021, and possibly not until 2016.

I am having a difficult time understanding how it isn't likely to be fully in place until at least 2021 and then possibly not until 2016. Who looks at these articles that are published by the main stream media to see if they make any sense?

A virtual fence! Are you kidding me? That means a fence that doesn't exist! I suppose that is supposed to stop "virtual invaders"…the invaders are real! I can see them, why can't you? I never thought I would see the day that something as ridiculous as this would even be seriously spoken about by our leaders. Say goodbye to what all of us over 40 once knew as America. To make it worse this is the second time that Homeland Security has proposed a virtual fence. How stupid can they get?

The new technology plan replaces a virtual fence project that cost nearly $1 billion before the Obama administration scrapped it earlier this year after repeated delays and glitches. It will be added to stationary cameras, underground sensors and other security infrastructure already in place.

Why all the stupid technology like you just wasted $1 billion for? Janet Napolitano is such a joke. This is the same thing that did not work and now the Department of Homeland Security wants to do the same thing again. The only thing that the virtual fence did was allow Boeing to earn the $1 billion and now they want to turn it over to a civilian contractor again. The President and Napolitano need to understand that securing the border is a military problem and place the troops on the border. It sure looks to me like our country is just putting out the welcome sign for all the more illegals. How many anchor babies can we afford because of our stupid politicians. The Department of Homeland Security and Janet Napolitano need to be abolished they are not only a joke but the laughing stock of the illegals and cartels.

Rep. Mike McCaul, R-Texas, balked at the idea that the high tech gear, which he said is already available to the military, would take more than a decade to be deployed.

Here's an idea: finish building the real fence, just like the citizens demand! We didn't ask for blimps. We didn't ask for drones. We demanded a fence and beefed up border patrol. You can't tell me our government is this stupid - they are intentionally acting against the wishes of the citizenry, usurping our democracy, and intentionally destroying out culture, all for the sake of a few poor future (illegal) voters.

This government no longer works for the people. It is time for a change.

"You are talking 10 to 15 years. It took us a decade to put a man on the moon," McCaul said. "I don't understand why it takes so long. You have a crisis going on down there. Everyone knows it. We know how dangerous it is in Mexico, we know how dangerous it is on the border. Why can't we ramp up this process?"

Bring the troops home to stop the invasion of this country by the Mexicans who are overwhelming the welfare system and the criminal system.

Mark Borkowski, Customs and Border Protection assistant commissioner for technology innovation and acquisition, said the new equipment could be bought more quickly if Congress allocated the money — the Arizona project is expected to have a price tag of about $755 million — but where to put what equipment has not been determined.

The Congress would probably allocate the funds if the Customs and Border Protection people would know what they were doing. When you ask for $755 million you need to itemize what the funds are going to be used for and where the equipment you are going to purchase is going to be placed and how it is going to be used. The funds are not the problem. It is the stupid people that do not know how to request large amounts of money from the Congress. Then again it could just be another ploy by the Democrats to blame the Republican members

of Congress. If I remember correctly, the Democrats controlled both houses of the Congress and had a Democratic President. There is no one to blame but the inadequacy of the Customs and Border Protection people.

"The question is where do we put the first ones and why do we put them there," Borkowski said.

If you would have answered your own questions the funding might have been provided.

A better question would have been where are we going to put all these illegals in the United States and when are the Democrats going to try and give them amnesty so that they can vote for the re-election of Obama.

He said Homeland Security officials are putting the new equipment in Arizona first because it is busiest Border Patrol sector in the country.

This is what the Obama administration wants. They don't want to seal the border. They want the votes from these illegals that are in hope of free benefits, education, healthcare, your jobs and citizenship. This is really what it is about. Obama wants the Hispanic votes, he is desperate because he is losing his base and the independents and conservative Democrats that voted for him last time will not be there in 2012. He wants to run the USA into the ground.

The virtual fence, which was officially abandoned in January, was initiated in 2005 and was originally expected to be fully in place by this year. Instead, only about 53 miles of operational "virtual fence" was put in place in Arizona at a cost of about $15 million a mile.

President Obama and the Department of Homeland Security need to take a page from Franklin D. Roosevelt's handbook. During the Great Depression, which is very close to where we are today the Works Progress Administration (WPA) employed millions in construction of public works such as: bridges, roads, dams, parks and schools. Is it that hard for Obama to understand that we should recycle this idea? Employ millions by constructing a border fence and America's

Highway parallel to the fence and these two projects will provide employment, security and stop the flow of illegals mooching off of our tax dollars. How difficult is this to comprehend?

I would be willing to bet that there are several thousands of armed volunteers that would be glad to secure our border in the mean time. This is ridiculous. Why don't they have a couple of predator drones on the border and a couple of fully armed black hawks and do what they did in Miami, if you don't stop, Shoot to kill. The politicians making the simplest things complicated. The drones would help spot and stop the illegals and the drug runners. The answer is so stupid, it's incredible. And they want to administer your health care. What a croc.

Use the border to train our military. It would be cheaper than the bases I trained on and would give them real life situations to train with.

What a joke! In other words, our border is wide open for the next 10 years...why? Because our politicians want it to be! Congress makes all the laws of this country and if they decided they wanted to secure our borders, they could do it in a week! Well, they don't want our borders secured...if they did, all it would take is a couple of million dollars of razor wire and land mines and as far as the man power to put it in place, I can guarantee there would be volunteers lining up to help for nothing! Why haven't we citizens marched to Washington, D.C. to demand our country be secured? The very last thing any politician wants to see is 500,000 angry voters outside his/her office...and why isn't our President doing his official duty? He swore an oath to protect us from foreign invaders of all kinds... if this is not grounds for impeachment, I don't know what is.

If 70% of our National Guard was NOT at war how long would it take to deploy enough of them to really secure the border? This is a lie and just a way to continue to allow illegals, dope dealers and terrorists into America as a pretext to pass tyrannical laws that do nothing but finance the government and it's about the final phase to complete their New World Order police state.

Take away the guns from the citizens of the US so that they can't defend themselves from the rush of Mexicans that just walk. Fill the jails with Hispanics that run gangs in every city in the US and let the US pay for it. Put up electronic devices so that we can see them crossing the boarder, but don't touch them because you might break the law, you know they have rights too... When is this country going to wake up and realize that our worst enemies are from within? One of them actually lives right in the White House.

Just ENFORCE our laws! Round them up and their anchor babies and kick them out. Allow the National Guard on the board to actually operate instead of watch and suggest. That will stop the illegals on BOTH borders. When I say round them up, I mean ALL illegals. English, Irish, Russian, SLAVS, Arab's, Mexicans, South Americans, Polish, etc. All illegals! Kick them out. ENFORCE the current laws. Quite playing politics with American lives you num nut politicians.

How many American citizens will be killed on American soil by illegals because our President and our Government refuses to protect us; ten, one hundred, a thousand, ten thousand? Since our Government does nothing, there must be an acceptable number of United States citizens that can be killed by illegals each year.

Wait until the desperate Democrats the party of the lie gives amnesty to 20 MILLION criminal illegal aliens and gives them "family reunification" there will be 50 million 4th grade educated, illiterates on the dole in 3 years of course all to vote for Democrats and handouts for life. Bye bye America, hello 3rd world country.

The Fence is cheaper and quicker......it can be done by the end of the year! I am not into trusting any technology to replace a fixed structure...add the fence then on top of that your wizard technology... then I might believe you're serious.

We should just relocate most of our military training grounds to the Mexican border. Vast areas of border would be covered just by the presence of the regularly used training grounds. They you just need the virtual fence between training grounds. This is the best, most efficient, and cheapest way to seal the border.

There are laws right now that are NOT being enforced by our government. Businesses are getting a free pass to hire as many illegals as they want. All the illegal has to do is show their FAKE SSN and FAKE GREEN CARD and the employer can hire them with no other questions asked. The government needs to pass legislation that will fine the employers and the landlords who rent property or sell property to the illegals. That would also include purchases of automobiles. Make the fines severe enough to make anyone that violates these rules will be put out of business. When the jobs and housing disappear the illegals will also start to disappear.

CHAPTER FOUR:

PROMISES, PROMISES AND MORE PROMISES

The American Citizens Political Action Committee would like to point out what the American citizens think about President Obama and his promise for more transparency in the government. During the campaigning Obama promised that this would be a totally transparent administration. The Obama administration is the most transparent administration I've ever seen. I saw right through them from the very beginning.

I agree that Obama is the worst President ever, has harmed this country and needs to be ousted. But unless the Republicans can put up a legitimate candidate, that everyone can get behind and support, the Obama political machine with its billions of dollars, illegal voting, busing in votes, the racist black votes and with the help of groups like acorn, the unions and black panthers he will get another 4 years. Republicans better get their act together and put up a candidate, unlike the last election. The Republicans need to be aware of the facts. Over 95% of the black voters voted for Obama and over 67% of the Hispanics voted for Obama. Another fact is that the ten states that have the largest union representation were for Obama and contributed 151 electoral votes to Obama. That is a major obstacle to overcome and the Republicans need to find a candidate that will present facts about what they are going to accomplish and how they are going to implement the policies to make sure that their promises are fulfilled.

PROMISES, PROMISES AND MORE PROMISES:

Here are the comments from average American citizens and what they think about the Obama administration's transparency and the policies that they are forcing the American people to live by. In some cases the comments are extreme but for the most part they are right on. They have not been altered in any way except for spelling and grammar. I hope you enjoy the comments and can get a clearer picture of what is happening in the United States government.

Me, too! Where the heck was everyone else? He mesmerized everyone with his teleprompter-aided speeches and became the most successful snake oil salesman of all time... We've had a lot of change: no jobs, inflation, a weaker dollar, a foreign policy which has made us the weakest we've ever been, social programs which waste money, so-called shovel-ready jobs which never appeared, an environmentalist policy which will bankrupt this nation and all who live within...err... except the Obama-ties...who have gobbled up all the government subsidies for ethanol and other ridiculous projects. Now, that's change you can believe in!

I can't wait until Act II to see what promises he makes and who's to blame for his policies...George Bush anyone?

We were promised Hope and Change we can believe in. What we got was nothing more than a Racist Street Thug from Chicago. He used the Racist Card to throw all the PC people off his true track. Had more voters checked into the liar's background as State Senator and US Senator, the only votes he would have gotten would have been from the other anti-white Racists in the country. He was almost non existent as a state senator and did even less as a US Senator. And now, we all know how worthless he is as President. He hides his past, refuses to talk about it, and calls us Birthers because we want to know the truth... For those of you that are sticking behind this blob of pond scum, I can tell you that as an American citizen it is not only MY RIGHT, it is also MY DUTY and MY RESPONSIBILITY to not only ASK but also DEMAND to know the TRUTH. I Have a real good feeling that if Obama doesn't come up with the truth, he can kiss the election goodbye. Too many people are more than tired of the Racist card and are sick and tired of the lies...too many lies and cover-ups...

Hands down, The WORST President we have EVER had. When the incredibly Liberal AP turns on Obama then it is becoming very apparent that he is a failure, complete and utter failure. We need to move forward from this guy. He has personally made this country a very divisive place to be. There has never been this much HATE for the other side before Obama. He has fostered the whole environment. It is time to stop worrying about the Party and concentrate on getting the country back on track. We simply didn't know ANYTHING about Obama when we elected him. We had to find out about him the hard way and we are paying a steep price for our ignorance. I don't care if a Republican or a Democrat leads this country AS LONG AS THEY REALLY LEAD.

Keep telling these liberals and Democrats. A blind man can see through the smock Obama is trying to pull over his head. This administration has done more to deceive and cover up than any other administration before it. He won't drill, he won't create jobs, and he won't share information with the rest of the country that may put him in jeopardy of losing his seat. He's literally Jimmy Carter and Richard Nixon rolled up into one. Only the illiterate can't see what a horrible job he's doing. He's already spent more in the last 2 months than Republicans are talking about cutting. And his cohorts are saying, "The Republicans are cutting too much!"

Think about this, CBS even agrees:

"On the day he was inaugurated, the national debt stood at $10.626 trillion. It had increased $4.9 trillion during President George W. Bush's eight years in office. The posting today shows the debt at $14.128 trillion; that's a $3.5 trillion increase in the 25 months Mr. Obama has occupied the White House."

He even got caught red handed, along with Harry Reid and Nancy Pelosi for hiding an additional $105 billion in the Obamacare bill. Nobody knew what was inside the almost 3000 page bill. Pelosi was strutting around like an old hen talking about how you have to "Pass Health Reform So You Can Find out what's In It." Not even 2-3 weeks before then, she was popping off at the mouth about Transparency of their process! This administration is a total farce. Seeing them in office for an additional 4 years, forget about it, I'd rather see this country in a civil war than to deal with their shenanigans again.

No Leadership

No Responsibility

No conscience for consequence

The only surprise here is that he still has so many supporters talking up his "successes". The "N" word is of more concern than illegal immigration yet it is fine to mock a soldier's demise. Far too many Americans fear being called racist so they sit back and remain quiet about his Chicago style politics. His so-called greatest achievement has half the nation's states suing on the grounds it is unconstitutional. The worst part of it all is that he may well win a second term because of all the money that will be spent by unions and other groups he has catered to. Any remaining negatives in the country will be recycled and blamed on old reliable, George W. Bush.

"The end justifies the means" Is the Liberal motto. Say and do anything to get into power, and then do what you want. This is no surprise to any conservative. The liberals do this all the time! Anyone with a brain knew not to vote for Obama, and that he was lying his way into office. Even people that voted for him hate him for duping them. He was a great salesman wasn't he? Now even the liberal media that made him is getting the shaft, go figure! LOL!

While the world is in horrible shape OBAMA just plays golf and has lavish dinner parties at around $1500 dollars a plate. He says all the right things and then seems to do the opposite. OBAMA'S words are empty it is so true that if he tells you its day it's really night.

Then the unions seem to have been taken over by the radical left wing the Communists. The communist party even took out the permit to gather in Wisconsin. What the hell happened? A very slow takeover of American politics by the Communist party just like over seas. News flash it didn't work over there. It failed so they are here trying to take over this country.

Tomorrow, or next year, or sometime later this century the truth about Barack Obama will trickle out. And when that happens, "Barack Obama" will be exposed as America's fraudulent president. Obama can be compared to a magician applauded by a gullible audience. There are three basic components involved in any magic trick: an assurance of truth, misdirection, and deception. We have an irresponsible egocentric evil man occupying the Oval Office. Obama certainly isn't transparent about his Birth Certificate and other Presidential Information for the public to see. Right away people should have seen how truth telling Obama is and was going to be. Obama the liar.

Obama can't afford to be transparent. As he has said, "an informed people are an obstacle to the implementation of his agenda".

President Obama summed it the best; "…Now, I am a President that can't get anything done…" This President has divided the nation, as it is racist to speak against his policies, and though he can be as brutal as he wants to be, everyone else has to be nice and smile while Obama bullies them.

President Obama is thin skinned, demonstrates no leadership abilities, and frankly has packed his administration with equally incompetent persons.

The Obama Administration has refused a FOIA for his birth certificate. Wonder what their reasoning was? It is outrageous what this President is committing and getting away with. This is what happens when you vote for someone you know nothing about because the media didn't do their job. Now you know something and hopefully you won't vote for this bonehead again.

Be still my beating heart!! You mean to tell me that Barack "Change You Can Believe In" Obama has not honored yet another one of the promises he made when he ran for office? Those who voted for this local community activist, part-time senator, Chicago political machine hack and Harvard educated elitist knew or should have known that this guy is a bag of wind and a fraud. He was meant to be a minister, not the leader of a nation. His sole mission as President

is to make sure that he makes this nation a province of France by the time he leaves office. **Please make sure that nobody lights a cigarette while standing next to him. The explosion from the gas coming out of his mouth would be enough to flatten every building East of the Mississippi River.**

When I am President I will use "tough, direct diplomacy" to keep Iran from obtaining nuclear weapons.

Concerning health care, "I will have the negotiations televised on C-SPAN, so that people can see who is making arguments on behalf of their constituents"

"When I'm President, I will go line by line to make sure that we are not spending money unwisely," His first budget included 7,991 so-called "earmarks" totaling $5.5 billion"

"I will post legislation online for five days before acting on it." He broke that pledge with his first bill. (Lilly Ledbetter Fair Pay Act).

"My administration will be transparent". Democrats in Congress and the White House have made multibillion-dollar deals with hospitals and pharmaceutical companies in private.

I will create 3.5 million jobs.

"All communications about regulatory policymaking between persons outside government and all White House staff would be disclosed to the public" It took several lawsuits just to get the White House to release the visitor logs. There are several caveats in the agreement to release these logs, one of which says they will not be released for 90-120 days of the visit.

I will eliminate all income tax of seniors making less than $50,000 per year.

No political appointees in an Obama-Biden administration will be permitted to work on regulations or contracts directly and substantially related to their prior employer for two years. ." Former Raytheon lobbyist William J. Lynn is the deputy defense. Jocelyn Frye, who is now director of policy and projects in the Office of the First Lady previously lobbied for National Partnership for Women and Families from 2001 to 2008. Many of the laws for which Frye lobbied are things Obama has supported. In 2008, for example, she was listed as lobbyist working for the Lilly Ledbetter Fair Pay Act. Another lobbyist is Cecilia Muñoz, now director of intergovernmental affairs in the Executive Office of the President, managing the White House's relationships with state and local governments. She has also been designated the administration's principal liaison to the liaison to the Hispanic community. Muñoz formerly lobbied for National Council of La Raza, a Hispanic civil rights and advocacy organization.

The whole Obama administration is trying to transform a rich nation into a poor third world nation and that change is WELL ON THE WAY and that is CHANGE THEY BELIEVE IN. Then everyone can look to government for a hand out.

The president who campaigned for a more "open government" and "full disclosure" will not unseal his medical records, his school records, or his passport records. He will not release his Harvard records, his Columbia College records, or his Occidental College records—he will not even release his Columbia College thesis. All his legislative records from the Illinois State Senate are missing and he claims his scheduling records during those State Senate years are lost as well. In addition, no one can find his school records for the elite K-12 college prep school, Punahou School, he attended in Hawaii.

Obama literally couldn't pass a background check for a GS-2 Clerical working for the Federal Government, but yet we can elect him leader of our country.

I agree. Obama has divided this country and taken us back almost 50 years and I for one do not believe it's been accidental or unintended. Now that I look back over his past 20 years with the shady characters he hung with, his 2 years in office has confirmed for me that he is not pro-America!

Can this country hang on for another year and a half? Maybe! Can we hang on for another four after that? I kind of doubt it. We need to get rid of the lawyers and put in a businessman or businesswoman who knows how to run things. Someone honest if that is possible.

It is time for the era of "poser victims" to end. This President has openly subterfuge relations between all types of people in this country. Obama is not only a bad President...he is not being challenged as one. Yes, he had to face many problems when coming into office. however, he looked the other way and rammed an unnecessary piece of garbage legislation down our throats, cowered before other countries in a way that has yet to be understood, divided relations within his own party, made blunders by not reacting or refusing to react, made unbelievable political and ideological appointees to big positions in government, all the while constantly campaigning for the next election.

Here's some advice for the voters that placed this tripe into office. Stay home next election or vote for someone else. This guy's not helping the United States......he's hurting it. We need solid progress on the reduction of the deficits, reducing the size and role of Federal Government in our lives and this guy is just piling on the additional programs and trying to fund it with money we don't have. Now that Japan has been devastated, the clamor for borrowed money for governments will get louder and more competitive. Japan will have the edge because of the empathy of their situation. The United States is responsible for it's own out of control spending. Imagine what would happen if that Tsunami had happened here. We must not re-elect this man that cannot stand by his own commitments to his electorate as well as make snap decisions. He is too inexperienced for this job and has no military experience...not to mention business, administrative, etc...The voters that put this plebian in office bought a ghost dream......and it's fading fast.

Several months ago a South Carolina politician got himself in trouble for calling Obama a liar. The national media did everything but pillory the politician. A fact check might now be in order about whether the South Carolina politician was the one telling the truth. If Obama had to tell the WHOLE truth, he would be able to say little. His latest distortions about domestic oil production, which he has done everything in his power to prevent, are a good example. His promises to have transparency were certainly a lie, as witnessed by the behind the scenes buying of votes to get the unread Obamacare legislation passed. His promises to include the Republicans were an obvious lie. His claim that he is not an ideologue is an obvious lie. His Cabinet and personal advisors are laden with individuals who are ethically challenged, nonpayer of taxes, outright liars and crooks such as the Whitewater/Rose billing records.

The Freedom of Information Act is clearly too broad, and these requests - half a million? - will further bog down a government already swimming in inefficiency. The government will tell us what it wants us to know, and historians will tell us later what we didn't need to know or that we shouldn't have known. Besides, it's not like Obama and his government is using underhanded political tactics to solve problems. Clearly problems are not being solved by this government and the bloom is off the rose with the American people - they're seeing President Obama for what he is: an inexperienced novice politician who can make good speeches while saying very little. I'm afraid we're stuck with BO in the White House for a while longer.

President Obama is hands down the worst President we've ever had. He uses strong arm tactics to get bills passed against the will of the American people. He and his administration have slowed down any possible economic recovery through the obscene spending in his first 2 years. He lacks leadership, integrity, and any form of courage. He is a complete fraud and now the American people will suffer from his Socialistic policies for generations. He must go in 2012 if we are ever going to have a chance for any form of recovery.

We might just find out everything they HAVE been doing and covering up if those documents were released. Having control of the House, Senate, and White House with oversight committees dominated by liberals has brought us to the point where one day we will wake up and ask ourselves, "What happened? How did this happen?" The media that gave this President a continued "pass" and did not do their jobs of investigative reporting and watching out for the people are likewise responsible.

That whole transparency thing was a big, fat lie...obviously. These creeps have the most sinister, hidden agenda I have ever witnesses in my 47 years. The truth only comes out after they pass one of their socialist bills and we get to actually read the trash ourselves.

Remember when Obama said that he promised us that ALL proposed bills would be posted online for 48 hours before any vote? Well you need to remember that LIE and all the other LIES that Obama told, just so he could get in position to fundamentally change America. Yeah, we see through you Obama.

I am completely mystified why the people that voted this arrogant, self-centered, self-serving and self adulating President in office can still sit at his feet and let him tread all over them. They seem to accept Obama's degradation of the American people by his overseas trips where he calls the American people arrogant, derisive and divisive. Eric Holder saying that the American people are cowards! And, for those who think Obama has clout with the foreign countries you are wrong! I have several foreign friends (was in Australia in July of last year) and they tell me their countries see Obama as a weak President and the United States as no longer a strong leader of the world since Obama became President.

The only thing open about the Obama administration is his mouth and when you see his lips moving you know he's lying. The man, who has nothing to hide, hides nothing. The fact that so much information is being denied means there should be more digging to get to what he's hiding and there's probably plenty. He knows his goose is cooked or he wouldn't be doing all of this since he took office.

Didn't anyone notice the deliberate lack of transparency when President Obama started creating "czar" positions to run the government outside of the government itself? Positions filled by people with dubious ethics, and obvious anti-American and big business interests? Barack H. Obama is a liar and a real POS that does not need to be in that job. His agenda has been done behind closed doors and even away from the Republicans and Tea Party legislators. Complete B.S! This is why he will never be re-elected to another term. If the Democrats do not get their way we have all seen what they do in Wisconsin. Obama is as vile and evil as they come.

I for one am glad that I was able to watch the debate over the health care bill on C-SPAN. I am also thankful that GITMO is now closed. I am particularly pleased that unemployment has not increased over 8%. I am proud that this president goes through each bill line by line, and removes all special interest spending. God bless all the troops who

were in Afghanistan but now they're all home. I am impressed that this administration is a pay-as-you go administration, adding nothing to the national debt. I am happy the surplus of our green jobs have eliminated our reliance on foreign oil and ended global warming.

I really hope the Republicans vote in a candidate that has the balls to very clearly and forcefully call out Obama on all his lies from the past election cycle in a debate. Chris Christie is the only one that comes to mind for me. If Christie runs, then wins, I bet they won't have more than one face-to-face debate. Town hall styles and so forth, but not a real in-your-face debate.

No need to think of consequences or of this country's future, Mr. Obama had that figured out in law school. Just vote the Progressive Party line and his hand picked managers will take care of everything. If Obama gets a second term he will go down the same path as his fellow progressive Hugo Chavez. Eventually the U.S. will no longer be the land of opportunity that draws people, who risk everything to be here. We will be a third world economy, whose citizens will risk anything to escape.

This administration once promised that negotiations over his health care overhaul would be carried out openly. Congressional investigators that requested details of meetings between White House officials and interest groups, including drug companies and hospitals, basically were given the brush-off by the administration citing confidentiality interests. In many cases stonewalling by the administration has made even Congressional oversight extremely difficult, if not impossible. New boss same (or even more secretive) than the old boss!

The Washington Times argues that "President Obama has intentionally hamstrung domestic energy production" and taken "deliberate action to block access to the nation's energy resources." And the Washington Examiner says "the President has effectively shut down" the energy industry in the Gulf of Mexico – a "key factor in the recent increase in gas prices as well as continuing high levels of regional unemployment."

Of course, opposition to American energy production is nothing new for Democrats. Interior Secretary Salazar famously told the United States Senate that he wouldn't support drilling for new energy even if gas prices reached $10 per gallon.

While reading news from a real news channel one of the President's aids stated recently that the President has said that he wished he was President of China. That way there would be no Republican Party, no Tea Party, no Democracy and no transparency. That way he could just tell millions of people what to do and they would jump to his bidding no matter how senseless it was. I think he is melting down, which would be a great day for America. Maybe he will depose Chavez and take over his country, now that would change I could voter for.

Democrat = corruption, bribery, spend the country into near bankruptcy, an unwanted passed vile and evil healthcare bill filled with pork and earmarks, special favors, strong-arming behind closed doors, if Barack Obama cannot get his way call in the slimy Bill Clinton to tell some more lies, and we have ours so who cares!

We should have an IQ test for voters. It is about time people elect officials on their content and character, and not the color of their skin. Half of the people that voted for Obama had no idea of what he stood for, but they knew he was a "brother".

Obama was elected based on a manufactured persona, a lie, put forward by the Democratic National Committee and the fawning media. And who is Barack Hussein Obama?

Obama is the first President in the history of the USA who is not a cultural American and it shows. No other President has ever run down his country to the world as Obama has. Obama has denigrated the people of America shamelessly and he has no idea of who we are because he is not one of us.

Obama was raised far outside of mainstream American culture. His upbringing was by communists who indoctrinated him from day one to be a hard-core Marxist ideologue. Obama was taught to loath the middle class and to use radical rules to attack it. From the time Obama was elected he has been tearing down the USA and the middle class which he fooled into voting for him.

Obama was billed to be all things to all people. A pseudo-mythical messiah-like figure that rose mysteriously with no background yet was a towering intellect that could solve all our problems. Obama is a man of slogans: he was "going to hit the ground running", and was "ready to lead on day one". He was going to be the post-racial President who would unite the USA and lead us into a new era of enlightenment and renewed respect in the world of nations. His inauguration was the "day the sea levels would begin to drop". Only now we know this all to be a farce.

To those of us who took the time to investigate Obama while the fawning media failed to vet him it comes as no surprise that Obama is a failure. Anyone who tried to point out his radicalism, his criminal associates, terrorist friends, his racist church where he sat for 20 years listening to hatred of America and Americans was branded as a racist. It turns out that everything Sean Hannity reported about Obama's past was true.

And now we know that Obama is a shallow self-serving man of little experience who constantly resorts to demagoguery of those who oppose his radical agenda. He makes denigrating generalizations of broad swaths of the population and makes it clear he is only the president of those who voted for him and support him.

We are much worse off as a nation than we were before Obama and have nearly 2 more years of this arrogant fool to endure. Let's all watch this impostor vacation and golf and travel the world in Air Force One at our expense while we continue without an inspirational leader and scratch our heads in wonder at the absurd Political Correctness that got us such a ludicrous President.

Sarah Palin is beginning to look real good right about now.

You have 535 people in Washington, calling the shorts, making the laws that we as American Citizens must follow, or be imprisoned. They are exempt from the same. They are supposed to be transparent, yet they do most of their bargaining behind closed doors. They set the taxes for us, but they are exempt from those taxes. Currently they are trying to re-set Medicare and Social Security, yet we have no say so in how they do it. They are handing out billions of dollars in aid to third world countries, and are conducting two wars, and may get involved in a 3rd, and we have no say so. They dictate what programs they want to finance (most are earmarks and pork) and tell us what taxes we are to pay to finance those earmarks and pork. You call that freedom. I call it a dictatorship, by a group of cronies and gangsters, with a scapegoat (Obama), being used as a fall guy.

When are the people going to accept the truth about America, that Obama has split up the United States worse then the Civil War or the War of Northern Aggression (depends on where you live what you call it). As a President he should be uniting our country not creating a wider division. This should be apparent to all people if you look around in our country honestly. He has set the Republicans, Democrats, blacks, whites, Hispanics, union & non-union, religions against each other and others I've probably missed (sorry). He has set the Senators against each other and the Congressman too. At both the state & federal level! When are the people going to accept the truth? These feelings of animosity will not go away in 2 - 3 years the damage has been done. I only hope it doesn't get worse, but I feel it will and hope that our great country can survive.

There was plenty of information available about Obama's corrupt background before he was elected stop making excuses. Now you're angry he is such a fake, corrupt and incompetent to lead? You're upset because Obama lies?

Character counts so does your personal beliefs and philosophy that is the bases from which one makes decisions. It was easy to see Obama would be dangerous and a huge failure from his history. Really someone who goes to a church 20 years that gives awards to Farrakhan and preaches God damn America, reparations etc.. Someone with the IQ of a turnip could understand that was all you need to know Obama was a total loser, and if that wasn't enough there was plenty more.

This is a bad sign of even tougher times ahead, the blind leading the blind, this is the kind of thing that created Nazi Germany, USSR, Communist

China etc. immoral corrupt people who are have no God or a phony Christianity , no real moral light to be guided by.

No shame, No conscience, No Morals...How would you expect transparency with a criminal administration such as we have. Mr. Obama, trust is the easiest virtue to lose and the hardest to regain. You should truly apologize to the American People for your "Hope and Change" ideals and seek redemption for the liar you are. Give up your political and socialist agenda, do something for America.

Obama's approval rating at an all time low of 37%, 79% think Gitmo should stay open, 68% favor repeal of Obamacare, 62% say government unions must be reigned in, and 73% disapprove of any bailouts of states or more stimulus. Obama is still not listening to the people.

Our whole 7th fleet has been exposed and has been ordered to retreat 150 miles off the Japan Coast. Radiation showing up 60 miles in all directions from nuke plants as of Saturday. This was even before the latest news that rods have been exposed. Meanwhile what does Obama do? ABC News' Tahman Bradley reports: The world is in crisis and where oh where is the leader of the free world? GOLFING AGAIN MAYBE? Plus before he has dinner with the left wing media event and cuts down Republicans once more, which he had skipped his first 2 years because he was on one of his many vacations at the time of the dinner, which had never before been missed by any other President. President Obama just could not wait for spring weather to arrive. For the second week in a row, the most powerful man in the world stepped away from the White House to hit the golf course.

Even as his administration and the U.S. military help Japan recover from a devastating earthquake, and as the world worries about Fukushima's nuclear reactor plus 3 more reactors about to meltdown, higher gas prices and he will not let us drill, he will not stand up against the Libyan leader who killed Americans or for the Libyan people, will not work on a budget to cut the debt, our soldiers fighting a war in a country where they are not wanted, yet the President could not resist taking advantage of the 48-degree weather in the Washington, D.C., area. The president left the White House Saturday afternoon by Marine One for a short trip to Andrews Base in Camp Springs,

Maryland. With cloudy skies, it's not the best weather for golf, but Obama loves to spend his Saturdays on the greens. Last fall, Obama went golfing darn near every weekend.

P.S. These are never quick "work on your swing" trips; usually the President plays 18 holes, as he did last week. The world is falling apart and "THE WORLD WONDERS WHERE IN THE WORLD IS THE LEADER OF THE FREE WORLD". Well he's on the golf course again after sending his Vice President overseas who was supposed to be in charge of working with Congress in reducing the debt or raising the debt ceiling once more so Obama can spend more money. Meanwhile the 1st lady is digging thru her new $1,000 purse paid for by the taxpayer and planning their 15th vacation trip since taking over the White House, all on the taxpayer's dime. The world is falling apart, gas prices and inflation are soaring, our militarily is being exposed to nuclear radiation as nuclear rods are exposed in Japan, Libya and Arab nations calling for a no fly zone, millions of US workers out of work, we can't drill for our own oil, etc, etc, and Obama votes present once again and plays golf for the 104th time.

Info on stock market swindles should not be secret. It only protects the politician's pimps. The commission investigating the financial disaster secretly turned a number of names over to the Justice Department. There the secret will probably be buried, secretly. But then, that's why it is kept secret. Government has no interest in transparency. They want to stay out of jail.

All Democrats spewed for a couple of years are that "BUSH LIED" - yet their boy is an even bigger liar, yet the Democrats say nothing now. Seems the Democrats are fine with lies - they just pick and choose who can lie and who cannot. They did a great job electing Obama - the greatest liar ever to sit in the White House. 2012 is coming - I personally am not buying a thing except necessities and am boycotting Obama and the Democrats.

"The end justifies the means" Is the Liberal motto. Say and do anything to get into power, and then do what you want. This is no surprise to any conservative. The liberals do this all the time! Anyone with a brain knew not to vote for Obama, and that he was lying his way into office. Even people that voted for him hate him for duping them. He was a great salesman wasn't he? Now even the liberal media that made him is getting the shaft, go figure! LOL!

You'd hide things too with friends like these. Obama's friends Louie Farrakhan and Jeremiah Wright only have had good things to say about Gaddafi and Sharia law. Their hoping after the next election to invite him and set up a beer summit with Obama and knows he'll like it better than having to sit down with a cop pig like the last time. They'll probably invite Bill Ayers to make sure they don't look prejudiced. Besides Jeremiah always had a soft spot for Bill after he tried to blow up the Fort Dix soldiers and their girlfriends in the 1970's. Some say this is where his famous "Chickens coming home to Roost" speech came from. Obama is hoping Mummy (Muammar this is what his friends call him) can help him find an Imam with ties to the Muslim Brotherhood to help set up the Mosque at Ground Zero. Now he wants the Muslim Brotherhood to takeover Egypt and the Suez Canal and see what they can do about that pesky Israel (Louie don't like their Gutter Religion). This crew will be taking bets on how long it will take to exterminate the poor Coptic Christians. Obama's told Mummy he's going to look the other way like he did when beautiful Neda was killed.

He was a liar from Day One. He just had the pathetic main stream media in his pocket and the white guilt vote. At least the people see now with their own eyes why not a single Founding Father was a Liberal. It's a failed ideology which preys on the ignorant masses looking for a free lunch. More than a 1/3rd of our population is now dependent on government handouts, but it's not high enough for a Liberal like Obama. That's why he is doing nothing about unemployment, nothing about foreclosures, nothing about energy etc. etc.

Obama's refusal to provide records on healthcare meetings should sound alarms. The obvious question is why? Why would the Obama administration who boasted open and transparent discussions of such a sensitive subject as healthcare close the door to the opportunity to present its factual case to the American people? Messaging anyone? Nope.

Complying with the records request from the House Energy and Commerce Committee "would constitute a vast and expensive undertaking" and could "implicate longstanding executive branch confidentiality interests," White House lawyer Robert Bauer wrote the committee. Translation: Nice try.

Before the Democrats rammed through the Obamacare bill (and don't think for one little old minute that our narcissistic President doesn't love that branding), Obama and White House officials met with several high-profile insurance executives as the Washington Post lists: The list included George Halvorson, chairman and CEO of Kaiser Health Plans; Scott Serota, president and CEO of the Blue Cross and Blue Shield Association; Kenneth Kies, a Washington lobbyist representing Blue Cross/Blue Shield, among other clients; Billy Tauzin, then head of PhRMA, the drug industry lobby; Richard Umbdenstock, chief of the American Hospital Association; and numerous others.

The most concerning is George Halvorson as he was the only executive to meet with Obama. And here is why: "There really are two Americas when it comes to health care — the fully insured, primarily white America and the disproportionately uninsured minority America," Halvorson wrote. "More than half of the total uninsured people in this country are minority. That fact alone should make the need to cover everyone in America a pure ethical imperative. This issue is not about economics — it is about equality. Universal coverage should be the next major civil rights issue for this country to face. Halvorson also wrote an article in 2007 equating health reform to the "unfinished business of the Civil Rights agenda." Halvorson discusses the disparities between the races and health care coverage and states: If we considered no other issue than racial and ethnic disparities, this nation's leadership — like the leadership of a number of states — should be moving this country down the path to an American form of universal coverage as quickly as possible. There is no more vital or meaningful way for us to honor and extend the great legacy of Martin Luther King Jr.

Again, Halvorson was also the only insurance executive to meet with Obama at that time. Why? Is it because Obama wants a single-payer system and sees himself as finishing the Civil Rights Movement, and

Halvorson has the same viewpoint and the most to gain via Kaiser Permanente? But, hey, there's nothing to see here, right? Or, is it that those meetings were, as Halvorson stated: "The real discussion this time, behind those closed doors, is about changing the way care is delivered. Not about the cost."

Now, that is confusing. According to former White House Budget Director, Peter Orszag, I thought that we were on an unsustainable path, so how could costs not come up in these meetings? So, if we now know that those meetings were about how our healthcare is to be delivered, wouldn't that be cause enough for alarm? Some questions that pop into my mind are: how are those changes going to be implemented, what type of practitioner has direct access to patients, who has the ability to refer to specialists, who orders advanced tests/images, who makes the medical decisions, what protocols are being set/followed and who sets them, and do patients have access to all available treatment options.

Unfortunately, the U.S. had to endure a perfect storm from 2008-10: President Obama, House Speaker Pelosi, and Senate majority leader Reid. These are the three of the most leftist figures in our entire federal government, and they were determined to wield their power without mercy. What we saw during this nightmarish period was a flood of big government bills signed into law. We probably won't even know the extent of the damage that has been caused for another five years. What we must learn is that you cannot elect far-left progressives to positions of great power. What a lesson.

Parties, lavish vacations, ignoring the law, all the czars, socialist agenda. I wonder if that is really what the Democratic Party is all about, what it wants to stand for. When the smoke screen faded and the campaign was over it was apparent that he was very transparent! He has tried to divide this country thru racial, political and the working class. He has hired an Attorney General, Eric Holder who hates white America, America period, and never misses an opportunity to say so, or act as though he does. I hope we can all heal from this administration when he is either impeached or voted out.

It depends upon how you define transparency. It is transparent that the President has failed to lead the Congress to address issues of importance to our Nation, such as addressing the deficit, addressing the massive debt and addressing illegal immigration. It is transparent that his program to address jobs was a lot of money with few jobs produced.

Here's a fun game...Who Said That!!

The rules are simple. I will give you a quote and you have to guess what great American said it. Your three choices are President Barack Obama, former Vice President Dan Quayle or former Alaska Governor Sarah Palin.

Good Luck

1) **"Let me be absolutely clear. Israel is a strong friend of Israel's."**

A. Barack Obama
B. Dan Quayle
C. Sarah Palin

2) **"I've now been in 57 states I think one left to go."**

A. Barack Obama
B. Dan Quayle
C. Sarah Palin

3) **"On this Memorial Day, as our nation honors its unbroken line of fallen heroes and I see many of them in the audience here today."**

A. Barack Obama
B. Dan Quayle
C. Sarah Palin

4) **"What they'll say is, 'Well it costs too much money,' but you know what? It would cost, about. It it it would cost about the same as what we could spend It. Over the course of 10 years it would cost what it would costs us. (nervous laugh) All right. Okay. We're going to. It. It**

would cost us about the same as it would cost for about hold on one second. I can't hear myself. But I'm glad you're fired up, though. I'm glad."

A. Barack Obama
B. Dan Quayle
C. Sarah Palin

5) "The reforms we seek would bring greater competition, choice, savings and inefficiencies to our health care system."

A. Barack Obama
B. Dan Quayle
C. Sarah Palin

6) "I bowled a 129. It's like - it was like the Special Olympics, or something."

A. Barack Obama
B. Dan Quayle
C. Sarah Palin

7) "Of the many responsibilities granted to a President by our Constitution, few are more serious or more consequential than selecting a Supreme Court justice. The members of our highest court are granted life tenure, often serving long after the Presidents who appointed them. And they are charged with the vital task of applying principles put to paper more than 20 centuries ago to some of the most difficult questions of our time."

A. Barack Obama
B. Dan Quayle
C. Sarah Palin

8) "Everybody knows that it makes no sense that you send a kid to the emergency room for a treatable illness like asthma, they end up taking up a hospital bed, it costs, when, if you, they just gave, you gave

them treatment early and they got some treatment, and a, a breathalyzer, or inhalator, not a breathalyzer. I haven't had much sleep in the last 48 hours."

A. Barack Obama
B. Dan Quayle
C. Sarah Palin

9) "It was ... interesting to see that political interaction in Europe is not that different from the United States Senate. There's a lot of I don't know what the term is in Austrian wheeling and dealing."

A. Barack Obama
B. Dan Quayle
C. Sarah Palin

10) "I have made good judgments in the past. I have made good judgments in the future."

A. Barack Obama
B. Dan Quayle
C. Sarah Palin

I'm sorry. This was a trick quiz. All of the correct answers are the same person. Each of these quotes is from President Barack Obama.

And now you know why he brings his teleprompter with him everywhere he goes...even when talking to a 6th grade class!

CHAPTER FIVE:

FACTS ABOUT THE 2008 VOTE RESULTS

The American Citizens Political Action Committee would like to present some facts that will support our contention that the main stream media and the unions are in a conspiracy with the government to control the elections. We need to change this for the 2012 elections. The Republican Party needs to do a better job of educating our younger voters by showing them exactly what the Republicans are going to accomplish and how they are going to go about the process. The Republicans need to show the younger voters how their policies are going to help the younger Americans. It is past the time to start "Taking Back America".

Hispanics voted for Democrats Barack Obama and Joe Biden over Republicans John McCain and Sarah Palin by a margin of more than two-to-one in the 2008 presidential election, 67% versus 31%, according to an analysis by the Pew Hispanic Center of exit polls from Edison Media Research as published by CNN. The Center's analysis also finds that 9% of the electorate was Latino, as indicated by the national exit poll. This is higher, by one percentage point, then the share in the 2004 national exit poll.

Nationally, all Latino demographic sub-groups voted for Obama by heavy margins. According to the national exit poll, 64% of Hispanic males and 68% of Hispanic females supported Obama. Latino youth, just as all youth nationwide, supported Obama over McCain by a lopsided margin – 76% versus 19%.

The American Citizens Political Action Committee believes that there is a direct correlation between the unions and the Democratic voting practices. Then you add the main stream media bashing all the Republican candidates it becomes perfectly clear that the unions are controlling the main stream media as well as the Democratic Party. This does not even take into consideration the millions contributed to the Democratic Party by the unions.

The following are the voting results from the 2008 election. The ten states with the strongest union representation voted Democratic in most instances. The results are as follows:

10. Oregon voted for Obama	978,605 or 57.1%
Oregon voted for McCain	699,673 or 40.8%
Electoral College Votes	7
9. Rhode Island voted for Obama	281,209 or 63.1%
Rhode Island voted for McCain	157,317 or 35.3%
Electoral College Votes	4
8. Michigan voted for Obama	2,867,680 or 57.4%
Michigan voted for McCain	2,044,405 or 40.9%
Electoral College Votes	16
7. Connecticut voted for Obama	994,320 or 60.6%
Connecticut voted for McCain	627,688 or 38.3%
Electoral College Votes	7
6. New Jersey voted for Obama	2,065,051 or 56.8%
New Jersey voted for McCain	1,545,495 or 42.1%
Electoral College Votes	14
5. California voted for Obama	7,441,458 or 60.9%
California voted for McCain	4,554,643 or 37.3%
Electoral College Votes	55
4. Washington voted for Obama	1,547,632 or 57.5%
Washington voted for McCain	1,097,176 or 40.7%
Electoral College Votes	12

3. Hawaii voted for Obama   324,918 or 71.8%
Hawaii voted for McCain   120,309 or 26.6%
Electoral College Votes   4

2. Alaska voted for Obama   122,485 or 36.0%
Alaska voted for McCain   192,631 or 59.8%
Electoral College Votes   3

1. New York voted for Obama   4,363,386 or 62.2%
New York voted for McCain   2,576,360 or 36.7%
Electoral College Votes   29

As you can see by the 2008 voting results the unions have dominated the elections due to their support, financial backing and the main stream media.

The following are the voting results from the 2008 election. The ten states with the weakest union representation voted Democratic in most instances. The results are as follows:

10. Oklahoma voted for Obama   502,294 or 34.4%
Oklahoma voted for McCain   959,745 or 65.6%
Electoral College Votes   7

9. Texas voted for Obama   3,521,164 or 43.8%
Texas voted for McCain   4,467,748 or 55.5%
Electoral College Votes   38

8. Tennessee voted for Obama   1,081,074 or 41.8%
Tennessee voted for McCain   1,470,160 or 56.9%
Electoral College Votes   11

7. South Carolina voted for Obama   850,121 or 44.9%
South Carolina voted for McCain   1,018,756 or 53.8%
Electoral College Votes   9

6. Virginia voted for Obama   1,958,370 or 52.7%
Virginia voted for McCain   1,726,053 or 46.4%
Electoral College Votes   13

5. Mississippi voted for Obama   520,864 or 42.8%
Mississippi voted for McCain   687,266 or 56.4%
Electoral College Votes   6

4. Louisiana voted for Obama   780,981 or 39.9%
Louisiana voted for McCain   1,147,603 or 58.6%
Electoral College Votes   8

3. Arkansas voted for Obama   418,049 or 38.8%
Arkansas voted for McCain   632,672 or 58.8%
Electoral College Votes   6

2. Georgia voted for Obama   1,843,452 or 47.0%
Georgia voted for McCain   2,048,244 or 52.2%
Electoral College Votes   16

1. North Carolina voted for Obama   2,123,390 or 49.9% North
Carolina voted for McCain   2,109,698 or 49.5%
Electoral College Votes   15

When you study these numbers it becomes clear why the unions are starting to worry about the states abolishing the collective bargaining and busting the unions. As the union numbers keep decreasing they are loosing the control over the American voters.

In addition, when you look at the following statistic you will become aware of why President Obama and the Democratic Party are not doing anything to secure the southern border. The Democratic Party needs to find a way to give amnesty to the Hispanics in order to continue to controlling the voter base in states like California and New Mexico. Here is the real number of how they voted in 2008.

The Pew Hispanic Center Analysis of the 2008 election results as reported by CNN showed the following:

67% of the Hispanics voted for Barack Obama and 31% for John McCain.

43% of the Whites voted for Obama and 55% for McCain.

95% of the Blacks voted for Obama and 4% for McCain.

I do not remember ever seeing these statistics being reported by the main stream media. They did not want the American people to realize just how biased and prejudiced that the black Americans are.

Another point that I would like to make is that 95% of the black voters were for Obama. That has to be the most racist voting that has ever occurred in the United States of America. There is no way that 95% of the black population could have realistically believed that they were voting for the most qualified individual for the presidency. Talk about total racism and you have it with the black community. Then there are the Hispanic votes that were 67% in favor of Obama thinking that there would be amnesty coming their way. That is not a good reason to vote for a candidate and the system needs to be changed.

WHAT DO PEOPLE FEAR MOST?

This is really pathetic, but darn funny when you think about it for a minute. Two magazines, *"Country Living"* which has a 95.99% white readership and *"Ebony/Jet"* which has a 99.99% readership did surveys on the following: What do people fear most? The results were very interesting to say the least.

Country Living magazine's top three answers were:
1. Nuclear war/terrorist attack on the United States.
2. Child/spouse dying.
3. Terminal illness.

Ebony/Jet magazine's top three answers:
1. Ghosts.
2. Dogs.
3. Registered mail.

No kidding…And these are the people who put Obama over the top in the 2008 elections. What else would you expect from this category of voters?

Then to go along with all of the above I'll share two of the famous quotes of history; one is great and one is just plain pitiful.

"My friends, we live in the greatest nation in the history of the world. I hope you'll join with me, as we change it." Barack H. Obama

"Life's tough, pilgrim, and it's even tougher if you're stupid." John Wayne

There needs to be legislation passed that will require all voters to meet certain qualifications. First and foremost the voters need to register to vote at least 5 days prior to any federal election. The registration will require proof that they are citizens of the district that they are voting in. This will include proof that the voter actually lives in the district. Then on Election Day the voters will be required to provide identification to prove that they are the actual registered voter prior to voting. Anyone that feels these requirements are unfair is just looking for a way to have illegal voters in the elections.

Professor Joseph Olson of Hamline University School of Law in St. Paul, Minnesota, points out some interesting facts concerning the November 2008 Presidential election:

Number of States won by: Obama: 19 McCain: 29

Square miles of land won by: Obama: 580,000 McCain: 2,427,000
Population of counties won by: Obama: 127 million McCain: 143 million

Murder rate per 100,000 residents in counties won by:
Obama: 13.2 McCain: 2.1

Professor Olson adds: "In aggregate, the map of the territory McCain won was mostly the land owned by the taxpaying citizens of the country.

Obama territory mostly encompassed those citizens living in low income tenements and living off various forms of government welfare."

Olson believes the United States is now somewhere between the "complacency and apathy" phase of Professor Tyler's definition of democracy, with some forty percent of the nation's population already having reached the "Governmental dependency" phase.

If the government grants amnesty and citizenship to twenty million criminal invaders called illegal - and they vote - then we can say goodbye to the United States of America in fewer than five years.

CHAPTER SIX:

RESPECT FOR AMERICA

The American Citizens Political Action Committee would like to share the input that Americans have regarding the respect for our country. First and foremost, the respect that America receives will come from the respect that the Americans and the world have for the President of the United States of America. The entire world is watching as President Obama keeps flip flopping on the issues that affect everyone in the world.

It is a disgrace to the people of the United States that President Obama left Washington for a so called state visit for 5 days while the world was preparing for the next war. What ever happened to the leadership of our Commander in Chief? President Obama ordered air strikes and the deployment of cruise missiles against Libra while on his vacation with family and friends in Brazil and other Latin American countries to promote greater economic ties and improve regional security. Why does Obama haul all of his family along if the trip is supposed to be about world leadership? What a lame excuse for not staying in the White House and acting like the Commander in Chief of our military should. Then there was a pressing problem with the staunchest ally that the United States has. Japan was suffering from the worst earthquake and tsunami of the last 100 years and then the problems with the nuclear reactors caused by the tsunami. These were real problems that needed immediate attention. The vacation to Brazil should have been postponed until the major problems of the world had been addressed. That was a total lack of leadership by President Obama and all Americans are embarrassed by his actions.

"The President does not have the power under the Constitution to unilaterally authorize a military attack in a situation that does not involve stopping an actual or imminent threat to the nation" This quote was from Senator and Presidential Candidate Obama, Dec. 20, 2007. The President sure has done another flip flop on his policies. The President is going to continue to say what ever he feels is going to pacify the main stream media and his liberal followers.

This is a quote from Lt. Col. Oliver North; "The bottom line is that Obama tries to please everyone. "He's done nothing but apologize for America, literally since he's been in office. And now, he's in a position where he has to be the commander-in-chief — and it is just beyond him," "If you try to please everyone, you will end up pleasing no one."

Obama arrives in Brazil, begins Latin America tour

That is the headline of an article posted by the Associated Press on March 19, 2011 from Brasilia, Brazil.

The photo that the Associated Press posted with this article shows the lack of any respect for the country that the Obama clan is visiting. In a foreign country you do not arrive in a halter top dress with your arm pits showing. It is not proper in most foreign countries. I have just taken a few of the paragraphs from the article so that the comments from the American citizens will indicate what the people think about the timing of the trip and where the people think that the President should be working.

By JIM KUHNHENN, Associated Press – March 19, 2011

Brasilia, Brazil – President Barack Obama arrived in Brazil on Saturday for the start of a three country, five day tour of Latin America to promote greater economic ties and improved regional security. The trip came against the backdrop of urgent issues elsewhere in the world, including the possibility of U.S. military action against Libya's Moammar Gadhafi.

Air Force One touched down in the highland capital of Brazil in an early morning mix of sunshine and raindrops with the president, Michelle Obama, and daughters Sasha and Malia aboard. Several hours later the president and Mrs. Obama met Brazil's newly elected President Dilma Rousseff at the presidential palace, the Palacio do Planalto, in an elaborate arrival ceremony featuring color guards and children waving American and Brazilian flags.

In his Saturday radio and Internet address Obama singled out the economic benefits of the trip, noting the rapid growth of Brazil and Chile, the second country on his itinerary. Obama said that the United States exports more than three times as much to Latin America as to China.

The trip risks being overshadowed by some ominous developments in earthquake ravaged Japan, where officials struggled to prevent a meltdown at a damaged nuclear power plant, and in Libya, where a defiant Gadhafi warned international troops Saturday that they would regret intervening. Obama departed Washington just hours after endorsing military action against the strongman's regime, leaving an array of military might at the ready and raising the prospect that he would have to authorize military action from a foreign land. Leaders from the Arab world, the United States and other Western powers were holding emergency talks in Paris on Saturday over possible military action as Gadhafi's troops swarmed into the one time rebel stronghold of Benghazi.

President Obama opted to depart for Brazil on schedule despite those international crises.

But as Obama and Rousseff were poised to meet, a disagreement between their administrations had already changed the dynamic of the trip. The Brazilian leader did not want to have reporters ask the two presidents questions – after the White House had already promised a news conference – so that event was scrapped. It had the potential effect of keeping the press from asking Obama about the Libyan crisis just as it seemed at its most dire time.

Still, Rousseff showed no qualms about distancing Brazil from the United States over Libya. As a nonpermanent member of the United Nations Security Council, Brazil was one of five countries that abstained from the vote Thursday that authorized a no-fly zone over Libyan air space. And she has not entirely abandoned the idea of maintaining a dialogue with Iran.

Here are the comments from average American citizens and what they think about President Obama leaving the United States while the country is facing major problems in the world. The accuracy of the following comments has not been verified. In some cases the comments are extreme but for the most part they are right on. They have not been altered in any way except for spelling and grammar. I hope you enjoy the comments and can get a clearer picture of what is happening in the United States Government.

Now we see what we got with all that Hope and Change. I blame the liberal media for not venting this joke of a President. He should have been disqualified before he showed up in Iowa. The press is still giving him a free pass. Wake up America.

Why can't you find this headline anywhere?

Violent protests and firebombing of the United States Consulate, signs saying "Obama go home" in Rio de Janeiro Friday ahead of President Barack Obama's visit to Brazil. Where has the respect for the President of the United States gone?

Where's the main stream media on this information?

On July 30th, even though Obama is against off shore drilling for our country, he signed an executive order to loan $2 billion of our taxpayer's money to a Brazilian Oil Exploration Company, which is the 8th largest company in the entire world, to drill for oil off the coast of Brazil! The oil that comes from this operation is for the sole purpose and use of China and not the United States! Now here's the real clincher…the Chinese government is under contract to purchase all the oil that this oil field will produce, which is hundreds of millions of barrels of oil. We have absolutely no gain from this transaction whatsoever.

It gets more interesting. Guess who the largest individual stockholder of this Brazilian Oil Company and who would benefit most from this?

It is American Billionaire, George Soros, who was one of Obama's most generous financial supporters during his campaign.

If you are able to connect the dots and follow the money, you are probably as upset as I am.

Not a word of this transaction was broadcast on any of the other news networks! Is this abject insanity or abject arrogance or an equal combination of both? How much more of this are you going to stand for?

President Obama will do anything to destroy the United States. We don't need enemies; our President of the United States is the most dangerous one we have. He supports other countries over the United States and helps their economy, but not ours, except to give entitlements and increase spending – which will kill us.

His attitude has gone from arrogant to disgusting with this country and its citizens. I have come to the conclusion that the man is a complete psychopath with his pathological lying and need to control everyone and everything from the food we eat to what kind of light bulbs we use in our homes. I don't know if America can survive two more years of this madman.

You are completely wrong on Obama supporting drilling because we produce more oil now than we did during the Bush years. Ask yourself how many permits have been issued since Obama has been president. Also go back and look when the permits were issued for all these rigs going now and you will see that some of them that haven't even been online very long were issued back when Clinton was still president. It takes too long because of the government red tape. Fact is, Obama does not support drilling and he is chasing this green city on a hill that doesn't exist yet. I'm sorry but the technology just isn't there. We can't just stop drilling though because special interest groups think it's bad. It's becoming a matter of national security now.

OBAMA STOPS WOUNDED
SOLDIER FROM SPEAKING!

Sent by Retired Vice Admiral Bob Scarborough, of Arlington, VA "I wanted to give you all some disturbing information on our wonderful President. I work with the Catch-A-Dream Foundation, which provides hunting and fishing trips to children with life-threatening illnesses. This past weekend we had our annual banquet/fundraiser event in Starkville. As part of our program, we had scheduled Sgt. 1st Class Greg Stube to come; he's a highly decorated U.S. Army Green Beret and inspirational speaker who was severely injured while deployed overseas and didn't have much of a chance for survival. Greg is stationed at Fort Bragg, North Carolina and received permission from his commanding officer to come speak at our function. Everything was on go until Obama made a policy that NO UNITED STATES SERVICEMAN CAN SPEAK AT ANY FAITH BASED PUBLIC EVENTS ANYMORE. Needless to say, Greg had to cancel his speaking event with us. Didn't you know if anyone else was aware of this new policy? You're just starting to see the Obama Nation. This is just how the Nazis did it in the 1930's – slowly, one step at a time. This should be read and shared with everyone regardless of party affiliation.

I'm sure we are being misled about the purpose of this trip. It's another family vacation and a chance to see how his investment in Petrobas is going.

If this is a state visit, then why take the kids and mother-in-law? I always take my kids and mother-in-law to important business meetings. I have an idea to reduce spending, rent out the oval office, its not being used right now. America sucking up to Brazil makes people wonder just what is being cooked up.

People in power do one thing...Make decisions in the best interest of themselves, their family and their friends. Doesn't matter about what party you're in, or what color you are, it's all the same. Would anyone of us be so different if given the chance?

By the way, why isn't he visiting Columbia – you know the folks who unlike Mexico got a handle on their drug lords? Just like he toured the

Middle East and bowed to them and apologized for whatever, but skipped the only democracy and our only true ally in the Middle East – Israel. He obviously doesn't have a clue.

How do you Americans tolerate such nonsense from your President? Your country better get a leader in office that actually will do something for the people. Mr. Obama has done nothing but set the stage to destroy your infrastructure as a top nation. The world is just waiting for your collapse. Don't let it happen. Wake up and act now.

Obama does his NCAA picks and then leaves for a Latin American holiday? Hope and change that I can believe in. Obama really has his priorities down. Unfortunately his priorities are not for the benefit of the American citizens.

All hail Barack Hussein Obama...the one man who believes that he occupies all three branches of government simultaneously. The man is clearly out of control and with each infraction...and with every usurpation of power...he gets bolder.

Guess who's with President Obama in Brazil? The Chief Executive Officers of George Soros biggest investments: General Electric, Anadarko Petroleum, Westinghouse, International Paper and Albright Stonebridge Investments. The United States main stream media and the English language press in Brazil won't report it. The Portuguese press is. Connecting the dots is getting easier by the day. Wake up America.

Another working vacation on our dime! If this is supposed to be a working vacation why is the entire troop tagging along with the President? Though Obama has not followed through with most of his 2008 campaign promises he does follow through for George Soros doesn't he? While he opposes drilling for our own oil he gives taxpayer's money to Brazil and its "Marxist" president to expand offshore drilling there? Yesterday the CBO announced he has far underestimated (lied about) the costs of his programs in the amount of trillions of dollars it will add to our national debt. Remember in November 2012.

Obama thinks that he is visiting another state of the United States of America. Remember his great comment which the great one stated: "I'VE NOW BEEN IN 57 STATES, I THINK I HAVE ONE LEFT". President Obama is even dumber than the peanut growing Carter.

Obama, the community organizer.

Obama, the State Senator that voted "present" 90% of the time (Why?)

Obama, the most liberal junior Senator of my lifetime.

Obama, the only President ever without a birth certificate.

Obama, elected President because he was black and had a great smile.

Obama, where are the million green jobs you promised?

Obama, the guy with friends like Rev. Wright and Bill Ayers.

Obama, the Socialist/Marxist and Muslim, and that's scary.

Please fellow Americans vote substance not fluff next time.

You're kidding me right? In the middle of when we are faced with high gas, high food, electric prices soaring, Obama goes on vacation? Then he plans another one in a few weeks to Ireland? This is just nuts. Hello, is there anyone out there trying to help Americans? Seems the one that was to build America up is either having a party at the White House, on vacation, playing golf or picking basketball teams. This is a joke. Though, if he had told us all what he was going to do before he was elected; I wonder who would have voted for him?

Another trip amidst the most turmoil our country has seen in over 25 years. We have a President that has resolved himself to Campaign for re-election in 2012, seeking favor among the Latino voters; rather than face the tough decisions at home! What with no less than 6 Muslim countries in turmoil, a natural disaster that has shaken the economic

and social core of one of our most staunch allies, souring domestic unemployment, currency issues that may well weaken the dollar to a historic low with no way out, an impending involvement in yet one more war front (Libya), skyrocketing national debt, unfinished 2011 budget that was due in October 2010; a faulted / over-optimistic 2012 budget proposal understating long term debt by $2.3 trillion; current out-of-control government spending on his agenda; and a nation that is the most divided it has been since the Civil War. Where is Obama? He is on a tour of South America? How nice! Where is the leadership that you voted for from our President? Is this the change (all of the above) you were wanting? And of course, your wonderful liberal-socialist main stream media is still promoting Obama without providing any true facts about the history of this President.

Did the main stream media mention that since it is business why are we paying for him and his family's tour? If this is a business of the United States of America why is the President dragging along his whole family?

Another reason to have an American for President! This foreigner cannot even operate a calculator so he can balance the budget. Yet has time to travel on an already over drawn taxpayer credit card. What a stimulus he'll make on the rest of the world. Most of the world already thinks that Obama is stupid and a vast majority of the Americans do too.

I thought the Obama's were all taking private jets? Michelle big "O" usually insists on private, first class accommodations, including a private jet that she recently took to Hawaii, poor Michelle big "O". It's so hard to be proud to be an American. She is such a phony.

Oh, man, can you hear the media if Bush had done anything like this when he was in office. Bush gave up golf after 9/11 but President Obama is oblivious to everything but what George Soros and the Chicago gods direct him to do. I guess we'll hear raves from the dress police about how gorgeous Michelle looks. She and the older daughter walk like they're stomping over cotton rows.

Michelle cover your arm pits, do you not know how rude that is in some countries to go sleeveless. And while you're at it follow some of your own advice about obesity. Lose quite a few pounds.

It's disgusting enough for Obama to bring his wife and daughters on this "vacation" but his Mother-in-Law and his children's God-mother too? Good grief has these people no shame at all? Why the need to bring his whole family of our dime...Shame, shame on you Mr. President and your mooching family.

Hope grandma and the kid's god-mother also enjoy this lavish vacation at our expense. Most assuredly Obama will keep close watch on his priority business at hand, the NCAA basketball tournament. Looks like Michelle has done the usual sleeveless dress-down to really impress the heads of state. This President takes another vacation every time world turmoil occurs so he doesn't have to do the job the Democrats elected him to do. Or, maybe he is doing their bidding. After all, he creates havoc everywhere he goes and leaves dissent in his wake. Looks like Obama's global jihad continues unabated.

Typical Obama reaction when he doesn't know what to do, he runs away to a foreign country to play golf. Every time there is a crisis, the boy goes on vacation. I will be so glad when 2012 arrives and we will once again have a President that knows how to lead and that would be anybody but this one.

The Democrat/Marxist Party lead by the one term mistake King Obama is going down in flames. The American people are finally waking up. The Democratic Party caters to the lazy, weak, cowardly, ignorant and irresponsible. It preys on the Liberal lemmings that are naïve and politically unsophisticated. It preys on students who have been brain washed by their Liberal teachers and professors. It preys on people who are incapable of managing their own money, or their own life for that matter. Most times these dregs of society seek out a cult to control them. But since the Obama administration, which consists of activists, racists, radicals, militants, terrorists, communists and other unpatriotic and anti-American scum, has come to power, these mindless dregs now have someone and something to worship and be controlled by (they also believe that as an added bonus, they will get a lot of free stuff). Socialism, Marxism, Communism has never worked and never will.

Maybe some of you have not been keeping up with business because you're too busy worrying about loosing your welfare check but Argentina and Brazil are the new and growth places to out source jobs too. They are cheaper than India now and you can bet the President is there to help that along. All you blue collar guys out there. NAFTA sent 50% of factory jobs off shore and to Mexico...brought to you by slick Willie Clinton! Now the white collar jobs are the target to cheaper markets. The Obama pledge during his run "I will stop out sourcing and provide incentives for companies who create jobs here". Did it happen? No! Liar in chief! Go look at the unemployment figures that are slanted by the government but you can add at least 60% to those numbers for the Americans that gave up looking for work.

Thank you Obama for leaving your Country in a time of financial crisis (no budget for our Nation) and during two wars, also during a period where military action may be used in another country. Thank you for spending our tax dollars on this family vacation which a portion came out of my pocket. And last but not least, thank you for leading America into the biggest mess we have ever been in during the history of our nation. You have shown your inability to lead, govern, manage and care about the people who live in these great United States of America.

Obama spends more time on vacation than any other president we have had and has time to play golf 3 or 4 times a week. Obama gets in the office by 9 A.M. and is out by 2 P. M., hey it must be nice! No wonder he now wants us to believe that he is going from left to center and will make an effort to get some work done with the new Congress, his overspending will have us going broke sooner than we think, and no permits for drilling in the gulf, but the Petrobras Brazilian projects get the go ahead, with our own money financing the deal, of course George Soros invested in Petrobras and you know how friendly the President is with his puppet master the big SOROS OPEN SOCIETY COMMIE.

Going on another apology tour in the time of Japan's problems, Libya's problems and he just came back from vacation...I'll tell you if Bush would have done 1/10th of what this bum does the main stream media would have torn him apart. I hope he's enjoying flying everywhere in Air Force One sucking up the taxpayer's money along with his over weight wife. This could be over in 2012 if true Americans get out and vote this community organizer out.

Here we go again. They aren't happy unless they are on a plane going somewhere they don't have to be. He has taken more trips than any other President ever. It would be really nice if the American people could take trips when we get a notice to or it gets too hard to handle at home. He loves to spend our money and it doesn't matter if the American people can buy food or not, he just has to go to some place we can't even think about going to just get us through these next two years and get him the hell out of our faces.

Just as one would expect from President Obama with catastrophic issues going on in Japan, the Middle East, and Obama heads for Brazil for a vacation on the taxpayer's calling it searching for jobs. Why isn't Obama searching for the jobs in the U.S., you know, the ones his billions of bail-out tax dollars were going to create? Here is another question. If this is his priority, is he that stupid? Or, is it true that he is facing reality and that he will definitely not be around in 2012, so he is soaking up all of the vacation trips before the end of his dismal stint in office? Will he do the right thing, for a change, and resign at the conclusion of his pseudo year of miscalculations, or will he get impeached first for his wretched leadership? Maybe the answer will be coming soon.

1. SPEND, SPEND AND SPEND! That's all Obama knows, after all it's not his money, now is it? Obama goes on another vacation costing taxpayers even more of their hard earned money. He did postpone 1 vacation though to pass his Obamacare to spend even more of your money. This dude just does not get the problem with spending and more spending.

2. Yesterday morning on CNN a reporter says fuel and food prices are up 84% since Obama took office! Old Ben, Obama and Tiny Tim say that there is no inflation? What? I guess they don't shop at the grocery store or fuel their cars/airplanes out of their own pockets, do they? We the taxpayer foot the bill and they have "PEOPLE" who wait on

them hand and foot to do that for them, you guessed it, paid for by the taxpayer. Only 19% of a barrel of crude goes to fuel our cars, close to 70% goes to fuel airplanes and ships on the ocean, and Obama and his Czars and all their entourage have used more than anybody over the last 2 years. Besides, just one day of air-traffic around the world does more to contribute to global warming than all gas fueled vehicles would contribute running 24/7 and 365 for a whole year.

3. Obama lies again! First it was no budget for last year and now it's a funny math budget for next year. How can you miss an extra trillion per year in spending? That is an extra $10 trillion over the next 10 year period. I thought Pelosi was delusional about having to pass Obamacare to see what was in it and Prince Harry saying Social Security was good for another 20 years after is has been robbed and left with loans to the Treasury for us taxpayers to pay and was also crazy for wanting taxpayers to pay for his "Cowboy Poetry Reading Festival" at "Brokeback Mountain" in North Nevada. Obama is even crazier for wanting to raise the deficit by $10 trillion; this man is crazier than Mad Dog Gadhafi. We are "BROKE" Obama. 50% of peeps in the United States pay no tax and 43% of the people in America are now living off the government while small businesses in America pay 25% of the taxes. But no this is not even enough, they are now protesting in the streets for the government to pay for their gas bills, electric bills, rent, food, provide them with a car, healthcare, provide them with a union government job for life with lavish pensions paid for by the taxpayers, etc., saying that all these things are a God given right. That is pure communism and has failed every time in history. If Obama was any kind of leader and did not dilly, dally, this no-fly zone could have been done 31 days ago when Obama first said Gadhafi must go and would have saved much destruction and many, many lives. Obama is the most inept leader of the free world we have ever had and that includes Carter. Obama is more worried about getting re-elected, basketball brackets, golfing and taking vacations on the taxpayers dime, spending increasing the debt, etc.; than jobs, nuclear meltdown, Mid East blowup, gas prices, inflation, national debt, food prices skyrocketing, etc. he is off to Rio on a vacation but he postponed his vacation before to pass Obamacare, but not this time as the world burns. CNN reports this morning that food and gas prices have increased more since Obama took office, then it did under 4 years

of Carter. Carter had to raise interest rates to 21% to stop inflation under his administration spending and printing of money. Soon we will see not only higher gas prices and interest rates, but long lines and rationing at the pump, just like under Carter. Carter is smiling through all of this because now the American people will not be saying that he was the worst president in the history of the United States. Thank you very much President Obama.

4. Fox news poll shows 65% do not want the United States involved in another war in Libya. France, Britain and Europe get oil from Libya, we do not. Let them fight this one! Well, you are too late the United States is already in the conflict in Libya. Hopefully, it will be a short one. Obama came on the news on March 21, 2011 that the United States will be turning over the command of the operations within a few days. Let's see just how much of a lie this turns out to be.

Obama should be in Japan, showing support for our ravaged friends. Not on vacation with his family. What an insult to the Japanese people. I am embarrassed by this idiot and hope that the Japanese people don't think we are all inconsiderate self absorbed liberals like our President. Meanwhile in Libya rebel fighters fight to the death because of Obama's irresponsible remarks made 2 weeks ago. "Gadhafi must be removed from power" and then he fails to do anything about it. Obama is the biggest idiot ever elected President of the United States.

We are concerned with the direction that the economy, unemployment, spending, immigration and lack of transparency with the current administration. It is time that the voting citizens voice their opinions and vote for representation that will vote for programs that are for "We the People, By the People and For the People".

CHAPTER SEVEN:

CREATING JOBS IN AMERICA

The American Citizens Political Action Committee believes that the most important problem facing the United States of America is the creation of new jobs for Americans. The people have watched since President Clinton and the Democrats passed the North Atlantic Free Trade Agreement (NAFTA) in January 1994. During the last few years the United States has seen the number of jobs being sent to foreign countries increase every year. Now, with the unemployment reported by the government in the 9.4% range we are wondering why there are not any jobs available in the United States. The federal government has been reporting the unemployment rate at 9.4% while every unemployed American knows that the real rate of unemployment in closer to 18% or 20%. The government conveniently does not factor in all the workers that have had to take a meaningless part time job to buy groceries.

What can America do that will create more meaningful jobs for our people? There are many different things that will all contribute to the number of employed Americans. We are going to try and break down the different items that will help Americans recover and find jobs. It is past the time to start "Taking Back America".

We will start with the easiest project that will create thousands of jobs in the shortest time frame. The United States needs to complete building the remaining 1300 miles of border fence between the United States and Mexico. This project will create jobs that will require a variety of different skills that the employees will be able to utilize when the project is completed. The United States could build the "Americas Highway" and rest stations along the border fence to make it practical to monitor and enforce our laws concerning the illegal entry into the United States. This will create jobs in the engineering field to design the fence. This fence will be designed for construction in sections and all of the sections will be exactly the same. This will make the construction much easier and the fence will look uniform for the entire distance. Then there will be the actual construction of the fence which will create thousands of jobs since it can be completed in sections instead of one long project. This will put many different crews on the project. This could also create a competition between the crews with prize money to the crew that completed their section in the shortest time and under budget. This will create jobs in the manufacturing of the components of the fence. It will create jobs in the transportation of the materials to the job sites. It will create jobs to support the crews that are doing the construction including lodging, meals, laundry services, convenience stores and many others. The building of the "Americas Highway" will require many different crews since it too can be completed in sections. This will require the manufacture of materials, transportation of materials, large equipment, earth moving equipment, surveyors and basically the same type of support personnel and services that are required to complete the border fence. Then we could have the rest stations placed about 50 miles apart so that the border patrol would have access to everything that a convenience store provides on a daily basis. These rest stations would also be used as tributes to the Presidents of the United States. Each rest area would contain information about one of the Presidents and would contain a statue of the President that was featured at the rest station. The United States is on the 44th President that would enable the 'America Highway" to honor all of the prior Presidents of the United States.

Going back into history we can see that these kinds of projects can be very successful. When President Hoover started the Hoover Dam Project on the Arizona and Nevada border it provided thousands of jobs for several years. The end result was that the city of Las Vegas was born and the dam provides electricity for millions of Americans. It was an engineering project that no one in their right mind would have tackled except that the United States needed the jobs.

Then there was the waste land known as South Dakota that did not have one thing to draw people to their state so an enterprising individual decided to carve Mount Rushmore into the side of the mountain. Now, South Dakota is a great tourist attraction and the state has been doing very well since.

There is no reason that this project to create "Americas Highway" will not end in having the same results since it will be an attraction that will honor every President that has been in office in the history of the United States. Americans would be glad to have the opportunity to work on the project and it will create jobs immediately.

The rules for the projects would be very simple. First, no one will be hired to work on the projects unless they are able to prove that they are an American citizen. That also means that green cards will not be allowed on the projects. Second, the unemployed will be offered the opportunity to work on the projects before other employees are hired. Third, if an unemployed refuses to work on the projects, they will lose their unemployment benefits unless they are physically unable to work. Fourth, the contractors that are hired for the projects will not be union companies. These are great projects to start "Taking Back America".

The problem that the American citizens are facing is that the government does not want the border secured. When we elect representatives that are concerned about America we will be able to move forward on this type of projects. Vote for representatives that are going to support securing the border. We can not afford any more illegals entering the United States.

The projects of completing the border fence and "Americas Highway" will do more for America than our politicians are willing to admit. All the politicians can see is the cost of the fence, "Americas Highway" and the rest stations. The politicians are not willing to look at the facts concerning the number of illegals that are entering into the United States every year and what these illegals are costing the local, state and federal governments.

The Conservative estimates of the annual costs of illegals in the United States of America are a staggering $350 to $400 billion per

year. It seems like a good investment to spend what ever it costs to stop this drain on the economy of the United States. Has anyone seen anything reported by the main stream media concerning the number of terrorists that have entered the United States through our unprotected southern borders?

I would love to be the first American to travel the length of the new "Americas Highway" and visit all of the 45 rest stations that are created. I am hoping that the 45th President the American people elect will support the securing of the southern border. It would be a wonderful way to see what the Presidents have contributed to the history of the greatest country on earth. We need to get started on these projects immediately.

Jobs can be created in the United States immediately for thousands of senior citizens and the youth of America. We can mandate that all employers are required to E-verify to make sure that all of their employees are citizens of the United States. When the illegals are eliminated from the fast food and restaurant jobs it will create several million jobs for the Americans. This should be a solution so simple that even a cave man can understand. There was the case of the Chipotle restaurants in Minnesota a few weeks ago. There were approximately 500 illegals working in these restaurants in Minnesota alone. When the illegals were fired all they would say is that they will go down the street and get a job at another restaurant. They all have their illegal identification documents and the other companies will hire them since they have experience.

The United States needs to start deporting all the illegals that are in the United States as they are fired from the jobs. Instead these individuals seem to just continue to live in America and enjoy the benefits of our wonderful country. If each of these employees is earning $1,000 per month in pay, they are likely to be earning $2,000 per month in tips if they are experienced. That means that most of these employees are not going to be declaring the tips and paying taxes on the money they earn.

These are estimates about 1.5 million illegals that are working in the fast food and restaurant operations. Each of these is taking a job from an American that would be able to do the same job. The feeling by the supporters of the illegals is that they only do the jobs that Americans will not do. That is an absolute propaganda play by the main stream media and the ACLU. Americans have done every type of work imaginable and will continue to do what ever it takes to put food on their table. We need to stop the dependency upon the government entitlement programs. By the way, Social Security for our senior citizens is not an entitlement program. Most Americans have worked the majority of their life and paid into the Social Security fund.

Another solution to the jobs market would be to eliminate all double dipping by the employees at all levels of the government. When an employee holds down a job after retiring from a government agency or the military of the United States and then becomes an employee of the government it takes away from the people that need the jobs. When the double dipping employees are fired they should not be eligible to receive unemployment. If these employees wanted to keep on working they should have remained on the previous job and not taken the retirement benefits. The double dipping is causing thousands of highly skilled Americans from becoming employed. Since the fired double dipping employees are not eligible for unemployment it will reduce the unemployment rate in the United States. These are permanent jobs for the benefit of all Americans.

Other projects that will create jobs in a short period of time will be in the development of the natural resources of the United States. The exploration for oil and gas reserves will create thousands of jobs in the oil industry. In addition, there will be jobs in the support industries as well. Just think about building a refinery in Alaska where the Alaska Wildlife Refuge Area (ANWR) is located. It would create permanent jobs and instead of using a pipeline to ship crude they could refine it and ship the finished products. This will provide jobs in the transportation industry, housing industry, service industry, supply industry and many more. This program will provide a permanent job solution that will benefit all the citizens of the United States. There are many other side benefits from the exploration of the ANWR in addition to the jobs that are created. The oil that is produced from this project will reduce the amount of crude oil that is imported from other countries. The net effect of reducing the amount of crude that is imported is that it also reduces the deficit spending that the United States is incurring every year. Now that the United States is also in a limited war with Libya there is going to be more pressure on the drilling for natural resources on land within the United States. When you can create thousands of jobs and reduce our balance of payments it sure seems like a great way to start "Taking Back America".

Then we can take the same approach to the exploration for natural gas and shale oil reserves in the Williston Bay Area of the United States. These exploration projects will create thousands of jobs in the Rocky Mountain Region of the United States. We need to develop our own resources since the United States is virtually broke. We can not afford not developing these resources.

Just think about building a natural gas processing facility and refinery in the Williston Bay Region. It would create permanent jobs and instead of using a pipeline to ship the shale and gas they could refine it and ship the finished products. This will provide the same type of jobs that developing the ANWR is going to produce. The products that are produced from these projects will reduce the amount of crude oil that is imported from other countries. The net effect of reducing the amount of crude that is imported is that is also reduces the deficit spending that the United States is incurring every year.

Then there is the most critical area of job creation. That would be to stop the flow of illegals into the United States and deport approximately 12 million that are taking jobs from the American people. Only about 2% of the illegals are working in agriculture in contrast to what the main stream media would like the Americans to believe. When we deport the illegals our job solution in the United States is going to improve dramatically. One of the benefits of deporting the 12 million illegals would be that they would not be able to send $25 to $40 billion in cash to Mexico every year. That would keep the money in the United States to stimulate our economy. About the only complaint would come from Wal-Mart since the majority of their customers are low income families from Mexico.

The situation of the illegals holding down 12 million jobs is not only hurting the unemployment numbers it is killing the United States economy as well. Take the 12 million illegals making an average wage of $20,000 per year. That means that $240 billion is taken away from the United States citizens and provided to the illegals. This is about as stupid as the politicians can become. The politicians need to understand that they were elected by the people to do a job for the people of the United States of

America. Stop the bleeding heart attitude for the illegals and start thinking about the American citizens. When the $240 billion is earned by the American taxpayers it is going to reduce the annual deficit of the United States. The revenue to the government from just the collection of Social Security and Medicare from these employees amounts to about 15.4% of the wages or $36.96 billion. Since a very large number of the illegals are working under the table, the United States government is not going to be able to receive those funds. It only makes sense to remove the illegals and employ the citizens of the United States.

What is the ulterior motive of the President and Democrats in not wanting to deport the illegals? Could it be that 67% of the Hispanics voted Democratic in 2008 and they want to maintain their voting base? Then I read an article a few days ago that there are 4 states that allow drivers licenses to be issued to illegals. How are the voting booths going to determine if they are illegal or not?

We have not touched upon the need to create incentives for the small businesses to create more jobs. They have historically been the reason that unemployment was low. The government needs to create some programs that will benefit the small business owners to justify the hiring of new employees. The prime reason that small businesses do not expand is that they can not afford the added costs involved with employees. The added cost of each employee to a small business is approximately 12% to 14% of the amount of wages that are paid to the employee. To keep it simple, if you pay an employee $10,000 the business has an added expense of $1,200 to $1,400 per employee. The small businesses will increase the number of employees when the government gives them a credit for the amount in excess of the actual wages for a period of two years. This will let the employee become more proficient and produce the extra products for the business to offset the added costs.

The government also needs to implement a payroll tax tariff on the large companies that are outsourcing jobs to foreign countries. This tariff would make the amount of wages paid to employees in the United States about the same as the wages that they are paying in the foreign countries. The tax would be paid directly to the Treasury of the United States on a monthly basis just like withholding on American employees. The funds generated by this tariff could be used to supplement the unemployment funds. The tariff would be calculated on the difference between the foreign wages and the wage scale in the United States. If the job pays $10.00 per hour in the United States and $4.00 in the foreign country then the tax would be $6.00 per hour or 150% of the foreign wages paid. Big business is going to start whining and you will hear it all across the country. That is just too bad and I don't think that the unemployed are going to do anything but laugh at the big businesses that are outsourcing their jobs.

The banks and mortgage firms could be required to hire a few thousand more employees so that they can start to straighten out the loan document mess that they have created.

I am sure that I have not covered all the possibilities for the creation of jobs in the United States. This is just a few of the possibilities that are available to create more jobs in the United States. To make these suggestions work it is going to take the President and Congress to acquire some courage. They have been ignoring the problem for way too many years. The representatives need to start thinking about solving the jobs problem now. It has been going on for way too long and it is time to start "Taking Back America".

CHAPTER EIGHT:

THE CORPORATE INCOME TAX FAILURE

The American Citizens Political Action Committee is going to present one of the major problems that have contributed to the annual deficit of the United States. The corporate income tax structure of the United States is corrupt and needs to be corrected. Major corporations are showing earnings of billions of dollars on their annual reports and not paying one penny in income taxes. The problems are caused by tax loop holes and they need to be closed.

One of the worst tax evasion practices of the corporations is the reporting of their income that is earned from operations in foreign countries. American corporations need to start paying their share of the income taxes so that the average middle class American can get a little tax relief.

According to the New York Stock Exchange market quotes reported at the close on March 26, 2011 General Electric reported earnings of $11.63 billion for the last fiscal year. The reporting system also reported that there were 10.61 billon shares outstanding and the projected earnings for the year are going to be $1.17 per share or $17.8 billion. Jeffrey R. Immelt the Chief Executive Officer made $7.69 million in 2010. I wonder how much income tax he paid. There were four other senior executives at General Electric that received over $4.5 million in 2010. These types of practices are an insult to the American taxpayer. Every American should forget about purchasing any products or services that are offered by General Electric. That would include watching NBC and CNBC. These are owned by General Electric.

I believe that President Obama appointed Jeffrey R. Immelt as the Job's Czar. This just shows another lame brain appointment made by Obama. Immelt has transferred over 23,000 American jobs overseas. It makes Americans wonder just how many other corporations have endorsed Immelt's policy of outsourcing jobs overseas. Wake up America and get our jobs back into the United States.

The activities of the large corporations such as General Electric just add fuel to the conspiracy theory that I have maintained. The programs that are presented by the NBC and their affiliates are so biased and geared to support Obama and the Democratic Party. One of the reasons is that they are promoting programs that will benefit them more than the American citizens. It is past time to start "Taking Back America".

The following article was reported on March 25, 2011 and after looking at the financials reported by General Electric on the New York Stock Exchange it makes one wonder where they received the figures.

G.E. paid no taxes on $5.1 billion in profits

By Brett Michael Dykes – Friday March 25, 2011 - 11:24 am ET

As Washington worries about the United States' growing deficit problem, there's mounting evidence the government is failing to collect taxes from wealthy individuals and corporations. A piece in today's New York Times by David Kocieniewski outlines how G.E. skirted paying any taxes on $5.1 billion in profits in 2010–in addition to claiming a $3.2 billion tax credit.

The main reason G.E. is so adept at avoiding paying taxes, Kocieniewski writes, is because it's compiled an all-star team of in-house tax professionals plucked from the Internal Revenue Service, the Treasury Department, and "virtually all the tax-writing committees in Congress."

G.E - whose slogan is "Imagination at Work"– has in-house, Kocieniewski writes, what is considered by many to be the best tax law firm in the world.

Their secret to success is a familiar one, though G.E. appears to have perfected it: "fierce lobbying for tax breaks and innovative accounting that enables it to concentrate its profits offshore."

In a regulatory filing just a week before the Japanese disaster put a spotlight on the company's nuclear reactor business, G.E. reported that its tax burden was 7.4 percent of its American profits, about a third of the average reported by other American multinationals. Even those figures are overstated, because they include taxes that will be paid only if the company brings its overseas profits back to the United States. With those profits still offshore, G.E. is effectively getting money back.

Such strategies, as well as changes in tax laws that encouraged some businesses and professionals to file as individuals, have pushed down the corporate share of the nation's tax receipts — from 30 percent of all federal revenue in the mid-1950s to 6.6 percent in 2009.

In an interesting twist, President Obama recently asked Jeffrey Immelt to be his chief outside economic adviser, and the company recently came under fire for being the manufacturer of the faulty reactors that sparked Japan's nuclear crisis in the wake of the devastating earthquake and tsunami.

Here are the comments from average American citizens and what they think about the current corporate income tax structure. In some cases the comments are extreme but for the most part they are right on. They have not been altered in any way except for spelling and grammar. I hope you enjoy the comments and can get a clearer picture of what is happening with the President of the United States of America.

The IRS could eliminate half of the audits they do, while focusing on one company like GE, and still get more money in assessments. But they won't do that, because they are scared of GE, and are not smart enough to figure out how GE works. Instead, they will continue to audit small businesses and individuals, and scaring people into paying small fines and fees.

In the United States we have a anti populous corporate bureaucracy in which the government is run by multinational corporations (such as GE) by buying Congresses and Presidencies with millions in campaign contributions (bribes), that are an extremely small portion of the billions of dollars in profits these multinational corporations reap from their efforts at bribery.

It is anti populous in that the tax burden is shifted from the multinational corporations and their owners, the rich, to the middle class and the poor, or us working people. Besides free pass tax laws, corporate profits are enhanced in other ways, such anti-citizen efforts by your political representatives and trade agreements that shipped your jobs elsewhere. Deregulation efforts allow corporations to harm citizens and so called "tort reform" that protects corporations from being sued when they do harm citizens. Collusion between the military the corporations and politicians bring on wars so that your tax dollars can be wasted needlessly by blowing things up (including your tax dollars) overseas.

The enemy of the people of the citizens of the U.S.A. is the current form of government under corporate control. Both Democrats and Republican collude in this travesty.

More proof that we need government regulations on these companies that want to be in the U.S.A., but not pay taxes. They need to choose; either pay fair taxes or leave the country and not is allowed to sell anything here. If I made $5 billion, I doubt I would be allowed to keep all of it and not pay any tax; absurd!

Both parties are just two factions of one larger Corporate Party, which is dominated and controlled by the corporate interests that donate heavily to both. That is why nothing really changes no matter which party is in power. The differences between the two parties amount to just a handful of social issues which will never be resolved anyway because they are based on belief systems. The ruling class in the U.S. remains firmly in power no matter which party is elected. They only bother to hold the elections to provide the illusion that there is a democracy left. The real power happens behind the scenes in Washington D.C., the statehouses and local government buildings. The elections are only a false front designed to give you the illusion that you somehow have power and are participating in the decision-making process, when in reality you have no part in it.

Political cronyism, nothing more...blame the Republicans AND the Democrats. They have been bought and paid for by these corporations and superrich, the lobbyists see to that. Offering up sex, money, and power the elected representatives sell their vote, sell WE THE PEOPLE out. The government that is supposed to represent you and me no longer does... And who's to blame? We are, we have let this happen, we have not held up our end by keeping government honest and working for us. Most are too wrapped up in their own lives and phones to see what is happening around them. It is time to wake up and educate you, and fight back...before we become slaves to these elite powerbrokers.

Americans need to vote for the politicians that are willing to consider reforming the tax code. I don't care if it's Republicans or Democrats. I don't care if it's the flat tax or the fair tax or cutting out all the loop holes in our existing code. But we, the voters, are the only ones that can do it. The same should be said about term limits! This is brought to you by the company that lobbied government (state & fed) to make citizens replace light bulbs in their homes with GE's expensive mercury filled crappy light bulbs in the name of "Green" quite a lucrative money maker for GE - losing proposition for America - then they can't even pay taxes. Wake up America - It's later than you think!

By not paying taxes, the vampire corporations are increasing the incomes to the top 1%, and impoverishing the rest of us by making us the sole bearers of tax burden.

But believe it or not, there is something that ordinary citizens can do: tax the corporations yourselves. If every citizen withheld from spending $1 a day for each member of his household, this would amount to $120 billion a year. Withholding $8 per day saves $1 trillion a year. This will hurt them the same way they hurt us.

Use the saved money to support food coops or neighborhood businesses. Remove your money from the banks and put it into member-owned credit unions. Become part of the underground economy - learn a craft or trade, and sell it informally to your friends and neighbors. Grow your own food, bake your own bread, and teach your children to do it. Give up your cable access; it's a wasteland anyway. And stay away from the shopping malls; even the most hardened shoppers know deep down that consumerism is a dead end. Develop some kind of spiritual life instead - you know it will make you feel better.

Multiply the GE fact by the number of major corporations in this country doing the same thing and then recognize why the country is "Broke" The union busting going on right now is empowering these companies even more. We must persevere and stand up for ourselves. The first thing we can do is to not buy their stuff. If we don't buy what they make they lose power. Research the companies whose products you buy and if the company record is one of bad deeds that hurt us. The biggest thing we can do is build businesses that don't poison the earth while providing jobs that address our need to sustain human beings on planet earth. We must displace old energy technology. Wind and solar power and an electric car in every garage for the around town. Eventually batteries for these cars will deliver 500 miles on a 5 minute charge and be fully recyclable. We have to get going building the world we want so were not stuck with the only one they want to make us think is available. It's on us to build the world we want and neuter these self serving entities. If we build to a purpose rather than for profit our end results will demonstrate that fact. It's up to us.

It's not just tax credits that get them off the hook. I suspect that they have enough "offshore" entities and subsidiary corporations that this alone qualifies them for paying no tax. Most, if not all the biggies do this. It's actually encouraged by the US GOV so don't fall for the rhetoric coming out of D.C.

By the way, it's all perfectly legal. This is also a major reason for jobs being shipped overseas. It's just flat out cheaper and it increases the bottom line which is: making their shareholders billionaires instead of just paltry millionaires. It all comes down to one word. GREED!

And we wonder why this country is such a mess? Unlike greedy companies and the wealthy lawmakers, WE the people are double, triple, and quadruple taxed on EVERYTHING - first on the pittance we earn, then our property, then our toothpaste and toilet paper, then on gasoline, then on propane/natural gas, then on electricity, then on fast food, then on dry cleaning, cell phone usage... and it goes on and on...TAX TAX TAX all of the working poor, but corporations get handed a free pass. How is that even remotely AMERICAN? It's NOT what our founding fathers envisioned - it's what they wanted us to be free of!! I can't even stand to read these articles anymore. It's become a giant hopeless pit of corruption in this country and there's not a damn thing anyone can do about it.

I remember when the economy was taking a dive; CNBC analysts were saying GE shares were not only safe but a good bet. Result was they plunged and everyone who invested in them lost their savings. Then I read that GE owns the NBC network! It is time to wake up and see who is feeding you news, who is feeding you candidates, and who is stealing the sovereignty of the United States away from the citizens.

Trickle down economics was and still is a failure. The proof of this is that there were 7% more millionaires created last year than the year before. That further bolsters the belief that the rich continue to get richer and the poor get taxed. Contrary to the most well meaning politician's intents, there is no program that they can come up with that will actually be of help to lower income families without the rich finding a way to skim the cream off the top and directing it to their own pockets.

If you reference the original article, no one has really done anything since Reagan for these tax loopholes.

http://www.nytimes.com/2011/03/25/business/economy/25tax. html?hp=&pagewanted=all

President Reagan supported a change that closed loopholes and required G.E. to pay a far higher effective rate, up to 32.5 percent.

That pendulum began to swing back in the late 1990s. G.E. and other financial services firms won a change in tax law that would allow multinationals to avoid taxes on some kinds of banking and insurance income.
"By the time the measure — the American Jobs Creation Act — was signed into law by President George W. Bush in 2004, it contained more than $13 billion a year in tax breaks for corporations, many very beneficial to G.E."

"Since 2002, the company has eliminated a fifth of its work force in the United States while increasing overseas employment. In that time, GE's accumulated offshore profits have risen to $92 billion from $15 billion."

GE and all other corporations pass costs on to consumers whether there are any costs involved or not. Your health insurance goes up by double digits every year, and Republicans only want to blame health care reform for the increase. These corporations should have all stocks and bank accounts frozen until the government collects a fair tax. Any one that squawks about it goes directly to jail and forfeits all assets.

SOLVING THE FEDERAL DEFICIT

The United States can change the pattern of deficits every year by altering the corporate income tax structure of the country. I have used the closing reports on March 26, 2011 by the New York Stock Exchange to show the amount of income taxes the corporations would have to pay if the policy of taxing the income reported by the corporations to the Security and Exchange Commission in their annual reports. If it is the proper amount of income to entice the shareholders to purchase the shares then it should be equally as proper to have the taxes collected on that stated income. For our chart we have only selected corporations that have reported in excess of $1 billion in their latest fiscal year earnings reports. The payment of these income taxes is not going to change the amount of money that these corporations are earning for their annual reports. Taxes come from retained earnings and are not an operating expense to the corporation.

Corporation:	Reported Income
General Electric Co. (GE)	$11,630,000,000
Boeing Co. (BA)	3,310,000,000
General Motors (GM)	6,170,000,000
American Int'l Group (AIG)	1,580,000,000
Dominion Res., Inc. (D)	2,810,000,000
Apple, Inc. (AAPL)	14,010,000,000
Amazon Com., Inc. (AMZN)	1,150,000,000
A. T. & T. (T)	19,860,000,000
Apache Corp. (APA)	3,030,000,000
Bristol Myers (BMY)	3,090,000,000
Baxter Int'l, Inc. (BAX)	1,420,000,000
Citi Group, Inc. (C)	10,510,000,000
Chevron Corp. (CVX)	19,020,000,000

Comcast Corp. (CMCSA)	3,640,000,000
Cisco Systems, Inc. (CSCO)	7,770,000,000
DirectTV (DTV)	2,200,000,000
Deutsche Bank (DB)	2,310,000,000
Dell, Inc. (DELL)	2,640,000,000
Dow Chemical (DOW)	2,310,000,000
DuPont (DD)	3,030,000,000
E-Bay, Inc. (EBAY)	1,800,000,000
Exxon Mobile (XOM)	30,460,000,000
Google, Inc. (GOOG)	8,500,000,000
Goldman Sachs (GS)	8,350,000,000
Halliburton (HAL)	1,840,000,000
Hewlett Packard (HPQ)	8,760,000,000
Honeywell (HON)	2,020,000,000
Home Depot (HD)	3,340,000,000
Intel Corp. (INTC)	11,460,000,000
Int'l Bus Mach (IBM)	14,830,000,000
Johnson & Johnson (JNJ)	13,330,000,000
J. P. Morgan Chase (JPM)	16,410,000,000
Kellogg Co. (K)	1,250,000,000
Kimberly Clark (KMB)	1,840,000,000
Loews Corp. (L)	1,290,000,000
Eli Lily & Co. (LLY)	5,070,000,000
Morgan Stanley (MG)	3,840,000,000
Microsoft Corp. (MSFT)	18,760,000,000
Marathon Oil (MRO)	2,570,000,000
Oracle Corp. (ORCL)	6,140,000,000
Pfizer, Inc. (PFE)	8,260,000,000
Pepsico, Inc. (PEP)	6,320,000,000
Phillip Morris (PM)	7,230,000,000
Sysco Corp. (SYY)	1,118,000,000
Time Warner (TWX)	3,588,000,000
Texas Instruments (TXN)	3,180,000,000
United Parcel (UPS)	3,490,000,000
Visa, Inc. (V)	2,970,000,000`
Yahoo, Inc. (YHOO)	1,230,000,000
The Total Reported Earnings	$325,686,000,000

The taxes that these corporations should be paying are approximately $113.99 billion at a 35% income tax rate. Of course we already know that General Electric did not pay any income tax. This is just a few of the corporations that have reported incomes in excess of $1 billion on their annual reports. I am sure that that there are many more but you can get the idea of what we are looking at. I do not have any way of knowing for sure the amount these corporations actually paid in income taxes. I would be willing to bet everything that I will ever own that they did not pay any where near the amounts I have shown. Another area that needs to be investigated is the taxes that foreign corporations are paying to the United States. It is past time for the corporations to start paying their fair share and help return our country to prosperity. Not only are the corporations not paying the taxes they have continued to the problems that the United States is facing because of the policy to outsource jobs from America. It is past time for the American people to start "Taking Back America".

The problem that the American citizens face is where are we going to find the politicians with enough courage to take on the established policies and look out for the people who are paying the majority of the taxes? We need to elect politicians that will stand up for the people and start to think about balancing the annual budget and reducing the federal deficit.

CHAPTER NINE:

THE PRESIDENTIAL EMBARRASSMENT

President Obama has become the laughing stock of the entire world with his lack of leadership. Obama is the Commander in Chief of the United States military and chooses to place our troops in harms way without any consultation or approval from the Congress of the United States.

Obama indicates that the United States is not at war. I find it hard to believe that we have flown over 113 of the 175 shorty missions over Libya and have launched over 150 missiles against their installations and that is not an act of war. These operations were to make their air and ground troops ineffective against the rebels. Not to mention the attack on Quadahfi's government compound.

Obama is stating that this is just to make sure that Qadahfi's supporters are not killing innocent people. Does Obama really think that all these missiles and air attacks are not going to kill anyone?

President Obama has statet that he wants to protect the citizens of Libya from the attacks of Qadahfi. If that is really the case then why are the troops bombing everywhere in Libya. How about bombing where Qadahfi is holed up and just get rid of him once and for all. Without Qadahfi, the loyal troops will not have their leader and peace can be accomplished. Where is the President's courage? Bomb Qadahfi's hideouts and get this war over with.

Obama is trying to make sure other countries are taking the role of leadership. No wonder, Obama does not have any idea what military leadership consists of. After declaring the war Obama took off on a vacation to Brazil and other countries. Obama states that he is in constant communications with the military leaders of the United States while he is away.

White House officials told Democratic and Republican congressional aides Tuesday, March 22, 2011 that the United States is not at war with Libya and, without laying out a timeline, that the President hopes to hand over control of coalition military operations in the next few days.

We're just bombing them because there was nothing else to do other than Samba and look in the mirror. Obama has become a total laughingstock of the world. The unfortunate part it is effecting the standing of the United States as a nation. We are becoming a total laughingstock! Our Military is becoming a total laughingstock! Our economy is becoming a total laughingstock! Our credibility is becoming a total laughingstock! Our money is becoming a total laughingstock!

And the main stream media, academia and Liberals tell us to "Thank Obama". I am not ready to say thank you. It is past time for the citizens to start "Taking Back America" from this embarrassment of a President. Make sure that you look at the credentials of the candidates before you vote in the 2012 election.

"The President does not have the power under the Constitution to unilaterally authorize a military attack in a situation that does not involve stopping an actual or imminent threat to the nation." Senator Barack Obama, December 20, 2007 - Between that and Biden's call for Bush's impeachment for an illegal war...whoa...down the memory hole!

We've got checks and balances, folks. You can count on Vice President Joe Biden to lead the charge. As Joe himself said while a U.S. Senator, "I don't use words lightly."

"Ladies and gentlemen, I drafted an outline of what I think the Constitutional limits [garbled] have on the President with the War

Clause. I went to five leading scholars, Constitutional scholars, and they drafted a treatise for me that is being distributed to every Senator. And I want to make it clear, and I'll make it clear to the President: that if he takes this nation to war in Iran, without Congressional approval, I will make it my business to impeach him." - Joe Biden Now that's playing hardball, Joe! I'll guess we'll just have to let the chips fall where they may. Does that mean that we will see impeachment proceedings started by the Vice President?

When will Joe Biden draft Articles of Impeachment for the House and Senate like he threatened in 2007 for Bush? Joe "situational ethics" Biden By the way, has anyone seen or heard from Biden since Obama declared the war against Libya?

I have just included parts of the article regarding the unanswered questions about Libya.

Unanswered questions about Libya

Glenn Thrush, Abby Phillip – Thu Mar 24, 5:31 am ET

It's hard to find a precedent for a president ordering U.S. military forces into action, then heading off for a five day tour of Latin America, but that's just what President Barack Obama did when he approved the deployment of air and naval assets to establish a no-fly zone over Libya.

His homecoming gift is a barrage of questions about the military action Obama aides refuse to label a "war."

Obama was asked the most obvious question — what is the U.S. endgame in Libya? — several times during his trip? His answers seemed deliberately obtuse: To stop a humanitarian crisis and, hopefully, drive Muammar Qadahfi's from power, while at the same time ceding leadership of the effort to countries with a direct regional stake in the outcome — France and Arab League nations — sooner rather than later.

But here are four more questions, whose answers will likely determine whether Libya is a foreign policy success or failure for Obama:

"It is very dangerous to have confusion about command and control. If people's lives are at risk and you're using military forces, you need to have a rather clear understanding as to who's in charge and who's making the decisions," former defense secretary Donald Rumsfeld, who knows a thing or two about the hazards of poor planning said.

"And these unusual debates that are taking place about who's going to be in command, what military official is going to be in command, which country, I think have to be worrisome for people."

The larger problem, warns Scott Carpenter of the Washington Institute for Near East Policy, is that the U.S. wants to cede leadership to France while still shaping the operation — classic back-seat driving.

"The administration is trying to cobble together this diplomatic coalition post facto while you already have planes in the air," he said. "Trying to lead from behind is hard. ... It's very difficult, and it takes time, and it's fragile and you have to work very, very hard at it."

Again, Clinton remains confident. "NATO will definitely be involved," she predicted, "It's moving forward in the right direction, and we will have what we need in the next few days." In a related story Secretary of State Hillary Clinton isn't planning on quitting her job anytime soon, she said in an interview Tuesday, even as reports suggest she was frustrated by President Barack Obama's approach to the crisis in Libya.

"I will stay until the beginning of the next term, because I know it takes a while for people to get appointed and confirmed," said Clinton. "Obviously, there needs to be a seamless transition with whomever President Obama decides to appoint after he is reelected, which I am confident he will be," she said.

Clinton's comments came just days after she denied wanting to run for president or vice president or wanting to serve in the Obama administration beyond 2012, which unleashed a flood of reports from insiders who say she was discouraged by the president's reticence to responding to instability in Libya under Muammar Qadhafi's regime.

Obama's decision to authorize military action was made on short notice and without even the most cursory consultation with congressional leaders beforehand. A coalition of progressive Democrats immediately raised questions about the constitutionality of committing U.S. forces based on a U.N. resolution alone — and Rep. Dennis Kucinich (D-Ohio) has even threatened Obama with impeachment.

But the more serious threat comes from the right. Senate Minority Mitch McConnell (R-KY) has been stone silent on Libya, leaving it to elder Indiana statesman Dick Lugar, the ranking Republican on the Senate Foreign Relations Committee — and normally an ally of Obama's on international issues — to question the lack of an endgame for the Libyan mission or a dedicated revenue stream to pay for it.

And House Speaker John Boehner (R-OH), who was reportedly infuriated that he was only briefed on the mission by an Obama subordinate on the day the U.N. Security Council resolution passed, seems intent on confronting Obama directly on the issue.

"I and many other members of the House of Representatives are troubled that U.S. military resources were committed to war without clearly defining for the American people, the Congress, and our troops what the mission in Libya is and what America's role is in achieving that mission," Boehner wrote Wednesday in a less than friendly welcome back letter.

"In fact, the limited, sometimes contradictory, case made to the American people by members of your administration has left some fundamental questions about our engagement unanswered. At the same time, by contrast, it appears your administration has consulted extensively on these same matters with foreign entities such as the United Nations and the Arab League."

Here are the comments from average American citizens and what they think about President Obama being an embarrassment to the United States. In some cases the comments are extreme but for the most part they are right on. They have not been altered in any way except for spelling and grammar. I hope you enjoy the comments and can get a clearer picture of what is happening with the President of the United States of America.

The four questions we should be asking:

1. Why do national leaders who order unprovoked bombing campaigns or invasions not face murder charges?

2. When a President violates his oath of office and commits the nation to war without the consent of Congress, why is he not impeached?

3. What is the difference between Libya's tyrants shooting rebellious civilians and Yemen's tyrants shooting rebellious civilians?

4. Are the rebels in Libya really on our side?

His homecoming gift is a barrage of questions about the military action Obama aides refuse to label a "war."

Aircraft attacked Hawaii on 07 Dec 1941, FDR called it a day that will live in infamy and an act of War. By Obama's definition an air and missile attack against Washington D.C. would not be an act of War?

"Because liberal wars depend on constant consensus building within the (so-called) international community, they tend to be fought by committee, at a glacial pace, and with a caution that shades into tactical incompetence,"

Our brave fighting men and women deserve better leadership than Obama. It's time to bring them home. Obama is not a Commander in Chief. Obama is not a leader at all. This community organizer is out of his league, Time for our congress to do the right thing. He has done more damage in his time in the White House then any other 4 Presidents did in their entire time on office combined.

I just read where Obama is giving billions to Brazil for oil exploration, but his moratorium has cost the gulf south oil industry over 100,000 jobs! Funny, Associated Press is writing about that. All we're told by Obama is that oil production is the highest in 7 years. That's a LIE!

But Obama's critics — many of whom don't buy in the birther theory that he was born outside the United States — still note a pattern of secrecy surrounding much of Obama's life before he entered politics. They note that Obama never has unveiled many key documents that presidential candidates traditionally release to the press and the public. For example:

During the presidential campaign, Obama released just one brief document detailing his personal health, while the Republican opponent John McCain released what he said was his complete medical file totaling more than 1,500 pages. The Obama campaign eventually released some routine lab-test results and electrocardiograms for Obama.

Obama refused to offer his official papers as a state legislator in Illinois and did not produce correspondence, such as letters from lobbyists and other information, from his days in the Illinois Senate.

Obama did not release his client list as an attorney or his billing records.

Obama declined to release his college records from Occidental College, where he studied for two years before transferring to Columbia University.

Obama's campaign refused to give Columbia University, where he earned an undergraduate degree in political science, permission to release his transcripts. Such transcripts would list the courses Obama took, and his grades.

Obama's college dissertation, reportedly titled "Soviet Nuclear Disarmament," has disappeared from Columbia's archives.

Obama did not agree to the release of his application to the Illinois state bar, which would clear up intermittent allegations that his application to the bar may have been inaccurate.

Obama has not released records from his time at Harvard Law School.

During his campaign for president, Obama promised he would make his White House "the most open and transparent administration in history."

Obama gives South American companies owned by George Soros $2 billion for Oil Exploration. While only 1 Permit has been approved for Oil Exploration within the U.S. in a year. Sure other countries can drill for oil off the coast, but U.S. cannot! Russia is working with Cuba drilling 54 miles off the coast of Florida now.
"It's hard to find a precedent for a President ordering U.S. military forces into action, then heading off for a five-day tour of Latin America, but that's just what President Barack Obama did when he approved the deployment of air and naval assets to establish a no-fly zone over Libya." Yeah, a sane person might wonder "why am I not hearing more about this, how does he get away with this stuff?" This is what happens when truth becomes less important than one's political agenda

Let's see first why didn't Obama go before Congress and get Congressional approval? The President is not authorized to use United States military without Congressional approval. That's one question

not addressed but who would expect the mainstream Propaganda Central to address issues of what the Federal Government can and can't do especially since the corporations that own them also now run Washington D.C.

This is one big mess folks. WHAT THE HELL ARE OUR LEADERS THINKING, DRINKING, OR SMOKING? Three polls I saw, show 93%, 73% and 64% oppose us going to war with Libya and oppose Obama spending all this money getting us involved in another war while Americans suffer. I have seen no-one, except the rich insider DC folks supporting this war on the backs of the taxpayer's dime. THERE THEY GO AGAIN, DC ELITE NOT LISTENING TO THE AMERICAN PEOPLE YET AGAIN. Obama and Biden have stated several times that Bush should have been impeached for going to war. Funny how the left wing media and code pink types with no massive street anti-war protest are totally absent when it comes to war and the shoe is on the other foot! Why should some political panel be ordering our troops into harms way and conducting a war using our taxpayer dollars? This whole thing has been a "FUBAR" from the very beginning. Only 24 civilians reportedly killed before we went to war spending billions and we have thousands being killed in other Arab countries and we do nothing. What about over 35,000 people killed along our southern border since December 2006 (more than in Afghanistan and Iraq combined) including nearly 1300 Americans and Obama allows only $600,000 more to protect our borders while spending over $2 billion in going to war with Libya where we have no business in a civil war. Heck we don't even get any oil from them. Anyone who thinks we need to be spending billions going to war with Libya while folks here at home have no jobs, food, gas, clothes, and all those costs, including home energy cost, have skyrocketed the largest amount in 37 years, has got to be literally insane.

Obama has violated the US Constitution and should be impeached - if anyone has to intestinal fortitude to do it! A US President can only order military action with approval of the US Congress - unless there is a national emergency from abroad - an attack against our nation or an attack on our military forces anywhere in the world. What ever happened to the "checks and balances" and constitutional law? Obama seems more dedicated to socialistic international concerns than the welfare and interests of the United States! Wake up idiots!

Where's Code Pink? Cindy Sheehan? Where are the liberal protesters with tape over their mouths that say "peace"? The cries of war for oil! The shouts over no exit strategies! Accusations of meddling where we don't belong! The citizens of Burma, Darfur, Yemen, Iran, Egypt, The Ivory Coast, and Palestine must be scratching their heads right now. Obama and those of you who rallied for Bush to be impeached (and in some instances even hung on a cross) should be ashamed of yourselves for such a blatant act of betrayal of your own "convictions". Silently whining?

The four questions that I have for Obama! 1) How was your spring break vacation in South America? 2) How is it you start a war while out of country, I thought you had a "transparent administration"? 3) What are your plans for this war, more oil? Just thought it would fun to do while on vacation? Haven't given it much thought? 4) Have you considered leaving office, because you lack of leadership skills is very apparent?

We are dropping bombs and killing people and Larry, Moe and Curly are in charge. We must demand impeachment of this Marxist who has no interest in this country other than to apologize and use taxpayer's money to pay back and bail out his friends. The height of corruption! The White House and Democratic Party look like they took a playbook out of the Bell, California way of doing things.

Obama was asked several times during his trip the most obvious question — what is the U.S. endgame in Libya? His answers seemed deliberately obtuse: 0bama did not have a teleprompter so he could read a prepared speech written by someone else. The suit is empty and the idiot is at a loss when it comes to what to do.

Obama clearly doesn't care what anybody else thinks. 0bama is in so far over his head he doesn't even know what he thinks so why would he care about what others think? Everything 0bama has touched has been a failure and as usual 0bama is consistent. Send this failure home. As Oprah said "he (0bama) is still learning" that is just what we need a President who after two years is still learning and will not listen to anyone else. We have a failed presidency and the idiot is still in the driver's seat.

When does the no fly zones start over Yemen, Bahrain, Saudi Arabia, Iran, North Korea and China. All these countries are doing the same thing as Libya to suppress the people. We can't justify going in to Libya, attacking a sovereign country and then turn a blind eye to all these other places where the same things are happening. We prop up corrupt governments and are afraid to step up to the ones that can fight back all the while, these other governments steal our technology and continue to develop more powerful weapons to one day use against us and our allies. Get ready people, World War III might not be as far off as you might think.

What did Obama say? Only a few days! Oh, forgot he was starting a vacation in South America claiming to be doing diplomatic work. Right, play soccer with the kids, golf and sight seeing. Do you still believe his lies? Obama runs every time something major happens. The President is vacationing and golfing, while our troops are in danger. If you check you will find every other President stopped their vacations and trips when major problems arose. Remember when Obama said: "I am going to keep fighting every single day, every single hour, every single minute, to turn this economy around and put people back to work". Recently, he was heard saying the following: "FORE!!"

Obama broke the law and didn't get the approval of the Congress before authorizing his war, and that is impeachable offence, now why isn't the Congress pushing for that? We see Biden had enough courage to say Obama was wrong, but he shut up quick when Obama returned. Impeach Obama for treason.

1.) He said this was to create a no-fly zone. So, when did tanks and personnel transports start flying? What does trying to assassinate Gadhafi by bombing his living quarters have to do with a no-fly zone?

2.) No approval from Congress for this mission. Even Bush went to Congress to get approval before military action. Clinton went to Congress before the Bosnian action. This President turns his back on the constitution every chance he gets.

3.) Sending our troops into harms way and then immediately taking off to help Brazil get more oil exploration and jobs for their people. It doesn't get much more stupid than that.

Well sir, Obama said we are not at War with Libya, No sir, Obama and the Democrats are just Killing Libyans with kindness and understanding is all, their thinking is asinine, totally, just get real.

Obama gets a pass…this really isn't war. This is a joke. Obama is a joke. Look at him…he was locked out of the White House. He'll get a pass on that too. They should have thrown away the key and never let Obama back in the White House. Then they could give the people that locked Obama out a medal.

It will be hard to find a precedent for a President to have such a low credibility within the country, such as Obama. He is lacking all skills to lead, not just as a President, but as anything. His administration's total disregard of the wishes of the country is evident. Am seriously starting to believe he is the Manchurian Candidate.

The latest development in Libya is that the pro Gadhafi forces are burning the United States flags in the streets of Tripoli. The respect for the United States has fallen to a new low since Obama took office.
Obama has lied since he started running for President in 2007 - he continues to lie and his lies are so unbelievable you can't trust anything he says about anything.

He vacillated back and forth for over a week before he announced the no-fly zone. Hillary was in France, Gates was telling him to stay out of it - and he made the decision to 'support' the coalition no-fly operation after 'careful study, discussion and planning'! Now Hillary and Gates are going to appear before Congress next week to explain what the mission is, what our participation (leadership) means, and indicate what will tell us the mission is complete?

I've got a better idea - have Obama appear before Congress and explain why he entered this war without Congressional approval, how much this war is costing us, and how long it is going to last. I don't believe he is capable of testifying before Congress without telling more lies –

then the House of Representatives will have a good solid reason to start impeachment proceedings; the last time I checked it was still a felony to lie to Congress.

The hypocrite Obama hammered the last nail in the coffin of hopes for a second term. His warmongering and hypocrisy surpassed that of George Bush. His claim of saving lives to market his war is foolish because he did the reverse in Bahrain. In Bahrain, he authorized the killing of the innocent Shiite majority by the Saudi Wahhabis and the hooded US marines to gain the support of corrupt Arab dictators in his adventure in Libya. His rivals, the doll Clinton and the wiseman Biden will be pleased to see him humiliated, and what is left of his presidency will be very difficult. He started his term with a hint of peace, dignity and honor but gradually lost these features.

Our current illustrious leader is neither illustrious nor a leader. He actually has NO skills, NO leadership ability, NO capability in any WAY, SHAPE, or FORM. He is a hollow raised as a Muslim, lied about everything to get where he is, empty shell of a politician. If it's not on his teleprompter after having been polished to a micro finish by his democratic socialist spin doctors he can't reply!

Libya's Civil War is now OBAMA'S WAR...He picked it...He started it, He owns it...And no one else wants it... so he plans on handing control over to an International Committee that will oversee NATO's supervision of the War...So now we are in a War without Congressional Approval and our Military might and Lives are to be Commanded and directed by an International Committee, not the Pentagon nor a U.S. Commander.

NATO is Commanded by the U.S. Commander in Chief Atlantic Fleet under his hat as Supreme Commander NATO and the lions share of troops and equipment are U.S. Military...So how does that lessen our involvement? How many NATO Ships and Planes will be ours? Germany has pulled it's Navy out of the Mediterranean. France has one aircraft carrier and England has none. The Arab League is most conspicuous by its udder lack of involvement. Sounds like this is just Political Smoke and Mirrors?

I would support both the UN and NATO on the condition that our military and funding do not exceed that of any other Nation participating AND that Foreign Aid be stopped to all countries that do not support the effort with military and/or funding, including the Arab League which has been absent since they called for the No Fly Zone.

WHO are the Rebels we are supporting? WHAT is their Political Ideology? Will they be better or worse for Libya or more importantly for the USA? 20% of Al-Qaida fighters killed or captured in Afghanistan came from eastern Libyan Tribes. A week into this shooting War and no one knows who the Rebels are ... Kind of scary considering they will have Libya's Chemical Weapons if they win.

7 days into OBAMA'S War and we still don't have a clear definition of the "Mission"? Support the Rebels? Overthrow the Government? Protect innocent civilians from whom...attacking Government forces...attacking Rebel Forces...or both?

Because liberal wars depend on constant consensus building within the so called international community, they tend to be fought by committee, at a glacial pace, and with a caution that shades into tactical incompetence. Gives you a nice warm fuzzy feeling about this War doesn't it?

Professor OBAMA could have benefited from reading a little History before he committed our Nation to this War ... "Never, never, never believe any war will be smooth and easy, or that anyone who embarks on the strange voyage can measure the tides and hurricanes he will encounter. The statesman who yields to war fever must realize that once the signal is given, he is no longer the master of policy but the slave of unforeseeable and uncontrollable events." Sir Winston Churchill

When did the mandates of the UN over rule U.S. Law and the Constitution? When is Obama going to address Congress?

President Barack Obama's intervention in Libya's civil war has not only failed to win the approval of a majority of the American people, according to a Gallup poll conducted Monday, it also earned the lowest public approval rating of any U.S. military operation polled by Gallup over the past four decades. In fact, it was the only U.S. military intervention polled by Gallup that received less than majority approval from Americans.

I am a person of color who voted for Obama as President. I was not an undivided supporter of Obama from the start though. What I perceived as a major red flag was that he raised an enormous amount of money when he was campaigning but did not seem to have the least scruples about having that entire amount being spent on his own personal cult without any concern for the poor. This seemed very strange for a person of color with honest motives. I must say that when it was time to vote I did not trust him completely, but since so many others seemed to do, I figured it was just me.

Then there were the usual nonsensical criticisms like he supposedly would not be American and be socialist or a Muslim. After two years Obama it is more than clear one does not need to make up such fake criticism in order to be critical of him, since the man is plainly incompetent and deceptive. He certainly is not stupid. He knows well how to build out a personal, self-serving cult but in a way that he can usually get away with it, as most of the things he does superficially look like he wants to 'improve' things. He was going to close Gitmo and he was going to end the wars. The guy simply has no balls. He is a weakling, a coward, and a complete fraud. I am deeply ashamed to have this guy as the President of my country, and I am deeply ashamed I voted for him. The fact that this guy is now President is partly my fault. If there is anything I could do to correct the consequences of my own stupidity, I would do it.

Few people have as much talent as Obama being able to mask his huge ego somewhat by a smoke curtain of fake humility. His supposedly peace-mined views that landed him a Nobel Prize are just one of the results of his deceptive behaviors. When it comes to lying Obama has shown to be able to offer some fierce competition to Nixon. Only, Obama's ego won't make him spontaneously resign, despite his incompetence.

It is beyond belief how this guy pushes the entire country into more uncertainty and financial distress. Sure, America has made mistakes before, grave mistakes, and yes Bush is responsible for various major problems, but that what Obama is failing to do or is doing wrong, he cannot blame on Bush. It's hard to blame one's own incompetence on the incompetence of someone else. Moreover, the Bush era is gone, and yes Bush got away with a lot. We cannot do anything about that anymore. Obama is still there and Obama makes a mess so big, that there is no doubt the country would be better off without him. It is one problem after another. Obama will not stop unless he is stopped. I hope that at least the disgusting way of how he drew the US into this entire Lybian affair will not go away and will have the House and Senate put their teeth in it to the point he is impeached. Time has come for us to make an example that a President cannot get away with everything he does or doesn't.

Make no mistake…IT IS A WAR. A war the President illegally authorized. Worse yet, Obama is fighting it on someone else's terms. The "rebels" don't want our troops and the Arab League doesn't want our troops there. Our military depends on ALL branches to accomplish its objectives. So we either have NO OBJECTIVE or we are fighting with OUR ARMS TIED BEHIND OUR BACKS. My gut tells me THERE IS NO OBJECTIVE. Obama had another knee jerk reaction for POLITICAL REASONS ONLY. This time the consequences are war. Obama cannot justify MILITARY ACTION because there is no justification for it. Neighboring countries are killing protesters daily but we act only on humanitarian interests in Libya. Really! The entire region is ruled by dictators and we WON'T CHANGE THAT CULTURE. DROPPING POLLS and a HOT HEADED Secretary of State who acted unilaterally speaking for the U.S. in a flimsy, hastily pulled together coalition are the only reasons we bombed Libya. The Secretary of State has absolutely no authority to inject herself in military decisions.

Come on give him a break……don't you remember that he said in an interview on FOX…that he never got the easy things over his desk, only the hard ones……poor, poor, President Obama……what did you expect when you ran to be elected for President? Sometimes it appears that the only thing that you like about the position is the availability

of Air Force One. Oh and please Mr. President would you learn to wear a tie on appropriate occasions.

"Let me be clear, I will answer all those questions on Libya and Afghanistan and Iraq and Gitmo and sky rocketing gas prices and sky rocketing food prices and the lack of jobs, both old and new and aid for Japan and the Mexican drug cartel violence and our porous borders both north and south and illegal aliens and North Korean Nukes and Iran's nuke program and of course, any other questions you have as soon as I check out how I'm doing with my NCAA Bracket Picks and as soon as I get my tee time for Saturday settled. Thank you," Barack Obama, Whiner in Chief

Does this President really stand for anything or does he just do what he feels like at the time? First he is anti-war, now he's a hawk (sort of but not quite). He was the progressive crusader against Wall Street corruption, and then has lunch with all the fat cats he was going to jail. "If you don't for something, you'll fall for anything." Who would have ever thought Jimmy Carter and George W. Bush would look good in comparison?

Obama's true colors showing again…His loyalty is to the U.N. and world government and not to the American people. He didn't even talk to the Congress before allocating men, equipment and money to a mission with no definition other than to get started. If this drags on it should be the final nail in his one term coffin.

Obama is obtuse. He is also cold, uncaring, with no empathy for the people he is supposed to serve. He is on a power trip now that he is President, he believes that he is right and everyone else is wrong and stupid or both. This breach of the Constitution is inexcusable for someone who was once a professor teaching about the Constitution. A supposed expert on constitutional law – not!

Our last experience with a No-Fly zone didn't go so well. After the first gulf war, we basically enforced a no fly zone in Iraq for the entire Clinton presidency, at great expense to the US. Is this a prelude to an 8-10 year commitment followed by another protracted war?

Give the man a break he just got back from vacationing in Brazil right when he started a war and has another vacation planned in May to go to Ireland. Let the man get his bags unpacked and see how his college basketball picks are doing before you barrage him with silly questions. Remember, he made those picks while the Japan Tsunami was happening so he was a bit rushed while he made them.

How the Hell do we know if the rebels are Muslim extremist or not, remember when the Shaw of Iran was over thrown only to have a bunch of nut jobs twice as bad take over. What the hell could this knuckle head Obama be thinking, same old crap from him when the going gets tough he gets going to another country.

The administration has warned Congress that failing to raise the debt limit would lead to an unprecedented default on the national debt and wreck the national economic recovery. This is really rich; Obama bypasses Congressional approval before declaring war on Libya and then warns Congress. Give me a break. Raising the debt limit is not going to wreck the national economic recovery. Obama and his free loading family took care of that all by themselves. Libya, of course, but with the added twist of harsh criticism of the President's failure to bring in the Congress. And the budget battle, which I believe is much more likely than not to lead to a shutdown. Once again, the US takes a backseat to a foreign nation and now the importance of Congress has been relegated to second place as well. Everything in this country now ranks anywhere but first. And if he chooses, we may find out the reasoning behind his unsanctioned moves against Libya. Aren't we just the luckiest people on earth? IMPEACH this Obama fool now or there will be nothing left in 2012 to restore.

So Obama is scaling back Operations in Libya? If so, why is the US Aircraft Carrier USS Bataan, LHD-5, just leaving Norfolk for the Mediterranean? The Bataan is an Amphibious Assault Ship, with the primary purpose is to put Marines on the Ground with their Helicopters. Recently in an interview with Bill O'Reilly President Obama said that "people hated him because they don't really know him." Mr. President you are wrong. The people hate you because they do know you and what you stand for.

Our Congress better do something about what Obama is doing because it is an act of war. Since when do tanks and tents fly? Obama is killing just as many people. Obama has put us in the middle of the war doing the fighting for the rebels and they don't even know who they are. We will pay for his stupid antics just look at the pump and your store shelves its only going to get worse. We the people can't afford Obama anymore he needs to go and go now, impeach this sob

Just because NATO approves this military action, doesn't mean we have to do the job. We have no stakes in this war. Obama has been against the war in Iraq, but he is ok with a war with Libya? Saddam killed 100,000 of his on people for protesting, and wanting a change in leadership in Iraq. There hasn't been that many people killed in Libya while Gadhafi is the rightful government of Libya. They have a right to stop citizens from a revolution. Abraham Lincoln started the civil war to keep the south from succeeding. No other country stepped in when people were killed. We lost more soldiers in the civil war than any other war. Why did we get involved in this act of war with another government? We have no business getting involved in a civil war. There are other countries that have killed their citizens, why didn't we get involved in that? Why start a war with Libya, when we have more reasons to go to war with North Korea or Iran. To me we started a war, just like Russia did with Georgia. Iran government shot and killed protesters when they tried to over throw their government. Iran arrested many protesters and they have not been released, if they are still alive that is. It seems we are big bullies and we pick fights with countries that we can easily beat. We do nothing when Russia, North Korea, Iran, and China kill and torture their citizens. We had no business getting involved. The Arabs should be taking action not the West! They certainly can afford a war more than we can. Somebody should be paying us back for what we have spent so far on this war! We can afford a new war, but can't afford to pay teachers and other civil servants. Impeach Obama for starting an illegal war!

Another funny thing has happened. A Paul Shanklin parody has Obama phoning around trying to find someone to hand the Libya action off to. After calling Britain and France, he tries at home with Bill Clinton. Finally, as a last resort, he calls President Bush. Bush laughs, and says "When you're going to walk a mile in another man's shoes, make sure you don't step in the dung"!

It's hard to find a precedent for a President ordering U.S. military forces into action, then heading off for a five-day tour of Latin America". Actually, it's impossible to find such a precedent. It is also impossible to find a precedent for the United States electing a "community organizer" as President. Does anybody even know if he was successful at being a "community organizer"?

There is nothing "humanitarian" about what's going on in Libya, it's all about oil and money. We just dropped over $200 million dollars worth of ordinance on Libya making the producers of these arms that much richer and for what, to take a back seat. Obama's war will be a failure, just like his back door health care plan. His focus should be on domestic issues like jobs and illegal immigration, these issues are more important to the American people right now.

The next President will have so much to clean up after the mess this guy is leaving. He's made a bad economy worse. The Middle East is more unstable than ever before. Unemployment has seen no improvement... I hope the next presidential election brings voters who want the best President, not vote for a man or woman because they are a certain race, color or sex.

Is Obama hanging out with Marion Barry or what, what the heck is he thinking. China and the Russia are upset that we did this and are worried they might be next to have a political uprising in their own countries. It's time to de-escalate the issue and follow a political path. We need to start utilizing our own resources and get away from foreign fuel sources, this is the only way to stop funding the terror machine.

This man sees himself as an all powerful ruler and he doesn't answer to anyone he should be impeached. We have laws in place for that very reason so ONE man cannot take this country into war, he by passes the Congress every time he wants something done and they sit back and say you can't do that...but he does and he gets by with it. It is time for Congress to step up and do some smack downs on him.

Come on guys! We all now know that Obama is a speaker, not a leader. Clinton is running Libya. He had to take his girls and wife

on Air Force One (and guests) on **SPRING BREAK! A promise is a promise to the family—except PROMISES THAT HE MADE to the NATION don't seem to matter. I sure feel sorry for our military. Can you imagine making a private COMMANDER IN CHIEF? Obama was not even a private!**

Few Americans see Obama as strong military leader

Reuters – U.S. Air Force F-16 Fighting Falcons return to Aviano Air Base, Italy, after supporting Operation Odyssey. The lead line almost brought tears to me eyes. After spending four years at this military installation and wondering why we were there, I finally found out. It was to support Obama's military strategy.

By Arshad Mohammed – March 25, 2011

WASHINGTON (Reuters) – Only 17 percent of Americans see President Barack Obama as a strong and decisive military leader, according to a Reuter's poll taken after the United States and its allies began bombing Libya.

Nearly half of those polled view Obama as a cautious and consultative commander-in-chief and more than a third see him as indecisive in military matters.

Obama was widely criticized in 2009 for his month's long consultations with senior aides and military chiefs on whether to send more troops to Afghanistan. Critics called it dithering, but he said such a big decision required careful deliberation. He eventually dispatched 30,000 more troops.

But Obama is facing mounting discontent among opposition Republicans and from within his own Democratic Party over the fuzzy aims of the U.S. led mission in Libya and the lack of a clearly spelled out exit strategy for U.S. forces.

If the Libya mission becomes a foreign policy mess, mixed with perceptions Obama is a weak military leader, it could spell trouble for him in the 2012 presidential election.

The poll also found that 60 percent of Americans support the United States and its allies bombing Libya to impose a no-fly zone to protect civilians from Libyan leader Muammar Gaddafi's forces.

Seventy-nine percent of those surveyed said the United States and its allies should try to remove Gaddafi, who has ruled the oil-exporting North African country for more than four decades.

In the survey, conducted on March 22 from a nationally representative sample of 975 adults, only 7 percent supported deploying ground troops.

Of the 60 percent in favor of the Libya military action, 20 percent strongly supported it and 40 percent somewhat supported it. Twenty-five percent somewhat opposed it and 14 percent were strongly against.

In a sign of political division, the top Republican in Congress, House of Representatives Speaker John Boehner, on Wednesday sharpened his criticism of Obama, saying he was "troubled that U.S. military resources were committed to war without clearly defining ... what the mission in Libya is and what America's role is in achieving that mission."

"Everybody thinks Gaddafi needs to go but there is absolutely no tolerance for the idea of sending in ground troops," Clark said, citing U.S. fatigue with the Iraq and Afghanistan wars. "The idea of entering a third conflict like that garners very, very little support."

The majority of the people of the United States are against the war in Libya and we are engaged in the war without Congressional approval. Why does President Obama believe that he can make decisions placing our military at war without consulting the other branches of the government? Then while Obama is in Brazil, Secretary of State Hillary Clinton is making decisions for the Americans. Since when did a Presidential appointment have the authority to engage the military in acts of war? The United Nations can be heard but the United States still needs to take the proper channels before we engage our military troops and equipment in any war. It should be an impeachable offense and all parties involved should be removed from office and anything that they promoted or legislation that was passed should be abolished. Americans need to start "Taking Back America" before it is too late.

GOD BLESS AMERICA

CHAPTER TEN:

TRANSPARENCY IN THE WHITE HOUSE

I must say that this current administration is the most politically divisive force I have seen in my lifetime (and I'm pretty old). Perhaps some of it comes about because of political appointments without regard to qualifications. Certainly the election of the head of the administration was apparently not connected to any qualifications for the job.

I'm thrilled that the Department of Homeland Security and Napolitano is the first to be probed and hopefully fully investigated. There is no one in Obama's administration more incompetent, incapable and more of an "Obama "yes" person than Napolitano and I am convinced she'd stonewall, lie and do anything possible to avoid complying with the previous requests. The security of America ranks at the top of our priorities but she doesn't have a clue of how to do her job or even know what is going on in the agency. Listening to this idiot, if you believed her, the border is secured, all problems and issues have been resolved and there is nothing to fear about the border situation. I cringe at the sight of her, knowing all we'll hear is generalized information that is a bald face lie and political rhetoric that is so weak, it's sickening. I wish the best to the committee and wish them all the success in the world.

The Declaration of Independence enshrines three basic rights: the rights to life, liberty, and the pursuit of happiness. The first ten amendment's to the constitution were put there to guarantee those rights because they knew that there were those that would try to take them away, but these rights are only guaranteed if we do not let others take them away and now we have because if one right is taken then they all are taken. When you give the government the power to protect you without keeping the right to protect yourself then the government can do anything it wants to you under the guise of protection that is why the 2nd amendment was put into place it was to empower you to keep your basic freedoms.

Insiders at the Homeland Security Department warned for months that senior Obama administration appointees were improperly delaying the releases of government files on politically sensitive topics as sought by citizens, journalists and watchdog groups under the Freedom of Information Act, according to uncensored emails newly obtained by The Associated Press.

The highly unusual political vetting was described as "meddling," "crazy" and "bananas!" It is the subject of a congressional hearing and an ongoing inquiry by the department's inspector general.

The Freedom of Information Act (FOIA), the main tool forcing the government to be more transparent, is designed to be insulated from political considerations. Anyone who seeks information through the law is supposed to get it unless disclosure would hurt national security, violate personal privacy or expose confidential decision-making in certain areas. People can request government records without specifying why they want them and are not obligated to provide personal information about themselves other than their name and an address where the records should be sent.

The Department of Homeland Security is having credibility problems? Who would ever believe such a thing? This is the department headed by Ms Janet Napolitano. While she was Governor of Arizona, she kept complaining to the Federal Government that too many illegal immigrants were entering the state from Mexico. Now she has become head of Homeland Security and immediately announced that things on the border with Mexico are all better. Are they? Hah! The only change has been Arizona's SB1070 which requires local and State police to verify the immigration status of anybody that has been arrested. There's nothing wrong with asking for proof of personal information, because police need to see some sort of Identification if they are arresting somebody. Have a valid Arizona driver's license? OK. Have a Green Card or equivalent? OK. Have a passport? OK. There is nothing wrong with the SB1070 law. It specifically prohibits profiling or arresting people for being brown. Now Ms Napolitano has cancelled the virtual fence that was $1 billion dollar waste of the taxpayer's money and has done nothing to complete a real border fence. That shows how much she cares about Arizona, the rule of law, and her oath to uphold the laws of the land, including the Constitution. Homeland Insecurity would be a better term for the agency.

We need to abolish the Department of Homeland Security. Since it's inception under the Bush administration it has been used as a tool to increase the police state. When we abolish the Department of Homeland Security the government will be able to cut $46.91 billion from the federal budget every year. The amount of savings was extracted from page 90 of the President's proposed budget for the fiscal year 2012. It has been a waste of the taxpayer's money from the day it was founded. It was only fears generated by the attack on the World Trade Center, the Pentagon and Pennsylvania that created the monster. At the time it seemed like a good idea but it has gotten out of control on what it is trying to do. Unfortunately, it has not done anything to protect the United States from the flow of potential terrorists and illegals entering into the country. Most of the functions of the Department of Homeland Security can be performed by existing branches of the federal government.

Here are the comments from average American citizens and what they think about President Obama and his transparency policies in the White House. In some cases the comments are extreme but for the most part they are right on. They have not been altered in any way except for spelling and grammar. I hope you enjoy the comments and can get a clearer picture of what is happening with the President of the United States of America.

When Homeland Security has political advisors, I have a real concern for the future security of our country. Too many people have died, usually to protect the good names of our politicians. Our freedoms as American citizens are fast being taken away under the guise of "homeland security" and fighting terrorism. It is time for all Americans to demand their rights back.

I remember Janet Napolitano when she was governor of Arizona and she looked the other way on immigration. Still does. Send her the first subpoena.

Our federal government is so clueless it's amazing. Homeland Security cannot even do the relatively simple job of securing our porous borders. All the American taxpayer hears from our over inflated government is one lame excuse after another. It's just plain sickening.

Homeland Security is telling a blatant LIE. The FOIA requests were ignored with no response most of the time, and if they were answered at all, there were long delays... Judicial Watch had to sue the Obama administration numerous times over the past 2 years for failure to respond at all to their FOIA document requests, and THEY are a group of lawyers. Just think what response normal everyday people get? None! It's time there were some repercussions to these high and mighty tactics.

Napolitano was appointed to Homeland Security purely to try to ram through amnesty. Now that amnesty is not going to happen, she should be replaced by someone more competent

Obama's notion of transparency at it's finest. It must be mentioned though, that a forewarning was given when he covered up his own personal documents and took so much trouble to obscure his past.

On many of Mr. Obama's policies, I disagree with him, sometimes strongly. On a few others, I support him. I don't feel he's done a particularly good job so far, though I acknowledge that he's had a very difficult 26 months to deal with and that the jury is still out. I have little time or patience for those who believe he's an America-hating, racist, socialist, wannabe dictator.

However, there is one aspect of Mr. Obama's administration on which my opinion has gone from hope to disappointment to frustration to exasperation, and which is now turning into full-fledged outrage.

Mr. Obama promised to change the way the federal government operates. In particular, he promised to be open, fair-minded, above partisanship and ideology, and to do everything in his power to change to tone in

Washington. Remember "there is no white America or black America…no red states or blue states…there is just the United States of America?"

On this account, he's failed miserably. With the possible exception of Richard Nixon, he's the most competitive and most divisive President of my lifetime. With no exception, he's the most ideologically blinded. For all of George W. Bush's failings, and I don't have enough room to list them all here, Mr. Bush never in eight years descended into the ugly, name-calling, finger-pointing, blame-gaming swamps to anywhere near the depths that Mr. Obama has plumbed in just 26 months. Even when Mr. Bush was giving one of his simplistic "us-vs.-them", "good-vs.-evil" speeches, at least the "them" and the "evil" comprised foreigners and hostile governments. The "good" and the "us" were always Americans – all of us.

For Mr. Obama, this equation has changed. The evil, the them, the "bad guys"…they're domestic. They're fellow Americans. Insurance companies are bad. Wall Street bankers are bad. Free market capitalists can't be trusted. Fox News isn't a "real" news service. All those "they" got us into "this mess". Even the Supreme Court got a shameful dressing down during the State of the Union address.

Ours was a country that was bitterly divided over the Bush years and which yearned for healing and unity, which Mr. Obama promised to deliver. Not only has he failed, but it's now sadly clear that his words on the campaign trail were completely empty. His intention was never to heal the left/right divide, but only to use it to further his own political agenda. Unfortunately, this AP story's revelation comes as no surprise, particularly the part where FOIA requestors had to be vetted as Democrat or Republican – aka, good vs. evil in the Obama universe.

I was sold a bill of goods in 2008, and I deeply, truly regret it.

It's just like the movie: The "Hunt For Red October". There was a Captain, of the Sub, and a POLITICAL OFFICER. And the Captain had to have every move he made, go through his POLTICAL Handler.

This is what you get when you elect a man, whose entire life is linked to the former Soviet Union.

His Marxist Father. His Atheist Communist Mother. His Communist Mentor (Frank Marshall Davis) and his Marxist Mentor. (Jeremiah Wright) His eagerness to "search out the Marxist Professors when I got to College". And, now, in the present, his Soviet Style Health Care, a COMMAND ECONOMY, Nationalization of Businesses, his use of CZARS to do an end run around Congressional oversight, a START TREATY (for old time's sake) and now this. Political operatives OVERSEEING every move, of every member of premier Obama's Administration. SIEG HEIL! I know that it's a NAZI phrase. But, if the shoe FITS.

The National Socialist Workers Party of Germany came to power in a time of a failing economy. They promised jobs. The "working man" would get what was rightfully his and those who had "stolen" that money and property would pay their fare share. That wealth should be redistributed to its "rightful owners".

They claimed to know what was "right" for the country. How to live! How to act! What to say! What not to say! What to believe! To assist in keeping tabs on folks, they implemented political monitoring.

They also killed 10 million people across Europe. You might know them better as Nazis. You see, the rhetoric is not new. What is new, though, is the ignorance of the American people.

Funny, the America hating Obama has done nothing significant to change the Patriot Act you speak of. You liberals complained about Bush implementing the Patriot Act whereas Obama has doubled the effort and further destroyed Constitutional rights and you idiot liberals are either clueless or purposefully ignorant about it. Or maybe it only matters when a Republican does it?

I bet the shredding machines at the White House have been working overtime since November. The Marxist Obama thought he could do whatever he wanted to and not have to worry about getting caught because his Marxist congress would protect him. News flash for the corrupt Marxist Obama… we are coming for you and there isn't a sink hole big enough for you to hide in!

How is it that a poor Indonesian/Kenyan/White/African American or whatever boy, who was raised by his Grandmother end up with an Ivy League education? Where did the Obama get his cash? I never once heard him speak of any significant legal cases that he argued in court? How's that for a FOIR? This Obama is a puppet on a string folks.

Obama gives whatever speech the Democrats hand him; and he's very good at it. The Democrats are the threat to America. They spend money as someone who has a credit card with no limit, and knows that they will presently have to declare bankruptcy.

The Department of Homeland Security follows the Obama administration's policy and has not withheld or edited any records that agency lawyers considered appropriate to release. Appropriate means anything you can sue them for and nothing the people will revolt over or would hurt Obama. This is more criminals protecting criminals while hurting and robbing the American people.

Issa, use your subpoena power and make everyone of these leeches upon society explain themselves before the American people, go straight to the head of the snake, The Queen Pelosi, make her squirm in the spotlight, she'll spill her guts (and not even know it). "We have to pass the bill so we can find out what's in it", priceless.

While we are discussing transparency and corruption in our government has anyone heard from Representatives Rangel and Waters? The government sure did a wonderful job of keeping these two Democrats out of jail. Any citizen would be spending the rest of their days behind bars if they had committed the crimes that these two have. I am not trying to be a racists but what would happened to these two had they been Republican and white?

Obama never said things would improve. He said it would not be the same as Bush's time in office. He was right, there's more secrecy, more spending, and more laws shoved down our throats. I feel for the morons who actually fell for his Hope and Change line.

The conspiracy theory seems to be right on because as a nation we are being challenged. The people we should fear, the people who want our guns taken away. There is a group of billionaires who are trying with all their money to influence all laws so they are protected. Check these people out look at what they are trying to do:

M Bloomberg advocates gun controls, open immigration, amnesty for all illegals, wage controls.

George Soros is for gun controls, open immigration, open borders, amnesty for all illegals and wage controls.

Rupert Murdock; advocates gun controls, open immigration, open borders, amnesty for all illegals, control of news, and news papers, wage controls.

Warren Buffett; supports gun controls, open immigration, open borders, amnesty for all illegals, control of all the nations rail systems, with tax breaks to rebuild the rail system. Intent to take most of the nations trucks off the road, ship all goods by container to centralized locations, with distribution from these points.

There are others in corporate America, too that are involved. People need to watch and listen to these people because they are trying to take over our Country, rebuke them at every point, they use their money and power to steer this country into profits for themselves. When the tax laws are restructured and these billionaires are required to pay their fair share they won't have as much money to corrupt our government.

This is just another secret Hussein Obama moment. Nothing happens where anyone can see it. It's all behind closed doors. But he PROMISED a "NEW TRANSPARENCY". Yeah, right. He's from Chicago where everything is secret because if it wasn't, they would all go to jail and that is precisely what should happen to Hussein Obama and his cabinet of corruption, lies and deceit. Go to Kenya Mr. President and take your crime family with you. I can't wait until all of this comes out in the Impeachment Hearings. I hope they speed that up around 6 months from November 2012…if we're all still in the White House by then? With him supporting the Muslim Terrorists in Egypt and Libya that is going to be in question.

Transparency, what a lie! This administration is the most corrupt in history. There are scores of people covering up the illegal agendas of Obama and his goons. Why, power and the change of our way of life. Why does this President so adamantly want to destroy our history and what our founding fathers set up as a model for our society, power and control of the people. He is a socialist radical who intends on destroying America from within. We all know it and no one in Congress has the guts to expose the truth. When will someone challenge the administration and shed light on the truth? We are waiting?

Tim Adams' (Honolulu senior elections clerk) statements conflicted directly with repeated affirmations by public officials in Hawaii that they had seen or had inspected Obama's birth records that would document his representations that he was born in the state. The issue of his birth is pertinent insofar as it plays a role in his status as a "natural born citizen" under the Constitution's requirement for presidents, a demand not imposed on any other federal office-holder. The Hawaii governor passed a law allowing public officials to ignore repeated requests for information on the birth certificate in question.

"But at the Homeland Security Department, since July 2009, career employees were ordered to provide political staffers with information about the people who asked for records — such as where they lived and whether they were private citizens or reporters — and about the organization where they worked." Big Bruthah be watchin' y'all!

".The most transparent administration ever" - another Obama lie!

Drain the swamp" - another Pelosi lie!

Fair and open government" - more Hairy Reid lies!

Nice to see the Democrats will say anything to get votes but will do whatever they want, once they're in. Glad the liberals are so righteous and forthcoming!

There is absolutely no end in sight to the depths of corruption that the dem/progresive/socialist/marxists will sink to? Our only hope is that honest, patriotic Americans will stop them and protect them and us from the horror that is their own corruption. They attempt to bankrupt the nation, try to foist the absolute fraud that global warming is upon us, the attempt to destroy our healthcare system through government control (social security, the post office, Medicare, medical, the budget, Amtrak and the very corrupted halls of the government are doing so well right?), lie, cheat, steal. Maybe gulags and re-education camps would not be such a bad idea for this swine.

So this is the most open and honest administration in years huh Obama. Is there a campaign promise he won't break? How about we GET RID OF THE DEPARTMENT OF HOMELAND SECURITY! We pay their salary and it appears their only job is to stop us from knowing the truth as to how our government is run. They spy on us and we pay them to do it, it is insane. We need to reduce the number of spy agencies, our government is out of control and it is up to we the people to fix it.

"Career employees were ordered to provide political staff with information about the people who asked for records — such as where they lived and whether they were private citizens or reporters — and about the organization where they worked. If a member of Congress sought documents, employees were told to specify Democrat or Republican." (AP 17 Mar 2011)
Now why is "political staff" gathering all that information? Are they making an enemies list? Why are they interfering with FOIA records requests? What are they trying to hide? Why is the Justice Department defending government (political appointees) efforts to withhold information? Why didn't Obama release the details of his Administration's meetings on Obamacare? Where's the transparency or does transparency disappear when you've got something to hide? Why is Homeland Security detouring "hundreds of requests for federal records to senior political advisers for unusual scrutiny, probing for information about the requesters and sometimes delaying disclosures deemed politically sensitive."

Wonder what Obama and his political appointees want to do with all that information they're gathering on requestors?

151

Of course this administration does not want anyone to have access to ANY files…the less we know, the easier it is for THEM to tell the public only those things they want us to know. It makes selling their liberal ideas and agenda so much easier if you are kept in the blind and don't know what they are REALLY doing…WAKE UP PEOPLE. Obama spent millions to block all his records of the past and that same practice continues with his presidency.

And you people actually think that the government will turn over the true and correct information? The only thing that the government will allow to be released under the FOIA is the version that the government wants to use. This is nothing more or less than more government propaganda that the news media reports as the "Truth". More lies to the American people.

Two great quotes: "They don't like to abide by the law or be reminded that they are breaking It." and ""The government should not keep information confidential merely because public officials might be embarrassed by disclosure, because errors and failures might be revealed or because of speculative or abstract fears," Obama said shortly after he took office." Obama says one thing, does another? I believe that is definition of liar and/or hypocrite.

THE NRA is fighting a new bill that would take our gun rights away totally right now in congress and is very worried about it, I don't know the bills number but it is very dangerous it would label certain individuals of terrorism even if they have done nothing wrong such as denying to renew your drivers licensees. Call the NRA and ask them what is the bill number. This is so the American people can call there congressmen to stop this its very dangerous bill, better yet join the NRA they need our help more now than ever what is your freedom worth because it is not free. Any one who knows there is something wrong going on and remains silent is part of the problem and not the solution step up to the plate and take action please I have, how about you or are you just going along for a free ride? Their is no free ride with this be a patriot do your part stop bickering and take action now.

We have a very big problem with Mexican gangs all over this country that the Government has put a lid on it not to mention the WAR at the border. She is nothing but a fat pig that takes orders from the very top. The whole department is a joke and should be ashamed the way they handle security in this country. The credibility of this department fell when Obama put worthless people in charge like he has every department in the Government, just a bunch of misfits like the President.

When are we going to throw these horrible people out of there? It has been clear all along that the security of this country is not a high priority for these people. They say anything that looks good in print and then do the exact opposite. They are walking all over the Constitution and nobody seems to care. They have one agenda and one only. That is to buy as many votes as they can by using the tax dollars of the working people. They look at illegals and see votes, they look at a single mother with 15 kids and no job and no education and they are paying her to raise those kids to be just like her. Votes mean power and they are getting as much as my tax dollars will buy. Why do you think that they don't want the budget cuts? There will be votes that they will not be able to buy.

The Obama Regime! Compulsive Liars Disorder! Such a person lies with unbelievable ease and seems to find comfort in it. Even if he is provided with hard facts, he would never acknowledge that he is lying. In fact, making him confess to his lies is next to impossible as lying feels right to him. A compulsive liar would feel awkward in telling the truth and would have no scruples of conscience about lying to one and all and about any situation however big or small.

There is way too much government, and it's driving America into financial ruin. We need to drastically cut the number of people the federal government employs, if the government waste had to be measured against a solvent business and accountability given for how our tax dollars are spent the CEO would be fired and probably a minimum 60% of the workers laid off to match how responsibilities would be covered in a business.

Government workers (the MAJORITY of them in any case) do as little as possible to get a check.

Why? Because it's all about funding! If a government organization does not use all of it's funding to complete a task, then they cannot request additional funds during the next budget. So the workers are encouraged to use every last minute and stretch jobs so that their organization can request additional funding from the next budget.

This has been going on for so long in many areas that organizations are over staffed and the staff is allowed to do as little as possible.

Add to that the nepotism and favor trading system by which many federal positions are filled and what we have is a financial nightmare.

The entire dog pile ought to be accounted for now and reported on, unfortunately the AP (all propaganda) is more interested in distributing lies about the economy than they are about changing America for the better and forcing our government to be responsible for the waste they encourage.

It now looks like the Obama administration is actively violating our nation's law and maybe it is time for impeachment hearings in the House. Freedom of Information is supposed to be for Americans and lack of it is for dictators or corrupt politicians. It sure looks like Obama is now fully a corrupt politician and needs to be corrected and/or removed. I sure wished that Joe Biden would show courage and stand up for America or leave this administration. So far on some issues the Republicans are sure making the Democrats look very incompetent in their work.

The funny thing about Homeland Security is that Bush, a Republican who supposedly advocated small government, started it and all of the so-called conservatives voted for it. We knew the Democratic National Committee would love to have a bigger government. Homeland Security employs some 200,000 people to do the job that the FBI etc used to do. What a waste. The more things change, the more they remain the same. America is a broken system and people like Obama are just another spoke in the wheel. What a joke. Is it time for a revolt?

What is Home Land Security? What is national Security? What is Border Patrol Security? What is Coast Guard? What is the National Guard? What does the DEA, FBI, BATF and all the alphabet soup groups do? We have more security in this nation than anywhere on earth and we still are not safe! Why don't we get rid of about 90% of this governmental pork barrel expenditure and let the original forces do their work. We have one security agency falling over another in any kind of investigation. No one knows who is doing what when. There is no control because each one wants to be in charge. Look at the border security situation. We have the Border Patrol working themselves to death and Homeland Security is spending their money getting in the way with the Justice Department telling everyone that if we catch anyone their are going to turn them loose. Maybe we need a new government! We will found it on the principals of the first one but keep control of this one away from politicians.

The man, who has nothing to hide, hides nothing. This whole administration is rife with subterfuge. No wonder Obama remarked the other day that he would rather be President of China than the USA. He said he had to report everything he was going to do instead of just doing it. Sounds about right, he would rather be a dictator than president is the problem and we don't need any dictators. The fact that people have to give the party the inquirer belongs to smacks of politics and nothing else so why are they hiding things from people of the wrong party? This President is the biggest mistake this country ever made and the more he talks the more people he convinces the people, but talk he must. That's all he can do.

Obama's administration is even LESS transparent than Bush's. Hate to say that, but it appears to be true. Becoming less and less difference between politics in this country and politics in Venezuela, Syria, Myanmar, the Ivory Coast, Cuba, or any other country where politics plays the decisive role. And just to be rhetorical, what GOOD has come from having Napolitano in the position of head of Homeland Security? Answer: absolutely none. Considerable harm as this article shows. If Obama can't even make sure his subordinates follow his mandates (for a more transparent government) the failure just shows his failure as a leader: hell, can't even keep his own house in order. Any good executive would have this woman on the carpet in ten minutes and, probably, out the door in fifteen. But, alas, doesn't work like that in politics where the cream quickly goes into the private sector and the dregs keep getting promoted.

This is a reflection of the elite, educated, liberal, morally bankrupt idiots that have been taxpayer financed into powerful positions. We are spending money educating people that are too shallow to handle the responsibility an education provides. Instead of merely being a read a book take a test; follow a communist professor requirement to get a degree. We need to evaluate the true reason for education. It should instill and test people for their ability to reason and make sound intelligent decisions. It should instill honesty, integrity, and a moral compass to follow existing law, and improve the ground they occupy.

What we have are losers that can only function as a mob. They speak one speak, follow those that destroy more than they build, and blame everyone but themselves for failure. They hide behind the media, kids, blacks, homosexuals, and blame conservatives for everything they screw up. They have locked the blacks into slum voting warehouses and are trying to put the Mexican illegals into the farm system to control them too. If the Mexicans don't figure this out they too will have their family structure become a mirror of what the slums our black population has settled for. If it's broke or failing look to a socialist, communist, liberal schooled idiot to be behind it.

Napolitano should be charge with TREASON, for not obeying the oath of office, "Protect and Defend the United States from without and within", she says that border cities are safe.........Lady, Tucson has the highest kidnapping rate of the whole nation, thousands of illegals have cross into our land, they are bringing whole families, men, women, children, the elderly, even the mentally ill, and they are getting our medical care, the women are having babies here, and they get instant Medicare, Food Stamp card, and housing assistance, without having to put one......one single penny into our system, where has your head been Napolitano.

It is obvious that there are a lot of concerns about the transparency that is in the White House and the federal government. It is past the time to start "Taking Back America". Make sure that during the election in 2012 that every vote is cast for the candidates that will start listening to the people and enacting the legislation that will benefit every American. It is not too late if all Americans start to be objective in their voting practices. Do not vote for someone because they are white, black, woman, Democratic or Republican. Vote for what the people want.

CHAPTER ELEVEN:

OBAMA'S LYBIAN ANSWERS

"The President does not have power under the Constitution to unilaterally authorize a military attack in a situation that does not involve stopping an actual or imminent threat to the nation." - Senator Barack Obama, December 20, 2007.

Where is Joe Biden now that Obama has entered the United States into another war? In 2007 the Associated Press reported that Joe Biden warned that he would impeach Bush for waging war without congressional approval. Biden forgot that President Bush did get congressional approval for the war in Iraq. When is Biden going to call on the Congress to start the impeachment process on Obama? The two esteemed leaders of the United States seem to be flip flopping on the issue of credible activities as long as they are the ones that are forgetting how the constitution actually is supposed to work.

Isn't Obama doing now, what he viciously criticized Bush for doing, with the Iraq war? The only difference I can see, is Bush actually went to the Congress ... Obama did not. The Secretary of State checked in with the Arab League, NATO and the United Nations. Why does it seem like the Secretary of State had more input on the decision than the President? The President did not consult the Congress of the United States prior to committing our military to action in Libya. Apparently the Congress does not matter to President Obama. The hypocrisy and arrogance that Obama is showing is staggering.

It was reported by Reuters on March 30, 2011 that President Obama has signed a secret order authorizing covert United States government support for rebel forces seeking to oust Libyan leader Muammar Gaddafi. The President's transparency just keeps on getting more muddy by the day.

Obama signed the order, known as a presidential "finding", within the last two or three weeks, according to four United States government sources familiar with the matter.

Such findings are a principal form of presidential directive used to authorize secret operations by the Central Intelligence Agency. The CIA and the White House declined immediate comment.

Obama, France, Britain and the United Nations for that matter, have involved themselves in affairs where they have no business. Libya didn't invade their neighbor nor did they threaten to. This is a civil war, a war internal to Libya, a war between civilian and government forces. Taking sides is what the United States, France, Britain and the United Nations are doing without knowing who they are siding with.

In the President's speech describing the Libyan war Obama failed to mention the rebels because he has no idea as to who they are. We're backing the "rebels" without knowing who they are, what they stand for, or what Libya will look like if they take over. Yet, we're blindly giving our support in the hope that it will work out the way we want. How can it work out the way we want when the President doesn't know what the objectives are in the first place? What are we hoping will work out? Instead of "Hope & Change", Obama has reverted to "Change & Hope"…Change something in "Hope" that it works out. What an incredibly arrogant administration we have.

The American citizens would like to know why President Obama has to lie. The President needs to start making sure that his speech writers start preparing the text of his speeches that are correct and not written just too appease the listening audience. When you learn to speak from the heart with feeling you will be able to discuss the problems honestly. America would like to see the President have a speech that he actually wrote and believed was the truth. Other presidents have written their own speeches and the reception was received by the citizens in a positive manner and believed in what the President said. Unfortunately, that is not happening with this President.

"Broadening our military mission to include regime change would be a mistake," Obama said on March 28, 2011. This is the same President that on several occasions had declared that Gadhafi must go. That would indicate that the President meant a change in leadership in Libya.

Obama is a walking contradiction. Much of his speech covered the same topics that Bush said to go to war with Iraq, only Bush said it not only to Congress for their approval to go to war, but to the American people. Obama also gladly accepted the Nobel Peace Prize. When was the last time you've heard of a Nobel Peace Prize winner bombing a country and killing its citizens without provocation. Obama conveniently changes his values, and his promises, when they're convenient. Obama launched his political career by opposing the Iraq War and why we went to war. Now he conveniently uses the same reasons we went to war with Iraq to justify his war against Libya, and doesn't even have the courage to use the word "war". When you bomb and kill people in another country that is a war. Obama's hypocritical allies who are opponents of the Iraq War are also conveniently silent as Obama conducts his unauthorized war against Libya. I certainly hope that Obama, and his hypocritically silent allies, all lose their re-election for the platform of lies and deceit they have been running upon. And Obama should give back his Nobel Peace Prize. He didn't deserve it the first time, and he certainly doesn't deserve it now.

There have been endless rumors that the rebels are, at the minimum, Al-Queda backed. If not Al-Queda! This would put us in a position of supporting militarily the people who committed 9/11 and who our troops have been battling for 10 years now. I don't know if that is true, but the rumor mill is running full force with the theory. He had an absolute responsibility to address that and define to who the "rebel forces" are. We are killing for them and have every right to know who we are allying ourselves with. He sidestepped that issue completely. It's not a small sidestep. His speech was eloquent as his speeches usually are. His speeches are what got him elected. Obama says glowing words with no substance behind them that deflect the mind and eye from the reality of events. I no longer listen to what he says in speeches. I listen for what he omits. And in this case, the omissions were enough to make me even more suspicious of what we are doing in Libya. Especially now that I've learned that Obama's own military advisers counseled against it. This means that exactly 2 people in America made the decision to go into Libya, the President and Hillary Clinton. And none of the rest of Americans really have any idea of who we are supporting, why we are, and when we will leave there.

Analysis: Obama doesn't mention Libyan rebels

By ANNE GEARAN, AP National Security Writer – /29/2011

WASHINGTON – President Barack Obama wanted to tell a hesitant America why he launched a military assault in Libya, and he wanted to describe it on his terms — limited, sensible, moral and backed by international partners with the shared goal of protecting Libyans from a ruthless despot.

Trouble is, the war he described Monday doesn't quite match the fight the United States is in.

It also doesn't line up with the conflict Obama himself had seemed to presage, when he expressly called for Moammar Gadhafi's overthrow or resignation. Obama's stated goals stop well short of that. And although Obama talked of the risks of a long war, he did not say just when or on what terms the United States would leave Libya.

Obama never directly mention the Libyan rebels seeking Gadhafi's overthrow, even though the heavy U.S.-led firepower trained on Gadhafi's forces has allowed those rebels to regain momentum and push toward Gadhafi's territory.

"We have intervened to stop a massacre," Obama said.

Ten days into a conflict many Americans say they do not understand, Obama laid out a moral imperative for intervening against a murderous tyrant, and doing so without the lengthy international dithering that allowed so much blood to be spilled in Bosnia. His address at the National Defense University echoed campaign rhetoric about restoring U.S. moral pride of place after squandering it in Iraq.

"Mindful of the risks and costs of military action, we are naturally reluctant to use force to solve the world's many challenges," Obama said. "But when our interests and values are at stake, we have a responsibility to act."

Gadhafi's forces have been largely pinned down and unable to mount a massacre since the first hours of the war, while U.S. and NATO warplanes have become an unacknowledged aerial arm of the rebels. Obama said the United States will help the opposition, an oblique reference to the rebels.

Over the weekend U.S. Air Force A-10 Thunderbolt aircraft, designed to provide battlefield support to friendly ground forces, flew attack missions for the first time in this conflict. The Pentagon also disclosed Monday that Air Force AC-130 gun-ships, low-flying aircraft armed with a 105mm howitzer and a 40mm cannon, had joined the battle. Those two types of aircraft give the U.S. more ability to confront pro-Gadhafi forces in urban areas with less risk of civilian casualties.

The Pentagon's lead spokesman on Libya operations, Navy Vice Adm. William Gortney, told reporters Monday that the U.S. military is not coordinating with the rebels. But he left little doubt that, by design or not, Western air power is propelling the rebels forward.

"Clearly they're achieving a benefit from the actions that we're taking," Gortney said. He displayed a chart that showed rebels advancing within 80 miles of Sirte, Gadhafi's home town.

If the purpose of the U.N.-sanctioned military action is to protect civilians, does that include pro-Gadhafi civilians who are likely to be endangered in places like Sirte that are in the rebels' crosshairs? If not, it is difficult to see the Western intervention as a neutral humanitarian act not aligned with the rebels.

The first goal of the intervention was to prevent a massacre of civilians in Benghazi, the eastern Libyan city where Gadhafi forces were threatening to crush the rebellion two weeks ago. Gadhafi said he would "show no mercy."

A U.S.-led assault quickly accomplished that first goal. A no-fly zone was established two weekends ago with little resistance. The U.S. and its partners then launched air-strikes on Gadhafi supply lines and other military targets not only near Benghazi but around other contested areas as well.

But the role of Western air power then went beyond that initial humanitarian aim, to in effect provide air cover for the rebels while pounding Gadhafi forces in a bid to break their will or capacity to fight.

Now U.S. forces are pulling back, handing much of the responsibility for the open-ended military campaign to allies, as Obama said they would.

"So for those who doubted our capacity to carry out this operation, I want to be clear: The United States of America has done what we said we would do," Obama said with clear satisfaction.

He meant that the U.S. had hewed to its stated role under a U.N. Security Council resolution that authorized force.

But he acknowledged that the U.N. mandate doesn't extend to Gadhafi's ouster, even if many of the nations carrying it out might wish for that. Obama was frank about the reasons why.

"Broadening our military mission to include regime change would be a mistake," Obama said.

It would shatter the international partnership he relies on for diplomatic cover and security backup. It would probably mean sending U.S. ground forces into yet another Muslim nation, something Obama has said he will not do in Libya. It would undoubtedly increase the risk to the U.S. military, the costs of the war and U.S. responsibility for shoring up and protecting whatever Libya might emerge, Obama said.

"To be blunt, we went down that road in Iraq," Obama said, where thousands of U.S. forces remain eight years after the fall of Saddam Hussein.

"That is not something we can afford to repeat in Libya," Obama said.

Getting rid of Gadhafi "may not happen overnight," Obama warned, in his first acknowledgement of the stalemate with the rebels that many analysts and some of his own military advisers suspect is coming. Gadhafi, Obama said, might well cling to power for some time.

The United States is considering arming the rebels, directly or indirectly, and U.S. officials say the U.N. resolution would allow that. Obama mentioned nothing about the possibility of civil war in Libya, or what the U.S. might do if the war grinds on for months.

Obama still faces questions about why Libya and not Yemen, or not Syria. One of his closest national security advisers, Denis McDonough, told reporters Monday that the administration doesn't "get very hung up on this question of precedent."

"We don't make decisions about questions like intervention based on consistency or precedent," McDonough said.

Throughout his address, Obama seemed to be answering his own criticism of past wars and past leaders who committed military force too hastily or too hesitantly.

The Nobel Peace Prize winner never used the word "war" to describe what's happening in Libya, but made a point of addressing what the conflict he chose "says about the use of America's military power, and America's broader leadership in the world, under my presidency."

His book "The Audacity of Hope" and his Nobel speech established the same predicates for U.S. military intervention — an allied coalition and use of multinational power.

"We know that the United States, as the world's most powerful nation, will often be called upon to help," Obama said Monday. "In such cases, we should not be afraid to act, but the burden of action should not be America's alone."

EDITOR'S NOTE — Anne Gearan has covered national politics and national security in Washington since 1999.

By BEN FELLER, AP White House Correspondent – March 28, 2011

WASHINGTON – Defending the first war launched on his watch, President Barack Obama declared Monday night the United States intervened in Libya to prevent a slaughter of civilians that would have stained the world's conscience and "been a betrayal of who we are." Yet he ruled out targeting Libyan leader Moammar Gadhafi, warning that trying to oust him militarily would be a costly mistake.

Obama announced that NATO would take command over the entire Libya operation on Wednesday, keeping his pledge to get the U.S. out of the lead but offering no estimate on when the conflict might end.

He never described the U.S.-led military campaign as a "war" and gave no details on its costs, but he offered an expansive case for why he believed it was in the national interest of the United States and allies to act.

In blunt terms, Obama said the response had stopped Gadhafi's advances and halted a slaughter that could have shaken the stability of an entire region.

"To brush aside America's responsibility as a leader and — more profoundly — our responsibilities to our fellow human beings under such circumstances would have been a betrayal of who we are," Obama said. "Some nations may be able to turn a blind eye to atrocities in other countries. The United States of America is different. And as president, I refused to wait for the images of slaughter and mass graves before taking action."

Here are the comments from average American citizens and what they think about the President's speech about why the American military was sent to war in Libya. In some cases the comments are extreme but for the most part they are right on. They have not been altered in any way except for spelling and grammar. I hope you enjoy the comments and can get a clearer picture of what is happening in the war with Libya and the actions of the President of the United States.

Obama really didn't address why he did not consult with the Congress as was required, and he should be impeached. All of the Middle East riots and protests started because of the price of food going up so much, and that is because of Obama policies. Quantitative easing raised prices of all commodities, including food and fuel, and we can see a huge difference here at home at the gas pump and at the grocers. Both are up the biggest share of 50%.

Middle East countries were unable to adjust to that, because many subsidize food and fuel, and not all of them reap the rewards of high fuel prices because they don't have oil, and if they gave higher subsidies and then prices went back down, they would be unable to sustain it, and you know how hard it is to give someone more money and then want it back, so there was no adjustment and the protests started. So it all comes directly back to Obama and his policies.

Another problem comes from inconsistency, asking some leaders to step down and leave, sending our forces in to fight for the rebels in Libya, even though we are on the same side as al Qaida there, and then ruling out intervention in other places where the problems are worse, and could become far worse.

It is also true that Obama has still not yet produced his birth certificate, as is required by our Constitution to become President, and he should be impeached. Obama has lost his legitimacy to lead, and should step down and leave. What he did in Libya was an act of unprovoked war, and should be held responsible for crimes against humanity.

This country needs to shed of Obama as soon as possible in any way that can be made to happen, before he forgets to consult Congress and commits another act of war that could start a wider conflict that will throw us into a depression, if he has not already done so, and Americans need to start hearing the truth, instead of half-truths and pure propaganda to make us feel good when there is nothing to feel good about.

Bombing Libyan forces was not a lot different from when Japan bombed Pearl Harbor, except that the Japanese just bombed us for a few hours, and we have been bombing Libya for weeks now, even bombing Gadhafi's personal compound, and I don't understand how that was protecting civilians...that was to kill Gadhafi, whether Obama wants to admit it or not. It's just another lie.

Impeach Obama, and find someone that can lead this country out of the trouble we're in, not further down a dead end road. Obama has driven the car off a cliff, and we need someone that can get us on the road again, and preferably someone that has a driver's license.

The idea of conducting warfare operations when you're not "in the driver's seat" is without merit. American servicemen and women putting their lives on the line for some alliance instead of under the direction of their Commander-In-Chief are wrong on so many levels. This is an administrative excuse to engage in deadly confrontation while escaping accountability to the American people and to the families of the brave soldiers. One very dangerous precedent and one we should not be willing to accept.

I think it is about time that the President of the United States starts taking care of America and stops trying to play god around the world. In case he has not noticed there is hunger in America, there is extreme poverty in America, there are incredible national problems in this country. Enough giving away of tax dollars now accompanied by borrowed dollars for which our4 future is at stake! How about suspending the so called help in billions of dollars to all those countries who then believe that we somehow owe it to them.

Mr. President, I am an American citizen first, a US Army Veteran, and a Black Man! How dare you take sides in this mess when you guys would not help in Darfur. Why did you not help there? You just lost my vote! If it's about helping the people that are being oppressed, what happened to helping those in Darfur? I will openly talk against you and your administration for getting involved in this mess, and not being true to your word. If you can't help one, then don't help the other. Are they not people too in Darfur?

Amazing, when Obama attacks a country that has made no threat to the US, has very little to do with our economy (less than 3% of our oil is from Libya) and Gadhafi is his friend, not a word from the liberals on how we are bombing children and killing innocent people. We do not even know who the rebels are. Why Libya? Syria, Iran and North Korea kill far more of their own people than Gadhafi and have been in a true civil war in their country. Why are we not bombing these other countries? Then when he finally makes a decision, he doesn't even have the balls to lead. He lets France of all people and now NATO controls our military. We are becoming the biggest joke. No wonder there is a cry to remove the dollar as the reserve currency. This will reduce our standard of living by at least 25%, but Obama, being ashamed of America, believes we deserve it......

I'm sure Barry will be at his best putting some really nice lipstick on this pig. But let's face it...do we even know who these rebels are? What do you think the odds are that once they 'win' they will look like nothing friendly to us? Many of them have actually FOUGHT against us in Afghanistan and Iraq.

Many have said that they welcome the air support, and it looks like we are even going to be giving them more weapons. What Poindexter is running this country, anyway? If we actually land troops on the ground the rebels would actually join Gadhafi's men to fight us. What does THAT tell you? The humanitarian thing isn't the issue otherwise we'd be in a dozen other countries right now.

And it isn't about the NATO and Arab League asking us to help. Since when does the President of the US take direction from foreign entities over consulting our Congress?

This man is a disaster. Obama is an unmitigated disaster of a President in every way. I have no idea how our country will survive him, or clean up this monstrous mess he is making in his ONLY four years in office. Obama is the worst President of the last 100 years.

Obama's strategy, in Afghanistan and Libya, is as clear as mud and getting worse. They're about as clear as Obama-care.

Yes he went to the UN, but did he go to the people who matter in THIS country and ask if he could go to war? NO he did not he went to the UN, Specifically Arab Countries to get an ok. He did NOT ask the Congress of the United States if it was ok. That is a stab in the back for the American people, because he did not ASK! He does not think that the judicial system works in this country.

Yep! It's more Change we can believe in. When that call came at 3 a.m., Obama put it on hold; pulled a Jimmy Carter and woke up his daughters' to ask, Sasha, Malia, What should I do? These are my "brothers"; and you know, I wrote in my book, when it comes down to these times, I will stand with my brothers. Oh me, Oh my, I'm the Peace President, can I wage another war. I better "sleep" on this a few days. The Republicans may have run the car into the ditch, but they had the keys; a GPS and called AAA. They also knew how to put it back in Drive and Drove the Democrats out. Obama on the other hand, has been asleep at the wheel; put it in "R" for "renege" and has been doing so since Day 1. The media got their darling, and they are now remarkably silent. All they can do is talk about the Tea Party…which is the only Party that can and will "Win Back the Future".

I have yet to understand why any Country at all expects the United States to stand and help them, when they hate us and everything we stand for, but when they need help who do they ask/demand should help. We are helping the entire world but not our own COUNTRY. WE NEED TO CLOSE THE BORDERS AND CLEAN UP OUR OWN COUNTRY FIRST, NO HUNGER IN AMERICA, GOOD EDUCATION, NO ILLEGALS, NO FOREIGN AIDE! Term Limits on Congress, and all laws should be voted on by the citizens since we can't truly trust our own government anymore to protect us and look out for our best interest first!

March 28, 2012 (AP) Obama did not seek congressional authority before he took military action in Libya, nor did he consult closely with congressional leaders, sore points for lawmakers on both sides of the aisle.

Has anybody seen or heard from Reid, Pelosi or Biden Lately?

This was the same Obama who voted against Iraq when the majority of Congress supported Bush. The difference was: Iraq was already under UN sanctions and broke every one for over a decade. Iraq was under a no fly zone for over a decade and was shooting at our jets for years. Every nation in the West had their intelligence agencies saying that Saddam was building WMD. The opposition in this country, including the Clintons and Kerry all said pre-invasion, that Iraq had WMD. Bush went to Congress with his case, long before going to the UN.

So here we have Obama beloved by the left for his no-Iraq stance, invades another country while on vacation without a peep to the American people or Congress. Don't blame me, I voted for the war hero.

The poor man is absolutely clueless. In hiding all weekend trying to determine what to tell American people. Blah, blah, blah…nothing new - he's a lost soul and has led us into another Middle East mess. Our soldiers deserve our support. I certainly hope we can get them home soon. We need them HERE - NOW. We need to get rid of the illegals, close our borders, rebuild our infrastructure and TAKE BACK OUR COUNTRY.

Obama has NO BUDGET, but still can borrow money from China for missiles to use in 3 wars. He is definitely showing his inexperience as Commander in Chief. He better start taking care of the American people or he may be sharing a room with Gadhafi.

Why are we helping rebels with admitted ties to Al Quida? What happens when Al Quida has the money from the oil in Libya to wage war on the Christian nations? But then according to Obama we are not a Christian nation.

The War Powers Resolution of 1973 (50 U.S.C. 1541–1548) was a United States Congress joint resolution providing that the President can send U.S. armed forces into action abroad only by authorization of Congress or if the United States is already under attack or serious threat. The War Powers Resolution requires the President to notify Congress within 48 hours of committing armed forces to military action and forbids armed forces from remaining for more than 60 days, with a further 30 day withdrawal period, without an authorization of the use of military force or a declaration of war. The resolution was passed by two-thirds of Congress, overriding a presidential veto. Well the Congress didn't authorize it, we are not under attack, so where is the serious threat to the United States?

Obama, you are a betrayal to who we are, you hate my country, my flag and my Constitution. Leave America out of Libya's trouble and you go back to the Middle East where you came from. If America would keep there nose out of all these foreign countries problems, maybe then we could solve more problems in our own backyard

'Defending the first war launched on his watch, President Barack Obama declared Monday night that the United States intervened in Libya to prevent a slaughter of civilians that would have stained the world's conscience and "been a betrayal of who we are." Yet he ruled out targeting Moammar Gadhafi, warning that trying to oust him militarily would be a costly mistake.'

Here we go, thousands die, and then restoration of status quo ante bellum, the pattern of all European wars before 1914. 'No regime change in Libya', then why are we there? Leaving a wounded Gadhafi in power would guarantee a reactionary terror and slaughter the likes we've never seen. Lt. Col. 'Queer-Daffy' is a madman who would mass murder his own people to stay in power, which is exactly what would have happened if NATO had not intervened. There's something definitely wrong with this section 8 that the king in Tripoli would have riffed out of the army had it not been for his coup. Then there's our killer clown, Obama, spends every dime on a failed health care system about to be repealed and declared unconstitutional, and a people are fighting for their very lives against a deranged dictator, and he abdicates America's role as a world leader to say he doesn't care, let them get massacred, its all NATO's problem. Some world leader!

Another issue that Obama did not address was WHO are the Rebels that we are supporting? WHAT is their Political Ideology? Will they be better or worse for Libya or more importantly for the USA? 25% of Al-Qaida fighters killed or captured in Iraq came from eastern Libyan Tribes. Ten days into this shooting War and no one knows who the Rebels are and what their goals are... And the President will not address the issue.

More importantly the President did not address is what is his exit strategy was to get out of Libya?

So is the President saying that his Foreign Policy is that he will use Military force to support UN or "International" Mandates that he supports and that Congressional Approval is no longer necessary?

He didn't adhere to his Constitutional oath when he unilaterally chose to bomb a sovereign nation. He has subsequently murdered civilian non-combatants in Libya via the missiles that he chose to launch at them. He is not only now open to investigation and impeachment trials, but he is also guilty of war crimes and should be tried as a war criminal. Sorry, you can't have it both ways. If it was not an act of war, then there should have been no bombing.

Our government needs to stop pretending it can police the world and our President needs to stop acting like a dictator by ignoring the Constitution and ordering military action without congressional approval. When will these war-hungry politicians stop? How many of our troops need to die? How many civilians do we need to blow up? How broke does this country need to be? How many enemies do we need to make? It needs to end now. Obama is worse than Bush, and THAT'S saying something. Also, the President forgot to mention that the United States is part of NATO. We're not going anywhere.

The man currently sitting in the Oval Office has no authority to declare this military conflict without the approval of Congress. He didn't get it and we all know what he did. If any Republican had done this, the Democrats would be up in arms over the illegality and screaming about it endlessly…look at what they did over Iraq and George Bush got the authority to engage in a military conflict and went through Congress getting the approval of the majority of Democrats. And they still screamed about it. This time, the American people are furious that this country has no business in a third war in the Middle East with all those unknown consequences. The same consequences that Jimmy Carter has had interfering in the Middle East will happen to Barack Obama as well. Not to mention everything else that he's done that has been unconstitutional. Obamacare tops the list, one issue out of many he has no constitutional authority to enact. There isn't enough space to go into the countless things this Oval Office occupant has done that he has no authority to enact, but he's done it anyway…we'll see just how much damage his continuing presence in the White House does. But it's considerable in just over two years. And more is coming. Just how much outrage will the American people have to endure? And how much economic slavery will the American people put up with?

Obama delivered his speech in such a phony, forced manner of speaking that it made me want to vomit…and what he said was so clichéd, it also made me nauseous to the point of wanting to scream and throw things at the television set. His speech writer should be terminated immediately. Obama's presidency should also be terminated immediately. He is lying … we all know he is lying… and that our sole objective in Libya is to orchestrate control over their oil supply. This has to stop. What are we, as a nation, going to do about this? Our government is acting in whatever way best serves the interests of the wealthiest of the wealthy. They aren't listening to us at all.

Obama has no authority to start a war. That is an exclusive power of Congress. The administration claims this is not a war. Would it be a war if another country was bombing us?

What a joke. "We will not target Gadhafi." Targeting Gadhafi should be the priority unless we want to be back there in 5-10 years, with a situation that looks similar to the Iraq War. But that's okay; the American people are used to his empty ignorant policy and promises.

Obama and his cronies need to go. The idiot says we don't want a regime change. So why are we there helping the rebels? I have no clue what our elected officials are up to other than spending our money that we don't have. It is becoming clear they know what they are doing. Guess we are borrowing money for this too. Would somebody please tell me what "our government" is doing? Aren't they supposed to represent the citizens of the United States? Get us the hell out.

Obama is completely insane. There is no justifying what he did other than start a war illegally without congressional approval. The United States was not in any danger from Libya. Obama just wanted a reason to finance and support the Muslim brotherhood rebels in Libya. This is something that the United States should not be involved in. Congress needs to impeach Obama and stop this craziness.

If he was still in the Senate, and a President, Democrat or Republican, came before them and asked permission to do this…he would have voted "NO". This is the most arrogant, pretentious, hypocritical

173

President ever. This country is disintegrating before our very eyes. Not one good thing has come from this administration.

We really need some real leadership. Someone who does not have a law degree! Someone who gets that we need to take care of our own people first. Get rid of these so called civil servants that have not heard the American people cries for years. They have given away our jobs, demanded that it was for the betterment of Americans. I'm not seeing it. We have more folks out of work struggling to make a living. It's time to put some new rules in place. If you want to sell to America, it has to be made in America. Get rid of those foreign cars. Stop supporting folks who do not care about you and me. BUY AMERICAN... Stop thinking that you're above all this before your job is given away. WAKE UP!

Have any of you called the elected officials of the United States? You can call the White House comment line at 202-456-1414, or call Harry Reid at 202-224-3542, or Boehner at 202-225-6205, or the wicked witch of the west Pelosi at 202-225-4965. You can give these numbers to your family and friends, and tell them to call. I call once every other day, they know me by name but I have never seen them. Now that is letting them know that someone is watching them, but I need and Army of people to keep them busy.

I am a legal immigrant that hates illegal immigrants, I learned the English language, I am a Combat Vietnam Veteran, and a United States Citizen. So, why do let all these illegals tell you what they demand, stop them in their tracks before they demand more form your tax dollars! Let them know it is not about race, it's about economics do not let them play you for a fool.

Why would anyone think they could impeach a black dictator? If he was white he would be gone a long time ago; we are losing more of our Constitution every week, no Republican or Democrat does anything about it. Unfortunately, it looks like are country as we new it is doomed thanks to a dictatorship led by Obama and the Muslims, Get your guns or run for your life

This is the first "President" to put our Army, Navy, and Air Force personnel directly into military action against a sovereign nation

without Congressional approval. Even his Vice President has proclaimed such action is impeachable. Come on Congress –IMPEACH THE MAN FOR THIS UNCONSTITUTIONL ACT, RELIEVE HIM OF OFFICE, AND DEPORT HIM TO SOME COUNTRY OF HIS CHOICE, like maybe wherever he was born.

After listening to the President's speech that came out of both sides of his face and hearing a least one lie, "I went to Congress". Who the heck wrote this speech, it couldn't have been the President. How can he mess with his Muslim Brother like this? Oh yea he had to, due to public and International pressure, otherwise he would have never attacked his own country meaning Africa. Oh he was so patriotic sounding, bull hockey this man doesn't give a rats behind about the moral fiber of this country. Take this speech with about 20 lbs of salt and vote him out in 2012.

What a lair! Just say we went to war to get rid of Gadhafi. He needs to be killed. You don't use A-10 Thunderbolts Warthogs and C130 Gun Ships to enforce a "no fly zone". They are used for close air support, taking out tanks, armored vehicles, and troops. Obama do you think the average American doesn't know what those planes are used for and are stupid. I forgot the peace loving liberal lefties would not know. Hey guys, they are use to kill troops.

It would have been a betrayal of who we are? When was the last time you took a good look at this country and its people, Mr. President? Thanks to your fantastic job of running this country into the ground, screwing the majority of its people and only taking care of the rich (including yourself) and in general driving us all to the brink of (and a lot of us actually) not making ends meet anymore we already have not been who we are for a long time now. It is time to think of us first to bring us back to who we are. Get to work!

More contradictions! First we are the leader, and then we turn leadership over to someone else who has full control of the United States military. Obama says we went into war because he will not stand by to see civilians slaughtered, yet how about Rwanda, and the other African countries that committed genocide. How about Syria! Yet he doesn't know how much this is costing! Give me a break. Obama is just campaigning, he has never stopped. Glad he will be

gone in 2012. Obama doesn't even know who the rebels are? What a total lack of leadership from the Commander in Chief. I am so sick of this garbage. No specifics, just rhetoric. Bye Barack, just don't destroy what's left of this country on the way down.

Obama saying "I' did this and "I" did that is a joke! Every sign you see in Libya says "VIVE LA FRANCE"! The Libyan people KNOW that from the start the French were on their side, while Obama just like with the oil spill disaster waited and waited, and waited 30 days, like a deer in the headlights without a clue what to do! PURE INCOMPETENCE!

The COUNCIL ON FOREIGN RELATIONS IS DESTROYING THIS COUNTRY AND EVERY SINGLE MEMBER INVOLVED IN OUR GOVERNMENT HAS committed perjury by violating their oath describes in article 6 clause 3 of the constitution (18 USC 73 section 1621), Aided and abetted in criminal activity by voting for or executing unconstitutional legislation (18 USC sections 2 and 3), are in dereliction of duty and should be REMOVED FROM OFFICE by article 3 section 3 AND for THIS USC 7311 - Sec. 7311. Loyalty and striking U.S. Code - Title 5: Government Organization and Employees An individual may not accept or hold a position in the Government of the United States or the government of the District of Columbia if he - (1) advocates the overthrow of our constitutional form of government; (2) IS A MEMBER OF AN ORGANIZATION that he knows advocates the overthrow of our constitutional form of government;

The following are notable members of the Council on Foreign Relations.

Barack H. Obama, Michelle Obama, Madeleine Albright, Eliot Abrams, Howard Baker, James Baker, Michael D. Barnes {former democrat congressman from Maryland), Joe Biden, Josh Bolton (former chief-of-staff to George W. Bush), Rudy Boschwitz (former R Senator from Minnesota), Sandy Berger, Michael R. Bloomberg (Current Mayor of New York City), Bill Brock (former Republican United States Senator from Tennessee), Erin Burnett (CNBC anchor), Tom Brokaw (journalist at NBC), Howard Berman (Congressman from California), Edgar Bronfman (president of the World Jewish

Congress), Ethan Bronner (deputy foreign editor of The New York Times), Zbigniew Brzezinski (National Security Advisor to President Jimmy Carter), Stephen Gerald Breyer (United States Supreme Court justice), Jonathan S. Bush, George H.W. Bush, George W. Bush, Marvin Bush, Barbara Bush (First Lady), Jimmy Carter, Frank Carlucci (16th Secretary of Defense under Ronald Reagan), Dick Cheney Warren Christopher, Bill Clinton, Hillary Rodham Clinton, Henry Cisneros, Mario Cuomo, Katie Couric, Chris Dodd, Michael Dukakis, Mervyn M. Dymally, Lawrence Eagleburger, Roger W. Ferguson, Jr. (former vice-chairman of the Federal Reserve), Dianne Feinstein, Geraldine Ferraro, Tom Foley, Robert M. Gates, Dick Gephardt, Alan Greenspan, Bob Graham, David Gergen, Mikhail Gorbachev, Newt Gingrich, Ruth Bader Ginsburg, Tenzin Gyatso (14th Dalai Lama), David A. Harris (director of the American Jewish Committee), Michael Hayden (Air Force general, former director of the NSA and CIA), Gary Hart, Frederick Iseman, Angelina Jolie, Vernon Jordan, Thomas Kean, Sr., Nancy Kassebaum, John Kerry, Henry Kissinger, Paul R. Krugman, Jim Leach, Jim Lehrer, Joe Lieberman, Lewis Libby, John McCain, Bud McFarlane, George McGovern, George J. Mitchell, Walter Mondale, Robert Mugabe, Benyamin Netanyahu, Heather Nauert, Sandra Day O'Connor, Stan O'Neal (CEO of Merrill Lynch), Henry Paulson, David Patraeus, Kitty Pilgrim, Colin Powell, Eric Prince, Condoleezza Rice, Dan Rather, Charles Rangel, David Rockefeller, Jr. John D. Rockefeller, IV, Charlie Rose, Diane Sawyer, Dan Senor, David Stern, Jeffrey D. Sachs, Karenna Gore Schiff (daughter of Al Gore), Brent Scowcroft, George Shultz, Walter B. Slocombe, George Soros, Jonathan Soros, Lesley Stahl, Yitzhak Shamir (7th Prime Minister of Israel), Donna Shalala, Eduard Shevardnadze, Adlai Stevenson III, George Stephanopoulos, Stansfield Turner (former head of the CIA), Ted turner, Richard Thornburgh, Fred Thompson, Paul Volcker (former Chairman of the Federal Reserve), Barbara Walters ABC News journalist, Vin Weber, John C. Whitehead, James D. Wolfensohn (former president of the World Bank), Paul Wolfowitz (former president of the World Bank), James Woolsey (former Director of CIA), Paula Zahn, James Zogby, Robert Zoellick (President of the World Bank)

What you do is look through Obama and imagine the community organizer and his links with the domestic terrorist as he speaks. Then it all makes sense that his actions are based on politics. If he isn't a wolf in sheep's clothing I don't know what is.

I wonder why he did not bring up the fact that both Obama and Clinton lifted economic sanction against Libya who we are now bombing. This doesn't seem to be getting much publicity. But then again just like his basketball picks he guesses with no real clue.

In the never ending battle between Good and Evil the USA is now on the wrong side. Hussein Obama watches True Freedom Fighters in Iran get slaughtered by Islamic Fanatics and does nothing. More True Freedom Fighters are getting wiped out in Syria by more Evil Islamic Fanatics who control Syria and Hussein says nothing. Hussein Obama self righteously demanded our long time friend Umbra's resignation. Obama routinely kicks Israel in the face. For the first time in history America is now on the wrong side. Obama's Legacy will not only be the "Destruction of our Economy", but also dooming America's Soul with his partnership with evil worldwide. The enemy we face sits in the White House. His name is Barack Hussein Obama.

But then again, what do you expect from a person who doesn't even begin to understand other people's cultures. I.E. like Mrs. Obama hugging the Queen of England, Mrs. Obama going over to India and standing in line ahead of her husband and then to top it off shaking hands with the officials of that country. Someone needs to teach the Obama's etiquette in the business world. It's the number one rule of thumb and he claims he was on a business trip representing this country. Go figure.

Who told the Lybian rebels that the U.S. would defend them? The CIA? They were obviously led to rise up by someone. Gadhafi cracks down on the people and our President says "We can not let this happen. It would betray who we are as a people." This is all B.S.! When did we care about Sudanese slaughtered by the millions for decades? We need Congress to hear us! STOP DO NOT LET THIS PRESIDENT do this!

I think the excuse for the attack is absolute nonsense. The slaughter of civilians is happening all over the world in more war torn countries that actually need assistance (Sudan anyone? Hundreds of thousands

have died and been displaced with not even an official word of support from the US, save for George Clooney and Angelina Jolie). Why the support for the rebels? How the heck did they get their arms? Who the heck are they and do they even like the West? For those who are unaware, is Libya a democracy? Not by a long shot, but this is the case in many other countries, where the situation for the people are substantially more dire. Libya was the ONLY country in Africa with a living index comparable to the West. The Only one! 80 percent literacy rate, 20 percent of the residents were foreigners, living and trading in the state. No one thinks Gadhafi is a good guy but this whole situation smells very fishy to me and for once, I think the President has told us a blatant untruth.

Wow, what a bunch of hocus pocus bogus! Obama has feed the American people and the world more rhetoric again. He just reiterated the same garbage he's been saying. Again the American people and our true domestic interest are not only put on the back burner, but have been taken off the stove completely. What happened to the question and answering part of this? He walked off like he was in a hurry to get to another White House party.

We are not for regime change, just destroying their Army and Air Force. Good thing is that once this is done, the gangs of rebels armed with AK-47s and Rocket Propelled Grenade's will be able to control large sections of the population by force. The last time we did something like this was in a country called Cambodia. It didn't turn out so good for the innocent civilians who were slaughtered like rabid dogs by the rebels with the guns.

Gadhafi's a bad guy no doubt just as Saddam was but destroying the ability of the government to control the rebels will leave us only two choices: Put large numbers of boots on the ground to prevent a massacre (Libya is a real large country) or roll the dice and hope the rebels have honorable intentions.

My argument is this? What if Gadhafi didn't give up his nuclear ambitions? Would we still be there? Why haven't we gone into North Korea, Cuba, China, Vietnam or Cambodia? All these countries have killing fields against their own people. I ask this final question. What if Texas decided to succeed from the US territory and declare them a sovereign nation? Would Washington allow this? What if they were willing to fight for it would we not send our Army against them? Would they be terrorists? Guess this is why so many countries seek nuclear abilities to prevent being oppressed by the outside world.

I think Libya will become another Yemen. I really think the world should be careful with what is happening with these Muslim countries rising up. Just like Afghanistan the first time against the Soviets we were used then and we are used now. Gadhafi was no threat to us. Many love him in his country. Many hate him why don't they leave then. Cannot we just stay out or abstain just one time like Russia and China does. Always we are upfront calling the shots.

President Barack Obama looks just like a little white boy that just got caught stealing your bicycle. OOOOPS! I was on vacation in Brazil and .Hillary and France decided to start the War. I did not do it.

I think it's time for us to stand up and start our own civil war against our government! Everyday we are loosing all our rights. We are letting the government waste our money, take away youth programs, cut back on our education system and other important programs! They keep saying we are broke and deeply in debt, but yet we can help every other country why we all suffer.

Something is definitely wrong here! At this rate we will become a communist country! The land of the free what a joke! Freedom as we use to know it is no more. Now its do this, don't do that or pay a fine! The government will do anything to take our freedom and money so they can give it away. It's time to stand up and fight back America.

Just wondering… who was he "trying so hard to convince" that he did the right thing? In my opinion, he acted a bit like Charlie Sheen. Obama just kept on talking, saying the same thing over and over, but not making any sense! His smug attitude during his speech proves he "knows he did something wrong". I'm not saying we should or should not be helping Libya, but he should have run it past his own country first, not the UN. They did not put this man in office - (some) of the

American people did. They should have been included in this decision. Talk about a dictator.

Does this mean Joe Biden will move to impeach him as he previously claimed? By the way has anyone seen Joe Biden lately? Except for the reporter that he locked in the closet so the reporter could not ask any embarrassing questions.

You got the no zipper zone, now shut up and leave. Get out of Iraq. Get out of Afghanistan and close the facility in Cuba, enforce the boarders, open deep water oil drilling to American companies not just to your buddy Soros and his oil company. We definitely have an anti American President, antichrist President. Keeping oil prices high so he can bring in trucks from Mexico and Canada to replace the truckers in America he is forcing out of business because he refuses to open deep water drilling to American companies. And will not go into the reserves to bring prices down. He would like Gadhafi to stay in power and quit shipping oil so as to keep prices high. He is out to bankrupt America and force a depression. Stop this jerk before it's too late. Impeach him, come on Congress do your duty.

When the Iraq war began there were a lot of people protesting the war, though we had a good reason to go into Iraq? We have absolutely no justified reason to be involved in Libya. Where are the protesters now? Obama spent more time picking out his NCAA basketball brackets than he did trying to explain before he left on his vacation, why we were getting involved in Libya. They are not our allies. The only thing they have we want is oil. The rebel fighters are nothing more than Muslim hoods and Taliban fighters. Obama is now supporting our enemy. Isn't that treason? Giving aide and comfort to the enemy? The penalty for treason is death.

This is nuts! Why are we selectively "protecting" people from "ruthless" despots? Syrians are being killed by their government so are Yemenis. Are we going to protect them too? The Arab World is finally opening their eyes and trying to determine for themselves which way they want to live their lives. Just because they want their current leaders out doesn't mean they want to live like us. Maybe they like being in a society that limits freedom and makes people face Mecca several

times a day to pray. Let them solve their own problems and focus on our own domestic issues.

CHAPTER TWELVE:

OBAMA CONTINUES TO CAMPAIGNE

Obama is already looking ahead at the next election and was advised to say these things, not actually do them. In reality, bio-fuels are a mistake since it drives up food prices. If he is serious, why did he grant permission to Brazil to drill in the gulf? But still keep the current United States drilling rigs silent?

So is it official now, that Obama is running his Re-election Campaign?

Now that Obama has lost all the Peace Activists by attacking a Country that was absolutely no threat to the United States of America. Perhaps the environmentalists are next when he opens up domestic drilling. There is no other way to cut our dependence on foreign oil by 33.33% in 10 years without drilling within the United States. Obama has lost all hopes of reality.

Even if we had an alternative fuel that was viable right now, it would take upwards of 15 Years just to get the whole countries infrastructure put in place for the distribution of this fantasy fuel. Obama is falling deeper into the fantasy world with his proposals. We need to elect a real President in 2012 that will come up with ideas that are realistic and practical.

I will give Obama this much: he is relentless. He said "the cost of energy will necessarily skyrocket under my plan" and this is one way to do it. Cut off domestic supply and then cut off foreign supply, and when you get a chance clean out the strategic reserve. That should just about put inflation over the top and bring nearly everyone into poverty. Relentless though he is, he doesn't have an original thought or understanding of either physics or business. Obama is just a puppet for the elitist whacko's he looks up to.

Obama wants to curb U.S. oil imports by a third

By Alister Bulll – March 30, 2011

WASHINGTON (Reuters) – President Barack Obama will set an ambitious goal on Wednesday to cut U.S. oil imports by a third over 10 years, focusing on energy security amid high gasoline prices that could stall the country's economic recovery.

Obama will outline his strategy in a speech after spending days explaining U.S.-led military action in Libya, where fighting, accompanied by popular unrest elsewhere in the Arab world, has helped push gasoline prices toward $4 a gallon.

Discussing the speech, the Democratic president said the country must increase its energy independence.

"What we were talking about was breaking the pattern of being shocked at high prices and then, as prices go down, being lulled into a trance, but instead let's actually have a plan," Obama told party activists in New York late on Tuesday.

"Let's, yes, increase domestic oil production, but let's also invest in solar and wind and geothermal and bio-fuels and let's make our buildings more efficient and our cars more efficient. Not all of that work is done yet, but I'm not finished yet. We've got more work to do," Obama said.

The White House says this is a deliberate turn toward energy security and will be followed by other events to highlight his strategy.

"He'll be laying out the goal … that in a little over a decade from now we'll reduce the amount of oil we import from the rest of the world by about a third," a senior administration official told reporters in Washington.

Obama will lay out four areas to help reach his target of curbing U.S. dependence on foreign oil – lifting domestic energy production, encouraging the use of more natural gas in vehicles like city buses, making cars and trucks more efficient, and encouraging bio-fuels.

U.S. LOVE OF DRIVING CHEAPLY

Analysts and experts said Obama's goal was ambitious, and not surprising.

"All U.S. presidents since the early 1970s have outlined ambitious plans to reduce their reliance on imported oil. It is not the first time and probably won't be the last," said John Sfakianakis, chief economist at the Banque Saudi Fransi.

Truly reforming U.S. energy use would involve sweeping changes, including possibly fuel taxes to encourage Americans to change their habits, analysts said.

"The whole U.S. model is based on you having your car and being able to travel from A to B cheaply," said Harry Tchilinguirian, the head of commodity markets strategy at BNP Paribas.

While polls show Americans have mixed feelings about getting entangled in a third Muslim country, with the United States still engaged in Iraq and Afghanistan, they are clearly worried by high gas prices before the summer driving season.

The latest measures of consumer confidence have also been dented by rising energy prices, which sap household spending and could derail the U.S. recovery if prices stay high enough for a long time, hurting Obama's re-election prospects.

A Quinnipiac University poll released on Wednesday showed that 48 percent of American voters disapprove of Obama's job performance, and 50 percent think he does not deserve to be re-elected in 2012, compared with 42 percent who approve and 41 percent who feel he does deserve to be re-elected.

Those were his lowest ratings ever, Quinnipiac said.

Voters also oppose the U.S. involvement in Libya by 47-41 percent, according to the survey, which was concluded on Monday, as Obama addressed the nation about Libya. It said voters say 58-29 percent Obama has not clearly stated U.S. goals there.

"The president certainly understands the extra burden that rising gas prices put on millions of Americans already going through a tough time," the administration official said.

Some analysts reckon Obama may tap America's emergency oil stockpiles if U.S. oil prices hit $110 a barrel. Prices were hovering just under $105 a barrel in late Tuesday trade.

Over half of the petroleum consumed by the United States is imported, with Canada and Mexico the two largest suppliers, followed by Saudi Arabia and Venezuela.

The Department of the Interior estimates millions of acres (hectares) of U.S. energy leases are not being exploited by oil companies and the White House wants that to change.

This argument also helps the administration push back against Obama's Republican opponents, who claim he is tying the hands of the U.S. energy industry by denying leases and restricting offshore drilling in the wake of the 2010 BP Gulf of Mexico oil spill.
"Part of our plan is to give new and better incentives to promote rapid, responsible development of these resources," the official said, but declined to go into greater detail before Obama speaks speech at 11:20 a.m. (1520 GMT).

In addition, the official said Obama will set a goal to break ground "on at least four commercial-scale cellulosic or advanced bio refineries over the next two years."

Here are the comments from average American citizens and what they think about the President's plan to reduce the amount of oil imported

from foreign countries by one third. In some cases the comments are extreme but for the most part they are right on. They have not been altered in any way except for spelling and grammar. I hope you enjoy the comments and can get a clearer picture of what is happening in the war with Libya and the actions of the President of the United States.

Why do they keep saying that people object to cutting fossil fuel, it is a pure hoax? If solar cells were made affordable to all households I don't know anybody who would not gladly do it to get rid of the yoke that utility companies have on us or at least cut our utility cost in half if they insist on being tied to the main system. Until the solar panels are under a $100.00 each its not going to happen since they are easily damaged by Hail and high winds, the lower middle class can not afford to pay thousands of dollars to buy the system only to have it destroyed in one storm and pay thousand again for repair parts. As for gas for our vehicle, we use on average one to two tanks of gas a month so not everyone in America is polluting the air just because they own a car.

Please feel free to correct me if I have the translation wrong: "The only way the transition to clean energy will ultimately succeed is if the private sector is fully invested in this future – if capital comes off the sidelines and the ingenuity of our entrepreneurs is unleashed," he said. "And the only way to do that is by finally putting a price on carbon pollution."

In other words, since we can't make clean energy affordable we will make sure you can't afford the energy you are getting now. And that's going to help our economy how?

Why now? Couldn't possibly be because of an upcoming election, could it?

Here we go again… As Rahm says "Never let a crisis go to waste"… They'll use this to push through cap and trade which is a sly way to break his promise not to raise taxes for the poor. BP is dealing with it the best they can and have pledged to clean it up and pay for everything. Oil companies have a tough dangerous job, they're not making brownies, and they're making propane, gasoline and jet fuel.

I never thought I would ever say this, but Obama is more incompetent than Jimmy Carter by a long shot. Barry is a complete and utter failure unless of course you like socialism and communism then he's doing what his ideology is based on, making citizens dependent on government totally. 2012 this man must be defeated to save this great republic.

Yep Obama......never let a crisis go to waste. You will use people and issues and crisis for your own agenda. You disgust me. You want an energy bill passed so you can tax the people in the United States and so you can mandate the energy they use and fine them if they don't comply. This is way too close to socialism for me. The building the size of government, mandating laws, paying your friends, lying to the people of this country and curbing the freedom. Obama is for taking money from the rich and giving to the poor. Obama wants total control of this country and that's not what our Constitution is about. He is a terrible example of a President of the United States.

This "GREEN" President has taken millions of acres of government land that is filled with oil, coal, and natural gas, and turned them into "national monuments", (which makes it impossible to drill or mine there) has denied permits for drilling almost everywhere, and has made it impossible to mine coal. (As he said in his 20008 campaign "coal companies will be able to mine coal but I will make it so expensive that it will be impossible to do so". And now Obama is just giving the public what he thinks they want to hear. Obama has no intentions of increasing domestic oil production, and he knows his green friends will spend so much time in courts trying to deny drilling permits that this is just more election year lies.

Let's see if I've got this right. Obama supports oil drilling off Brazil's coast.

"We want to work with you. We want to help with technology and support to develop these oil reserves safely, and when you're ready to start selling, we want to be one of your best customers" Obama 21 Mar 2011 in Brazil

But Obama opposes oil drilling off the United States coast. Obama's energy policies in the United States: a moratorium banning "all" drilling in the Gulf (lifted in Oct), new regulations, slowed permitting

process by the Department of Interior, increased costs to drill, increased taxation of oil companies.

Consequences of Obama's policies: oil rigs leaving the Gulf of Mexico (five so far), job losses in the Gulf's oil economy, numerous small businesses that service oil rig workers impacted, increased gasoline prices, increased heating oil prices.

I'm confused. I thought Obama was President of the United States. So why is Obama not investing our money in developing and discovering our energy resources (oil, natural gas), investing in American companies, creating American jobs?

Follow the money. Ask yourself one simple question. Who profits? George Soros (Democrat friend & fundraiser) profits as a major investor of Petrobras. Renewable energy companies profit (GE). Obama wants huge federal subsidies (your taxpayer dollars) for numerous renewable energy projects. (More friends) Obama and the Democrats profit. Pay real close attention to where these campaign contributions come from next election.

I truly believe the only reason Joe Biden was picked for Vice President is because he makes Obama look smart. America wanted an idiot for President, and man, did we get one!

It is my understanding that 2/3 of our off shore oil wells are not even being used partly because of Obama's drilling referendum. All he has to do to lower oil prices is undo what he did in the first place. He is part of the reason oil is so high. Now he wants look like he cares about high gas prices. Bull! All he cares about is getting elected in 2012. Not with my vote!

The Republicans drove the car into the ditch, Obama and the Democrats, pulled it out and are now driving that same car off a cliff. Just another crisis Obama is not going to let go to waste and push the Liberal agenda of "Green" when the technology simply doesn't support it yet.

Obama, when no one is producing anything and there are no jobs, no production, and every one is on welfare and Medicaid, the illegals will be eating us out of house and home, WHO is going to be left to support your lifestyle? If no one is working, and no one is paying income tax, where are you going to get the money to pay for your elaborate lifestyle?

You have not thought beyond being a community organizer and pandering to the corruption of the unions, Save yourself the disgrace of being impeached and resign, preferably today.

People need to get their heads out of the sand and pay attention on what's going on around them. Obama is doing his best to destroy America piece by piece in everything he attempts to do. His changes are not for the betterment of America.

"An end to oil company tax breaks". The most taxed industry in the USA, and they are going to tax it even more. Before you all jump on board this idea, just remember, "Corporations don't pay taxes, people pay taxes". If you think that any company just plucks money off the money tree to pay increased taxes, you obviously went to the same schools as Obama did. In a word for the mentally weak, an increase in taxes on anything is paid by us as consumers. We will all pay more, not just for gas, but every product associated with it and produced by it. (Which is pretty much everything).

Yea, I'm for alternative energy, but efficient alternatives are still years away.

Kill Cap and Trade now before we realize too late that it will cost jobs and money from us all. Study the candidates for the November elections, and vote for the candidate that will once again do their job and represent the majority of their constituents.

Obama, I was once given three wonderful words to live by in a crisis, Stop, Think, Act. You need to stop overreacting just because your handlers tell you it's what you should do. For once in your political life, lead from the front for Gods sake! Your new policy on off shore drilling is already costing more jobs than you can imagine, and will cost thousands more, very soon.

Absolutely everything and everybody the Community Organizers proposes supports or nominates is ultimately about raising taxes, increasing the size and control of government, and taking away individual liberties.

Rather than leverage our own resources, Obama will push technology that will cost 3 to 4 times more per KWH. Who will pay for the higher costs? Obama wants to do this so he can create more union jobs which are a lie as the manufacturing will go overseas.

Talk about bringing transportation to a halt - if we are going to cut down on imported oil and he won't let us drill into what we have here, I hope we all have strong, sturdy shoes because we'll be doing a lot of walking. What kind of fog is this program organizer walking us into? How long is he going to keep us in the dark about what our alternatives will be? Why must everything be kept a deep, dark secret? Frankly, if we knew more about some of his grandiose plans we might be able to head him off at the pass. I guess that's why they're secrets.

Cap and Trade is a big fraud. European cyber crooks sold $7 Billion this past year from the European cap and trade tax system, it's a scandal all over Europe. I support energy policy, but I don't support ANY carbon tax credits policy. It will hurt the poor most through increased food costs and loss of jobs, and just gives our irresponsible politicians another "social security slush fund" to spread around to their special interest buddies, buddies that are already rich. Its time to stop stealing from main street Mr. President, stop it!

Yeah right! He just handed $2 billion to Brazil's socialist state owned oil company for off shore oil drilling while hundreds of United States oil workers loose their jobs. Worse yet is George Soros, who spends a lot of time in the Oval Office bending Obama's ear and contributing tons of money to the Democrats, is a major investor with this Brazilian state owned oil company. Think about that! This to me is criminal conflict of interest, but where is the outrage from the left on this big oil deal? If this was Bush or another Republican they'd be calling for impeachment and jail time! Wake up people, Obama is an outright socialist who hates American. This action is just plain criminal.

10% unemployment, $13 trillion in debt…and Barry wants to drive a stake through the heart of the US economy with his carbon tax scheme. Brilliant!

So, let me get this straight. This bonehead president of ours is investing $2 billion of our tax dollars in the Brazilian government's owned oil company so they can drill off their coast; but does nothing to improve domestic production here in the United States.

Now all he wants to talk about is reducing our dependence on foreign oil imports. When will our idiot-in-charge realize that the only way to reduce our dependence is to replace the imports with domestic production?

I am now also hearing the same old argument that any drilling policy instituted now won't have any results produced for 10 years … well, well, well! I heard these same people using this same argument about 6 years ago when oil prices started rising then. Imagine if we actually started our own drilling program then, we would now be within months of seeing production occurring and we would have created thousands of jobs in the process.

PEOPLE OF THE U.S.A! Unless we start drilling here in the United States now we will forever be dependent on OPEC.

"Obama, a Democrat, accused Republicans of sitting on the sidelines while his administration worked to rescue the economy and, with November congressional elections looming, used his speech to lambaste the opposition party for opposing initiatives from health insurance reform to tax cuts."

There it is again and again and again – let's blame someone else for the problem and then I will cram my objectives down your throat.

When he eliminates the tax incentives expect your gas prices and prices for ordinary products like tires, computers, etc to go up. By the way did he give back the campaign contributions BP gave him? Of course not! How is the hope and change working for you America? Wake up and get rid of these socialist before it is too late.

We have more oil in Alaska and the Gulf than our country could ever use. The problem is we have all these retard liberals complaining that we would have to relocate Wally Moose in Alaska and take control of the waters where the Chinese and Brazilians are drilling in the Gulf. It's time to tell the "Save the Whale" butt holes to get out of the way and let our country grow.

I said when this all started that two coal mine collapses and an oil rig explosion inside of 10 days was way more than coincidence. Now the other shoe has dropped and the "see how bad fossil fuels are for the environment" drum is beating again. Can't get your healthcare bill passed? Turn a market correction in to a drawn out recession so that all of a sudden "tens of millions of Americans can no longer afford health insurance." Don't have the votes to put a Cap and Trade stranglehold on manufacturing and industry in America? Have a bill stalled out in the Senate to force out fossil fuels? Just cause some disasters in a couple of coal mines and oil rigs, and the votes will come running. THERE IS NO SUCH THING AS COINCIDENCE!

This guy is such a farce. He along with the other socialist, Nancy Pelosi, Harry Reid, & Barney Frank are why the world's economy is in the condition we are in right now. Obama wants to cut our dependence in foreign oil and he is solely responsible for the drop in production. No new drilling permits for any offshore drilling. The fault of the oil spill in the Gulf of Mexico belongs to Two Companies. BP for unsafe work practices, bad inflow test and Trans-ocean Off-shore for faulty BP's. If the BP's would of functioned as designed which are to cut the pipe the extended spill of millions of gallons of oil would of been shut in, Boy I can't wait for Nov 2012 when we can get this clown out of office.

Why is Obama crushing American oil companies and spending BILLIONS of AMERICAN tax dollars so Brazil can drill in the Gulf? Maybe it is because his controller and soon to be world dictator super socialist George Soros is a major stake holder in the Brazilian oil company? Nah, Obama the wonder-boy-god would never crush American companies and American jobs to help make even more trillions for his master George Soros.

Obama, just allow drilling in places now forbidden and build more SAFE nuclear plants. Keep all politicians, like Pelosi, from jaunting back and forth unnecessarily across the country in fuel devouring jets that are not full, make them fly commercial and coach like the average person. Get oil from Iraq at a discount or free for all the money we've spent on their infrastructure. Don't send money to places, like Brazil, where you announced money to help their oil industry, spend it on ours. I could go on all day but liberals like Al Gore and the environmental boogieman only understand.

In Spain, they found that for every one job created in so-called clean energy, they lost two jobs in traditional energy. Spain reported a net loss of jobs by a 2 to 1 margin. But Obama and the extreme environmentalists don't care about jobs. They intentionally want to downsize our economy and standard of living.

Before you push this Cap and Trade legislation Obama you and Al Gore should give up your money positions on this cap and tax. This will be a $10 TRILLION per year business. You and your buddies stand to make a lot of money on this scam. Call Glen Beck. He wants to talk to you.

Every single bill that gets passed has more "pork" in it than brains in those who pass it. The world laughs while the United States cries. The good news is that Osama bin Laden is happy. It won't make any difference what happens in November 2012 because the damage has already been done and no one is paying any attention. There has never been a government (or corporation) who can continue to spend more than it makes and still survive. Too many have tried and all have failed.

I may not be good at Economics but I think this is Obama's plan:

(1) Lower supply of oil plus high demand for oil plus low alternative to oil equals a higher price for oil.

(2) High oil price equals high gas price.

(3) High gas price plus transportation of raw materials and workers plus manufacturing needs equal a higher product costs.

(4) High product cost plus company's need to earn money plus Obama's plan to give higher tax to big companies equals a very high product price.

5) Very high product price plus middle class, low income and unemployed Americans equal a really screwed up American.

Anyone who hasn't recognized by this time that we have elected our second enemy President (the first being Chairman Mao's understudy) needs to wake up, Along with his entourage embedded in every facet of our government, the king of Acorn has done a terrific job at decimating our country at every level. It's not difficult to see everything Democratic commies have done for the last 100 years has been aimed at creating a progressive haven. Look to going from 4 car families to 4 loaves of bread a month. The misery index will climb and our saviors will become the elitist class who will keep you under their thumbs and run every aspect of your life. They have used the EPA to shut down California farmers putting hundreds of thousands of people out of work and reducing our food supply. They use the FED to thoroughly screw up of economy... print $600 Billion in paper. What did that do to the dollar? By the way, how does George Soros make his billion? Wasn't he the one that got Big Obama elected? Shutting down the voice of opposition on the net talk radio and Fox, dumbing down our schools to create a politically ignorant society... re-writing history, controlling most of the state-run media... wait a minute. Am I talking about the former USSR of the current USA?

I think by now everyone realizes that "green" and environmental" is the code word for loss of freedom and Socialism. Obama is tying up resources and forcing the cost of food and energy to skyrocket. He and others are engaged in a fierce economic sabotage of this country.

Chu (Obama's energy secretary" testified to Congress that Obama and he would like to see gas prices go to $8 to force Americans into the "Green" initiative. Electric cars, solar and wind! Problem is, planes, cars and trains can't efficiently use any of these and just like ethanol, the results of trying and to keep pushing these failed experiments means disaster to this country.

Obama is subsidizing General Electric with millions if not billions in "clean energy" money. Jeffrey Immelt made millions in bonuses and GE made $14 billion in profits, but paid no taxes. This criminal of a "President" is waging war on America and Americans for greed and power.

Colorado Springs Air force academy: 18 million dollar solar project with an expected life span of 20 years. The annual electric savings to the Academy was $500k annually. Do the math. We are spending $900,000 a year to save $500,000. BTW, all of the solar panels are from China. This is the TARP money hard at work. Google it, this is fact.

WAKE UP PEOPLE, THERE IS NO OIL SHORTAGE!

Fighting in the Middle East is not the cause of rising oil prices. The rising cost of oil is due to the Wall Street trader's speculation. If you take oil and gas off of the commodities trading list it would stabilize. We can thank our own greedy government for allowing this to happen.

Obama does not have any policy other than say what it takes to get re-elected, then defecate on America. That is all he has done for over 2 years. Increase domestic production on oil he says, yet his policies are just the opposite, and if re-elected he will go back to today's policies. He is a bald faced liar on his good days.

Isn't this the same President that just got back from Brazil promising to give United States taxpayer dollars for oil exploration in South America? Is it not also the same President who said while down there "We want to be your biggest customer?" It's like he doesn't even try to cover his lies anymore!

Windmills are a pipe dream. They are not efficient and relatively high maintenance and not reliable, solar panels are the same. They are very expensive and easily damaged. Electric Cars are not viable for most Americans. All of these industries have Democrat liberal investment politically and some (like Nancy Pelosi, Hillary Clinton and Al Gore) have a lot of personal money involved in the promotion of these and other so called "green" ideas. Our government is corrupt and driving

us down the tubes. We need to cut, and discontinue funding and reduce their power as much as we can or we will not leave much for the future of our children.

The liberal environmentalist created the worst possible scenario for the oil companies to drill in by, "DECLARING WE WILL NOT DRILL ON U.S. SOIL, WE WILL NOT DRILL ANY CLOSER THAN 50 OR 100 MILES OFF SHORE". And then they have the audacity to proclaim that the oil industry has socked it to us again. Washington and the bleeding heart liberals have socked it to us to create another of Rahm Emanuel crisis that the administration will not waste, a spring board for Carbon Cap & Trade. You know, where they nationalize the energy sector and raise the prices of every facet of energy consumption and production to get the increased tax base they need to create socialism along with health care reform and nationalizing the insurance companies and the banking and financial markets. Does no one recognize this Marxist socialist we have for a President yet?

I wonder who will pay for the carbon released by volcanic activity (remember we have a few here in the states). Iceland just spewed about 4000 power plant yearly emissions out in 48 hours. The only thing being done in Washington is creating work for law firms - not surprising since now the Congress (lawyers) are being led by a lawyer President.

I am witnessing the last throes of the Republic - and the beginning of the State. I guess that is change.

Absolutely hysterical…for two years, all Obama talked about was how we would become enlightened and energy independent once the electric car was made available. Well, it turns out that:

1. The electric car can go a whooping 30 miles on an electric charge, before it runs on GASOLINE.

2. The electric car is pretty much a box, and of little use for people who need a vehicle larger than a box.

3. The electricity for charging those electric cars comes from FOSSIL FUELS.

4. This is what happens when you elect an ideologue to occupy the White House, instead of a realist who takes a pragmatic approach to solving complex problems.

Wow, a speech about pie in the sky windmill and mass transit schemes to correct a problem Obama created by not allowing us to exploit our own natural reserves at the same time he invests in Brazilian exploration of our backyard. Just think if we had started to develop these resources last time gas prices rose exponentially. Remember "drill, baby, drill"? Back then the argument of the critics was that even if we started drilling immediately, it would not affect current prices. That specious argument aside, YOU HAVE TO START SOMEWHERE, SOMETIME! Enough of this egg-head "intellectual" and his energy "policies!"

There is a huge medical benefit to using a tourniquet. By stopping the blood flow in the "wrong direction", which would be out of your body, you can sustain someone's life long enough to repair the damages. Until the liberal Democrats and liberal media allow, and I say allow with unbelievable nausea, to become self sufficient with drilling and gas and oil production we will not get out of this situation. You can not simply flip a switch and become "green" overnight. We have resources here. While it may be a difficult decision for the bleeding hearts, drilling on our own soil or war and fighting over oil and foreign import politics, it is one that needs to be made. Become self sufficient with resources, bring our boys home, protect our borders, increase jobs, and get on with it. Fund a sector to do more research on alternate energy once these things are done. Until Obama, the dreamer and everybody needs a huge crowd gets the hell out of the way and lets the big people with jobs and responsibilities that we actually take care of make some decisions we are headed in the same direction.

Why does Obama think we will believe him after everything he has said to this point has been a lie? We still don't have a budget for the current fiscal year even though he had both houses of Congress, he is asking for us to go into debt by another $1.3 trillion in fiscal year 2012, illegally and on his own he has got us involved in another civil war

where we have no interest and will be spending billions. All of this crap he keeps throwing at us is a re-election smoke screen. I am beginning to think that he really wants to destroy this country because action speaks louder than talk and lies. He is the least qualified President who has ever held the office and has no governing ability. He should do us a favor and resign, or be impeached and removed from office.

I heard all this before: in 1976 Carter set up the Department of Energy to wean us from oil and coal. Today the Department of Energy is a $26 billion a year expense with 170,000 employees, hundred thousand contractors and the best they can show for is that we don't make a single light bulb any more in the United States. What's your carbon foot print on Air Force One Mr. Obama and what do you have to show for it? The left is always preaching water and while they drink expensive wine.

George W. Bush tried this shortly after being elected to his first term. He wanted to expand domestic drilling in the short term and work on alternate energy over the long term. Every organization from Green Peace to the Democratic National Committee had a fit. They said that Alaska is too "pristine" to drill more there. Let's see how those liberal organizations react when it is one of their own who is saying what every American knows needs to be said.

Oil will never go away! If you stand in the middle of any room anywhere, and look 360 degrees, you will see almost everything is a derivative of an oil product. Obama is following the lead of his favorite socialist George Soros. He follows his lead because Soros put him there. When Soros put $5 million into the Democratic Party to buy the people he really wanted there, you can know this is a Soros experiment. There are not many people in their right mind (either left or right) that elect the group you have there. Chuck Shumer, Barney Frank, Harry Reid, Nancy Pelosi, Obama and the list goes on.

I know everyone has been asking where Obama came from? I am not going to tell you anything. Look for yourself. Investigate the Hawaiian school systems! Investigate the names of Dr.'s available through the period of years Obama supposedly lived there. There is no record of this guy anywhere. He is a ghost. When he ran for the Senate, people did not know him, but he had a very well oiled machine behind him? Why would you put a person into a race with no recognizable name or face, and as Soros says, no recognizable attributes, and he wins! Soros laughs at us. His money will buy anything he wants in a corrupt system. It is time to get the thugs, criminals, the thieves, the liars, deceivers, out of our business and put someone in their place with some sense of business, willing to actually do the job required. I was not sure the Tea Party group would be good for America, but now I know they are for real. They want what the country was initially founded on, taxation without representation, we have it. The United States Constitution that will stand the test of time. IT IS TIME TO GET ALL THE CRIMINALS OUT OF THE WHITE HOUSE!

Gee, I guess Americans are stupid. You think if there was a profitable way to produce alternative power that big business would have swooped on it a century ago? Does Wall Street like profit? Where is the high dividend investment in green power? How did the energy companies miss the money? Ah, is there a little secret of how to do it and the government been hiding it? Like FDR's experiments in tidal power at Campobello Maine. Great power while until the tide ebbed. Obama knows how to make the wind blow at peak use hours. They know of a way to store power that no one else in the world has heard of. Do we use more lights on cloudy or sunny days? Obama's going to get Rahm on the energy council. Any day now ethanol will cost less and pollute less than gasoline. That oil spill? Maybe if they weren't forced to drill in the middle of the ocean they only would have had 500 feet of pipe instead of a half mile. What do I know? I didn't serve a half term as a junior Senator or play as a community activist.

"Over half of the petroleum consumed by the United States is imported, with Canada and Mexico the two largest suppliers, followed by Saudi Arabia and Venezuela." And all the conspiracy theorists keep crying that we're in the Middle East because we want to steal or control their oil. Hell, we don't even need their stinking oil. We just need to find a way to keep the speculators from doubling our prices every time some lunatic blows himself up.

What's the socialist up to now? Is he going to have barracks build next to the companies that still employ Americans? Is he going to outlaw vehicles? How about handing out refrigerator packing crates for people fortunate enough to have jobs? So they can live in the

alleyways next to the Wal-Mart stores or wherever they're working for peanuts. I know Obama is going to print a few more trillion dollars in paper money and give every citizen a small check. So he or she can stay home, listen to public broadcasting network, and wait for the next check to arrive. After all, Nancy Pelosi said unemployment checks stimulate the economy. Every day, this once great nation looks more and more like our only friend, France.

"The Department of the Interior estimates millions of acres of the United States energy leases is not being exploited by oil companies and the White House wants that to change."

Obama and his progressive/communist thugs are working hard each and every day to totally destroy the United States of America and bankrupt her people. They screw us over every chance they get with high taxes, mean green scams, and now the master plan to limit fuel. We are sitting on top of enough oil to last us for many years to come and yet we aren't allowed to drill for it but BP was and just exactly where were they selling all our oil before they spilled it all over the place.

This rhetoric is coming from the mouth of the idiot that halted all drilling in the Gulf of Mexico. What a liar. So much for civil discourse as Senator Charles E. Schumer briefly revealed his true face Tuesday as reporters listened to him instruct fellow Democrats in how to paint Republicans and House Speaker John Boehner as extremist Tea Party zealots in the budget debates. "I always use the word extreme," Schumer told his fellow Democrats. "That is what the caucus instructed me to use this week." Republicans were quick to blast the remarks.

Schumer, extremists, Pelosi "It just lends to the fact to what we've always known, that this is a political game," said Rep. Allen West on Fox News. "It's about gamesmanship, it's about maneuvering, and it really is about politics. It's not about doing what is best for the American people, it's not about reducing the size and scope of the federal government so we can get back to have long-term, sustainable economic and job growth. I think Charles Schumer showed his hand. Now it's up to the American people to realize what the biggest obstacle for us to move forward."

201

West added that Schumer, Harry Reid, and Obama want a shutdown so that they can use it to blame Republicans, and position themselves for 2012.

The brief peek behind the curtain came as Schumer was about to start a conference call with reporters on Tuesday morning, according to The New York Times. The No. 3 Democrat in the Senate was apparently unaware that many of the reporters were already on the line when he began revealing what passes as strategic messaging for Democrats.

After thanking his colleagues — Barbara Boxer of California, Benjamin L. Cardin of Maryland, Thomas R. Carper of Delaware and Richard Blumenthal of Connecticut — for doing the budget bidding for the Senate Democrats, Schumer told them to portray John A. Boehner of Ohio, the speaker of the House, as painted into a box by the Tea Party, and to decry the spending cuts that he wants as extreme.

A minute or two into the talking points tutorial, though, someone apparently figured out that reporters were listening, and silence fell, according to the Times.

Obama and his czars are intent on bankrupting the country. These are the worst tax and spend liberals in the history of the United States of America and that is why we have a 1.5 trillion dollar deficit this year. Vote these idiots out in 2012 while there still may be a chance to save the country from financial ruin.

Open up the gulf again to United States companies. This will allow the thousands of United States citizens who are unemployed or working low end jobs just trying to make a living, to return to work. It should reduce the cost of our fuel here as well. There are many other land based oil wells that are just sitting idle, but were working prior to the fiasco in the Gulf of Mexico. Get those wells pumping again!

Yes, use wind and solar power when those can be used. Why not? But the reality is, we still live on oil, we still need oil for daily living. Why can't we use our own oil for this? That does not include the oil from Brazil either. I will get down off my soap box for now, as I could go on and on.

Being in the oil and gas industry I for one would be glad to see America become less dependent on oil from other countries. I guess the question I have is this. If the refineries in this country are operating at or near capacity does it really matter where the oil is coming from? Seems to me if you wanted to reduce the price of a gallon of gas you would encourage the refineries to expand so that when and if production is increased we have the capacity to turn that in to fuel. It is basic supply and demand here. If supply is higher than demand the price goes down. So if you increased production and enlarged the capacity at the refineries the price of fuel may not decrease a lot but would certainly stabilize while the development of bio-fuels is continued.

Obama must have a tumor in his brain, because that's the only thing that can explain his illogical behavior. Everything he has done is the things you would do if you were going to destroy a country from within. Kill all jobs, spend faster than you can recover, go in debt to communist China, destroy the economy, destroy the dollar, kill oil drilling in the United States, ban the use of coal in power plants, start a war in Libya, and staff your cabinet with anti American subversives, Communists, and Fascists. EVEN STRANGER is the lack of concern by the press and the other Americans that are not brain dead. WE should be seeing civil unrest like we saw in Egypt, riots, protests, and demands that Obama resign and jump without a parachute. Why is America so complacent when the new House Republicans have failed in canceling the funding for Obamacare, and cutting Obama's reckless spending?

This guy is an IDIOT! When will Obama ever start to do what's right for our country and our citizens instead of what's right for a particular political party?

It's time to cut independence from imported oil alright...DRILL HERE, DRILL NOW! Create American jobs while at the same time gaining our independence from the INFERIOR leaches who continue to take advantage of our country's God given place in this world. PROUD AMERICAN here!

If anyone can tell me of anything in the GREEN field of energy that is AFFORDABLE to the common man I'd love to hear it. Read about the Nissan Leaf being an AFFORDABLE alternative to gasoline powered vehicles. I don't know of ONE person out there that agrees that a 35,000 dollar electric car is affordable to the common man, I make very good money and I'll be damned if I'd buy it, got better things to do with my $35,000. At any rate you still need a bridge to get from ONE side to the OTHER and fossil fuels ARE that bridge.

If not for lawmakers and socialist Democrats like Obama who are beholden to the green agenda and environmental groups stopping the drilling, the exploration and building of new refineries, we would already be halfway to energy independence. Why now? Obama sees the gas prices going up and his favorability going down in the polls. Obama has stated clearly that he would have preferred a gradual adjustment to $4.00 gasoline back in 2008. Prices were already rising and predicted to hit the $4 mark back in December of 2010. This was all before the unrest in the Middle East, but the Obama media spreads the talking point that higher prices are due to Libya. They fail to acknowledge the drilling ban by Obama in the Gulf. Why has this President been shielded from blame for his obvious attack on U.S. energy production? His administration was funding offshore drilling in Brazil but not here, why? Bush was held to account in media reports every single day and was accused of helping his oil biddies get rich. Bush is gone, they cannot pin high prices to him or Cheney any more. It's not Bush, so it must be Gadhafi. Obama always finds a finger to point and issue blame to. Too bad he doesn't point it towards himself.

It is great to know that the average American is able to remember the failures of past presidents and the President of the United States thinks we are too stupid to remember and tries to present the same failed policies as the previous presidents. President Obama, how about presenting something original that you can show the American people ways that your proposals are going to actually work.

Quit blowing smoke and stop the rhetoric. We already know you are going to run in 2012. Stop the campaigning and do some work on the 2011 and 2012 budgets. God help us if the blacks and Hispanics have enough votes to get you elected again.

CHAPTER THIRTEEN:

WAKE UP AMERICA

The Federal government under the leadership of President Obama and his loyal followers is going to bend over America and really give it to them this time.

The report by the Associated Press is really misleading when it states that the President has a bipartisan deficit commission. There is not a Republican in his right mind that will ever allow this proposal to become law.

Erskine Bowles and former Wyoming Sen. Alan Simpson, co-chairmen of President Barack Obama's bipartisan deficit commission proposed curbs in Social Security benefits, deep reductions in federal spending and higher taxes for millions of Americans to stem a flood of red ink that they said threatens the nation's very future.

The Republican lawmakers had better respond quickly and strongly to the commissions proposals. They include increasing the retirement age for full social security benefits from the current levels to 66 to 69 by the year 2075. The plan would also raise the regular Social Security retirement age to 68 by about 2050 and to 69 in 2075. The full retirement age for those retiring now is 66. For those born in 1960 or after, the full retirement age is now 67.

Besides social security Medicare spending would be curtailed. The tax breaks on many healthcare plans would be eliminated and the deduction for interest on the primary residence of the taxpayer would be eliminated.

The commission estimated that these changes would eliminate $4 trillion from the national deficit in the next decade.

This commission is proposing to make changes to programs that have been paid for by the taxpayers for most of their lives and are calling these programs entitlement programs. Mr. Obama these are not entitlement programs they are what the majority of Americans have paid into for 50 years or so and they are retirement programs. Your entitlement programs are the illegals that are bankrupting all levels of government. Those and the 99 weeks of unemployment would eliminate $20 trillion from the federal deficit during the next decade. Where are your priorities? I know, you are looking out for the Hispanic and uneducated to make sure that you will get enough votes for the Democratic Party. How about getting in the Oval office and actually doing some work?

Where in the world does the President find these brain dead loony's that are trying to make policy that will harm just about every citizen of the United States?

In addition to the social security plan increasing the age to full retirements the commission would adopt a program where the current recipients would receive smaller than anticipated annual increases. Just how are they going to lower the increases? The senior citizens of the United States have not received any increases for 2010 and 2011.

Then we have the commission wanting to eliminate the income tax deduction on the mortgages that the taxpayer pays. Why doesn't the government think that this should be considered increasing the income taxes of the majority of taxpayers? This is after the fiasco caused by Fannie Mae and Freddie Mac concerning the mortgage crisis? How many times are the Democrats going to present programs that are going to bury the taxpayers?

The commission acknowledged that these proposals were controversial and would be difficult to pass. No kidding? You want to have 58 million seniors and millions of homeowners bend over to pay for the Democrats spending sprees. Does anyone really think Obama and his committees have any inkling of what they are doing?

The commission stated that the debt is like a cancer on the United States that will truly destroy this country from within if we do not fix it. That is the only good thing that has come from the commission's recommendations. The way to fix the deficit is to cut the spending. President Obama' spending has increased the budget more in the two years he has been in office than all the cuts that are designed to hurt the elderly and working class of Americans.

The government reported separately Wednesday that the deficit for last month alone was $140.4 billion – and that was 20 percent lower than a year earlier. Wait a minute. If the deficit was $140.4 billion for a month that would indicate that the deficit for the year would be $1,684.8 trillion. The red ink for all of the past fiscal year was $1.29 trillion, second highest on record, and this year is headed for the third straight total above $1 trillion. Current deficits require the government to borrow 37 cents out of every dollar it spends.

When the President decides to quit slamming programs down the taxpayers throats like the healthcare, stimulus, cap and trade to mention a few we will be able to come close to a balanced budget. The Federal government needs to pass legislation that the budget will be balanced every year and what is in excess of the budget will be applied to the deficit.

Some comments from other taxpayers.

How about cutting some people from the Presidents 200,000 plus government workers hired since he took office? He already has cut benefits for social security and Veterans Affairs benefits for 2 yrs in a row. Government workers that are currently making $150,000 per year are given a $10,000 raise. This seems like it could be part of Reverend Wright's agenda against America. We need to vote the pension benefits out of the Presidents and Congressional payroll and make serving the people what it was meant to be, a service not a retirement.

This is such a crock. After working for 50 years, now they want to cut my benefits. The government is a bunch of thieving irresponsible politicians. I am sick to death of them all. There must be other programs that can be cut, how about welfare, and kick all those damned illegals out and quit giving them welfare and healthcare. Anyone who votes to cut Social

Security for our retired citizens is going to get their asses handed to them next election. Oh, and by the way, Social Security is not welfare or a government entitlement program, workers have paid into the system for all their working life, and there was no option to opt out, now they want to cut benefits, no way.

Easy, eliminate the cap on social security taxes which is currently $104,000 everybody below this pays tax on 100% of our income. Make it fair, eliminate the cap, and Social Security would be solvent for the next 75-80 years. Unfortunately that means members of Congress would also pay on 100% of the money we pay them. Probably not a go. Also repeal the 2005 law prohibiting the government from bargaining with drug companies for lower prices. According to then Vice President Cheney, this alone tripled the cost of Medicare. Drug companies are making lots though.

We have basically given our wealth to foreign countries. Bring American jobs home from overseas. Tax overseas profits earned by American companies. Tax imports from foreign countries like they do to our products. Rebuild the manufacturing industry in the United States. Force corporations and unions to work together to rebuild our country. Provide tax credits to Americans buying American products.

I'm really tired of hearing the phrase "entitlement" programs when folks refer to Social Security... we've paid these taxes for all our working years; they are not merely entitled to us, but owed to us. The lack of a raise for 2010 and 2011 is cruel and unusual punishment when based on "low inflation!" For example, butter is $2.98 a pound, milk over $3.50, and "on-sale" bread over $2.00 – how are seniors supposed to live on what we get from Social Security to say nothing about medical needs, shelter, etc. Cutting back and not giving cost of living raises smacks of "age discrimination" which is against the Federal Law. Again, I reiterate, seniors have paid these taxes and they were to have been maintained in a trust. I'm thinking the trust in the federal government is down the tube, based on these decisions.

This is the only country in the world that rewards law breakers. Stop giving free health care, jobs, driver's licenses, education, food stamps and social security benefits to illegals.

At the top of the list should be complete review and reform of the gold-plated compensation and benefit plans of Congress. Second on the list should be complete review and reform of compensation and benefit plans of all other federal employees. The objective in reforming these two areas would be to bring them into line with private sector practices. Then we could start talking about things like reducing federal employment followed by program expenditures, especially military and foreign aid expenditures.

Why don't they reduce the budget by doing away with retirement for federal employees? All the rest of the people working in the United States don't have entitlement retirement systems. How about a 401 plan where the government will give 3% and the employee can give 3%. That would be a good start. Next reduce the government work force and the salary range. A Federal Government employee makes on average $70,000 per year and the average Joe on working in the private sector only makes $40,000. Then there are the people who do nothing but get their dole from the government. Low cost housing, welfare, food stamps, etc. I know of a woman in Georgia who has 14 children and a husband no one can find. She receives $27,000 per year in food stamps that doesn't include federal free food, free housing, and a welfare payment for each child. Where is the Husband? It is time for Change. If the federal government takes away mortgage interest that would be a major tax increase for all home owning Americans and many will lose their homes or more will go into mortgage failure. Wake Up, I think the real Americans want Change less government and fewer taxes.

Of course, first lower Social Security then raise Medicare premiums, no Social Security cost of living allowance, raise the Social Security age to 70. That should put the old people on Welfare. Next, let's hit the young and old home owners that have a interest mortgage and take that away as a deduction. I've not seen one thing about taking something away from our government workers and legislators, or even stopping the money drain for the two wars that are bankrupting this country for the last 12 years. Is this a great run country or what?

And when is the government going to cut its expenses: lower their salaries, reduce inefficient head count and eliminate pork and earmark spending, sell unneeded real estate, put them selves on Social Security like the rest of us and eliminate their pensions. These should save far more than the $4 trillion.

Simply stop giving our hard earned tax dollars away over seas to any country with a hand out. We just promised millions to Indonesia where the volcano went off. Take care of America and Americans first and the rest second and third down the line. I AM TIRED OF SUPPORTING THE REST OF THE WORLD LET THEM SUPPORT THEMSELVES. I AM TIRED OF FASTENING MY BELT NOTCHES UP FOR THEM. Oh, and by the way Congress should take pay cuts and start living like the rest of America. HEY OBAMA STOP SPENDING MILLIONS ON TRAVEL; HOW MANY TRIPS HAVE YOU TAKEN NOW?

That will give everyone an idea of what America thinks of the commission's proposals. These were from 5 minutes of activity by the responding citizens.

The same day the President's commission on dealing with the deficit that recommended reducing the salaries of government employees by 10% the President proposed the following pay raise for government employees.

Fox News reported that President Obama has recommended an across the board pay raise of 1.4% for all of the governments 2.1 million employees. In addition, the report stated that the number of employees earning $150,000 or higher per year has doubled since President Obama took office less than two years ago.

Sure looks like the President is really trying to decrease the deficit by spending and more spending while punishing the American taxpaying citizens. This is really going to make the 58 million senior citizens that are living on Social Security happy. Not?

Then let's try and compute an example of how the commissions proposal to take away the tax deduction for mortgage interest. To make the example simple we will use a tax deduction of $10,000 in mortgage interest. This taxpayer would have had a $20,000 taxable income after the mortgage deduction. His income tax would have amounted to $2,169.00 if married and filing a joint tax return. If you eliminate the $10,000 deduction his taxable income would jump

to $30,000 and the income tax would amount to $3,669.00. The commission was recommending a 3% tax rate deduction. That would save this taxpayer a total of $900.00 on the $30,000 taxable income. Now this is so simple even a caveman can understand. The problem is that the President and his commission can not understand. Take the $3,669.00 and subtract the $900.00 difference in the tax rate and this taxpayer would owe $2,769.00. That indicates that the government has spun the facts. This taxpayer actually had an increase in income taxes in the amount of $600.00 or 3% on his taxable income of $20,000.

Besides hurting every senior citizen these types of policies are hurting every homeowner that has a mortgage. At the same time the President is recommending a pay raise for all government employees.

We need to contact our representatives in Congress and make sure that these programs cancelled.

CHAPTER FOURTEEN:

CAP AND TRADE RUMORS

We have received information that should be a major concern to every American. The rumors regarding the Cap and Trade bill came from contacts in Europe. I have no way of verifying the information. If it not true, I apologize to the American people. If there is any truth to the rumor the American people need to know about it.

We need to make sure that the Cap and Trade bill will never be passed. It is vital for the United States to understand the ramifications of this bill. It is not being promoted for the benefit of the citizens of the United States. It is however, being presented for the benefit of a select group of people that will gain billions of dollars in benefits. The primary benefactor this legislation is none other than Barack Obama.

We have criminals that are in Washington D.C. and they will be steeling from every United States taxpayer. This article may be longer than usual but please bear with it to the end. You may want to learn some of the dirty tricks and games being played out on all the rest of the taxpayers of the United States. It took the British Times to piece together some of the Obama cronies' crooked activities. The web of deceit is so huge that it is staggering. Read to the end, it gets better as you read. This is just another sellout of the American people by Obama's crowd. The last part is a definite shocker.

This is an interesting story put together from various articles and TV Shows by the British Times newspaper. It shows what Obama and his friends are really all about? It's not hope and change, it is all about money.

We warn you, the first part is a little boring, but stick with it. The second part connects all the dots for you (it will open your eyes). The end explains how Obama and all his cronies will end up as multi-billionaires. (It's definitely worth the read. You will not be disappointed).

A small bank in Chicago called SHORE BANK almost went bankrupt during the recession. The bank made a profit on its foreign micro-loans (see below) but had lost money in sub-prime mortgages in the US. It was facing likely closure by federal regulators. However, because the bank's executives were well connected with members of the Obama Administration; a private rescue bailout was arranged. The bank's employees had donated money to Obama's Senate campaign. In other words, Shore Bank was too politically connected to be allowed to go under.

Shore Bank survived and invested in many "green" businesses such as solar panel manufacturing. In fact, the bank was mentioned in one of Obama's speeches during his election campaign because it subjected new business borrowers to eco-litmus tests.

Prior to becoming President, Obama sat on the board of directors of the JOYCE FOUNDATION, a liberal charity. This foundation was originally established by Joyce Kean's family which had accumulated millions of dollars in the lumber industry. It mostly gave funds to hospitals but after her death in 1972, the foundation was taken over by radical environmentalists and social justice extremists.

This JOYCE FOUNDATION, which is rumored to have assets of $8 billion dollars, has now set up and funded, with a few partners, something called the CHICAGO CLIMATE EXCHANGE, known as CXX. It will be the exchange (like the Chicago Grain Futures Market for agriculture) where Environmental Carbon Credits are traded. Under Obama's new bill, businesses in the future will be assessed a tax on how much CO_2 they produce (their Carbon Footprint) or in other words how much they add to global warming. If a company produces less CO2 than their allotted measured limit, they earn a Carbon Credit. This Carbon Credit can be traded on the CXX exchange. Another company, which has gone over their CO2 limit, can buy the Credit and "reduce" their footprint and tax liability. It will be like trading shares on Wall Street.

Well, it was the same JOYCE FOUNDATION, along with some other private partners and Wall Street firms that funded the bailout of Shore Bank. The foundation is now one of the major shareholders. The bank has now been designated to be the "banking arm" of the CHICAGO CLIMATE EXCHANGE (CXX).

In addition, Goldman Sachs has been contracted to run the investment trading floor of the exchange.

So far so good; now the INTERESTING parts. One Shore Bank co-founder, named Jan Piercy, was a Wellesley College roommate of Hillary Clinton. Hillary and Bill Clinton have long supported the bank and are small investors.

Another co-founder of Shore Bank, named Mary Houghton, was a friend of Obama's late mother. Obama's mother worked on foreign MICRO-LOANS for the Ford Foundation. She worked for the foundation with a guy called Geithner. Yes, you guessed it. This man was the father of Tim Geithner, our present Treasury Secretary, who failed to pay all his taxes for two years. Another founder of Shore Bank was Ronald Grzywinski, a cohort and close friend of Jimmy Carter.

The former Shore Bank Vice Chairman was a man called Bob Nash. He was the deputy campaign manager of Hillary Clinton's presidential bid. He also sat on the board of the Chicago Law School with Obama and Bill Ayers, the former terrorist.

Nash was also a member of Obama's White House transition team.

(To jog your memories, Bill Ayers is a Professor at the University of Illinois at Chicago. He founded the Weather Underground, a radical revolutionary group that bombed buildings in the 60s and 70s. He had no remorse for those who were killed, escaped jail on a technicality, and is still an admitted Marxist).

When Obama sat on the board of the JOYCE FOUNDATION, he "funneled" thousands of charity dollars to a guy named John Ayers, who runs a dubious education fund. Yes, you guessed it, the brother of Bill Ayers, and the terrorist.

Howard Stanback is a board member of Shore Bank. He was a former board chairman of the Woods Foundation. Obama and Bill Ayers, the terrorist, also sat on the board of the Woods Foundation. Stanback was formerly employed by New Kenwood Inc. a real estate development company co-owned by Tony Rezko.

You will remember that Tony Rezko was the guy who gave Obama an amazing sweet deal on his new house. Years prior to this, the law firm of Davis , Miner, Barnhill & Galland had represented Rezko's company and helped him get more than 43 million dollars in government funding. Guess who worked as a lawyer at the firm at the time. Yes, Barack Obama.

Adele Simmons, the Director of ShoreBank, is a close friend of Valerie Jarrett, a White House senior advisor to Obama. Simmons and Jarrett also sit on the board of a dubious Chicago Civic Organization.

Van Jones sits on the board of Shore Bank and is one the marketing directors for "green" projects. He also holds a senior advisor position for black studies at Princeton University. You will remember that Mr. Van Jones was appointed by Obama in 2009 to be a Special Advisor for Green Jobs at the White House. He was forced to resign over past political activities, including the fact that he is a Marxist.

Al Gore was one of the smaller partners to originally help fund the CHICAGO CLIMATE EXCHANGE. He also founded a company called Generation Investment Management (GIM) and registered it in London, England. GIM has close links to the UK-based Climate Exchange PLC, a holding company listed on the London Stock Exchange. This company trades Carbon Credits in Europe (just like CXX will do here) and its floor is run by Goldman Sachs.

Along with Gore, the other co-founder of GIM is Hank Paulson, the former US Treasury Secretary and former CEO of Goldman Sachs. His wife, Wendy, graduated from and is presently a Trustee of Wellesley College. Yes, the same college that Hillary Clinton and Jan Piercy, a co-founder of Shore Bank attended. They are all friends.

Interesting? And now the closing... Because many studies have been exposed as scientific nonsense, people are slowly realizing that man-made global warming is nothing more than a money-generating hoax. As a result, Obama is working feverishly to win the race. He aims to push a Cap-and-Trade Carbon Tax Bill through Congress and into law.

Obama knows he must get this passed before he loses his majority in Congress in the November elections. Apart from Climate Change he will "sell" this bill to the public as generating tax revenue to reduce our debt. But, it will also make it impossible for US companies to compete in world markets and drastically increase unemployment. In addition, energy prices (home utility rates) will sky rocket.

But, here's the KICKER, FOLLOW THE MONEY TRAIL. If the bill passes, it is estimated that over 10 TRILLION dollars each year will be traded on the CXX exchange. At a commission rate of only 4 percent, the exchange would earn close to 400 billion dollars to split between its owners, all Obama cronies. At a 2 percent rate, Goldman Sachs would also rake in 200 billion dollars each year. But don't forget SHORE BANK. With 10 trillion dollars flowing though its accounts, the bank will earn close to 40 billion dollars in interest each year for its owners (more Obama cronies), without even breaking a sweat.

It is estimated Al Gore alone will probably rake in 15 billion dollars just in the first year. Of course, Obama's "commissions" will be held in trust for him at the Joyce Foundation. They are estimated to be over 8 billion dollars by the time he leaves office in 2013, if the bill passes this year. Of course, these commissions will continue to be paid for the rest of his life.

Some financial experts think this will be the largest "scam" or "legal heist" in world history. Obama's cronies make the Mafia look like rank amateurs. They will make Bernie Madoff's fraud look like penny ante stuff.

Could rumors like this have contributed to President Obama signing the following to law on the first day after he was sworn in as President? It sure smells fishy. Obama had to be writing the President's Executive Order 13,489 before he was even sworn in as President. Not to mention all the other missing records.

President Obama was sworn into office on January 20, 2009. It seems kind of strange that it only took him 1 day to pass an executive order to establish executive privilege to presidential records. What does the President have to hide? Why was it so important to make it one of the first acts of the new President?

Federal Register

Vol. 74, No. 15

Monday, January 26, 2009

Title 3 — The President's Executive Order number 13489 of January 26, 2009

Presidential Records

By the authority vested in me as President by the Constitution and the laws of the United States of America, and in order to establish policies and procedures governing the assertion of executive privilege by incumbent and former Presidents in connection with the release of Presidential records by the National Archives and Records Administration (NARA) pursuant to the Presidential Records Act of 1978, it is hereby ordered as follows:

Section 1. *Definitions.* **For purposes of this order:**

(a) "Archivist" refers to the Archivist of the United States or his designee.

(b) "NARA" refers to the National Archives and Records Administration.

(c) "Presidential Records Act" refers to the Presidential Records Act, 44 U.S.C. 2201–2207.

(d) "NARA regulations" refers to the NARA regulations implementing the Presidential Records Act, 36 C.F.R. Part 1270.

(e) "Presidential records" refers to those documentary materials maintained by NARA pursuant to the Presidential Records Act, including Vice Presidential records.

(f) "Former President" refers to the former President during whose term or terms of office particular Presidential records were created.

(g) A "substantial question of executive privilege" exists if NARA's disclosure of Presidential records might impair national security (including the conduct of foreign relations), law enforcement, or the deliberative processes of the executive branch.

(h) A "final court order" is a court order from which no appeal may be taken.

Sec. 2. *Notice of Intent to Disclose Presidential Records.*

(a) When the Archivist provides notice to the incumbent and former Presidents of his intent to disclose Presidential records pursuant to section 1270.46 of the NARA regulations, the Archivist, using any guidelines provided by the incumbent and former Presidents, shall identify any specific materials, the disclosure of which he believes may raise a substantial question of executive privilege. However, nothing in this order is intended to affect the right of the incumbent or former Presidents to invoke executive privilege with respect to materials not identified by the Archivist. Copies of the notice for the incumbent President shall be delivered to the President (through the Counsel to the President) and the Attorney General (through the Assistant Attorney General for the Office of Legal Counsel). The copy of the notice for the former President shall be delivered to the former President or his designated representative.

(b) Upon the passage of 30 days after receipt by the incumbent and former Presidents of a notice of intent to disclose Presidential records, the Archivist may disclose the records covered by the notice, unless during that time period the Archivist has received a claim of executive privilege by the incumbent or former President or the Archivist has been instructed by the incumbent President or his designee to extend the time period for a time certain and with reason for the extension of time provided in the notice. If a shorter period of time is required under the circumstances set forth in section 1270.44 of the NARA regulations, the Archivist shall so indicate in the notice.

Sec. 3. *Claim of Executive Privilege by Incumbent President.*

(a) Upon receipt of a notice of intent to disclose Presidential records, the Attorney General (directly or through the Assistant Attorney General for the Office of Legal Counsel) and the Counsel to the President shall review as they deem appropriate the records covered by the notice and consult with each other, the Archivist, and such other executive agencies as they deem appropriate concerning whether invocation of executive privilege is justified.

(b) The Attorney General and the Counsel to the President, in the exercise of their discretion and after appropriate review and consultation under subsection (a) of this section, may jointly determine that invocation of executive privilege is not justified. The Archivist shall be notified promptly of any such determination.

(c) If either the Attorney General or the Counsel to the President believes that the circumstances justify invocation of executive privilege, the issue shall be presented to the President by the Counsel to the President and the Attorney General.

(d) If the President decides to invoke executive privilege, the Counsel to the President shall notify the former President, the Archivist, and the Attorney General in writing of the claim of privilege and the specific Presidential records to which it relates. After receiving such notice, the Archivist shall not disclose the privileged records unless directed to do so by an incumbent President or by a final court order.

Sec. 4. *Claim of Executive Privilege by Former President.*

(a) Upon receipt of a claim of executive privilege by a living former President, the Archivist shall consult with the Attorney General (through the Assistant Attorney General for the Office of Legal Counsel), the Counsel to the President, and such other executive agencies as the Archivist deems appropriate concerning the Archivist's determination as to whether to honor the former President's claim of privilege or instead to disclose the Presidential records notwithstanding the claim of privilege. Any determination under section 3 of this order that executive privilege shall not be invoked by the incumbent President shall not prejudice the Archivist's determination with respect to the former President's claim of privilege.

(b) In making the determination referred to in subsection (a) of this section, the Archivist shall abide by any instructions given him by the incumbent President or his designee unless otherwise directed by a final court order. The Archivist shall notify the incumbent and former Presidents of his determination at least 30 days prior to disclosure of the Presidential records, unless a shorter time period is required in the circumstances set forth in section 1270.44 of the NARA regulations. Copies of the notice for the incumbent President shall be delivered to the President (through the Counsel to the President) and the Attorney General (through the Assistant Attorney General for the Office of Legal Counsel). The copy of the notice for the former President shall be delivered to the former President or his designated representative.

Sec. 5. *General Provisions.*

(a) Nothing in this order shall be construed to impair or otherwise affect: (i) authority granted by law to a department or agency, or the head thereof; or (ii) functions of the Director of the Office of Management and Budget relating to budget, administrative, or legislative proposals.

(b) This order shall be implemented consistent with applicable law and subject to the availability of appropriations.

(c) This order is not intended to, and does not, create any right or benefit, substantive or procedural, enforceable at law or in equity by any party against the United States, its departments, agencies, or entities, its officers, employees, or agents, or any other person.

Sec. 6. *Revocation.* **Executive Order 13233 of November 1, 2001, is revoked.**

THE WHITE HOUSE,

This was signed by Barack Obama
January 21, 2009.
[FR Doc. E9–1712
Filed 1–23–09; 8:45 am]
Billing code 3195–W9–P

We are concerned with the direction that the economy, unemployment, spending, immigration and lack of transparency with the current administration. It is time that the voting citizens voice their opinions and vote for representation that will vote for programs that are for **"We the People, By the People and For the People"**.

The excessive federal spending programs have to stop. We need a balanced budget in the United States. We need to enact programs that will reduce the unemployment and stop the illegals from entering the United States. The United States needs to be firm on completing the border fence and enforcing the laws with regard to illegals. There can not be amnesty for the 20,000,000 illegals that are already in the United States.

CHAPTER FIFTEEN:

THE WINNING PRESIDENTIAL PLATFORM

The American Citizens Political Action Committee is going to present some ideas for the presidential platform for the 2012 elections. We hope that the candidates that the committee will endorse will be backing and will present the ideas that we are presenting. The United States of America needs a presidential candidate that will start looking out for the welfare of the citizens of this great country. It is past time for the Americans to start "Taking Back America" from the politicians.

The United States needs to elect a President that has an agenda that the American voters want. We need to make sure that the next President is capable of doing what they promise during their campaigns. We need a President that is capable of speaking from the heart about their policies. We have had enough of the relaying messages via teleprompter. If the President does not know what they are talking about we do not need more information from the czars. When you speak from the heart it is easy to tell the truth. When you are using prepared speeches it is easy to fall into the trap of telling lies since you can not remember what was on the teleprompter the last time you spoke on a certain subject. America needs and wants a President that has defined programs and the courage to carry them out. We can not afford another President that will be flip flopping on the issues to placate the audience they are talking to. Honest, sincere, dedicated, knowledgeable, understands the constitution, enforces the existing laws and is committed to protecting and supporting the will of the people that elected them. It is not asking too much for the American citizens. We deserve to be guided by a strong individual and one that will earn the respect of the world for the United States of America.

I AM ENTERING THE RACE EARLY AND THIS WILL BE MY PLATFORM. IF THE PRESIDENT OF THE UNITED STATES WANTS TO COPY THE REFORMS THAT I AM PROPOSING THE UNITED STATES WILL BE AWARE OF WHERE THE PROPOSALS AND SOLUTIONS CAME FROM. THE PRESIDENT HAS MADE LOTS OF PROMISES BUT HAS NOT KEPT MANY OF THEM. IT IS TIME TO TAKE BACK AMERICA AND RETURN THE GOVERNMENT TO THE PEOPLE OF THE UNITED STATES.

As President of the United States I will recommend programs that have been presented by the people of the United States. I want the United States to return to what the founding fathers determined was best for the country. It is going to be by the people, for the people and not for the government. There will not be a promise of transparency. **There will be transparency.** The American citizens have been kept in the dark for too many years by politicians that are only presenting projects that benefit their special interests groups.

As a candidate for the office of President of the United States I am going to ask that the Republicans work on legislation that will correct the improprieties in the voting laws. The first piece of legislation that I am going to ask the Republicans to pass will be for the United States of America to adopt the English language as the official written and spoken language of our great country. The requirement to become a citizen of the United States is clearly stated that the citizen will be able to speak and write English. The government will then be required to print the ballots in English and no other language. If a voter does not have the capacity to read then they should not be making decisions about who should be elected President.

I will ask the Republicans to pass legislation that all voters must register in the district where they live at least 5 days prior to the election. In addition, the voter must present proof of their citizenship to the voter registration people. The time to be bussed to a voting booth to vote without pre registration needs to be stopped. The voter will also be required to show identification at the time of voting. Voting without proof of citizenship needs to be stopped. In the states that are allowing drivers licenses to be issued to illegals the proof of citizenship must be in the form of a birth certificate or passport. The voting policies need to be corrected prior to the elections in 2012. They have been abused for too many elections.

As your candidate for President I am going to recommend to the American people that we address the following problems:

First, the United States is facing a major problem with the federal deficit. I am going to recommend that the Government issues drilling permits to American companies to develop the natural resources that are located within the United States and offshore. The dependency of the United States on foreign crude oil is creating a huge deficit each year. I will fight the Environmental Protection Agency and work with them to come to an understanding of how some of the policies are jeopardizing the future of the Untied States. There are new drilling procedures that reduce the amount of land that is affected by the drilling and modern technology to prevent damage to the environment.

This policy will not only produce our own natural resources it will provide thousands of high paying jobs to American citizens. The United States has enormous natural reserves that are not being developed and I intend to change that. I believe that the American people want to become self reliant in the use of oil and gas products. We will create jobs in many of the support industries as well as the oil industry. This will create trucking jobs, housing development, food industry development and many more support activities. The parts for the exploration can be produced in the United States. The oil companies could build refineries close to the exploration sites to facilitate the production of the finished products. The price of gasoline for our automobiles will then start to decline. The price of crude on the international markets will decrease since the United States will not be required to purchase billions of barrels per year.

I am not against the alternative sources of energy. They need to be developed by private companies just the same as the oil companies will develop the oil reserves. The problem with the wind farms is that a vast amount of the products required to make the farm are

imported instead of creating American jobs. The costs of producing energy are many times the cost of energy produced by oil and gas. The government is providing billions of tax payer funds to establish wind farms and that type of funding needs to be controlled.

The tax credits and depletion allowances need to be adjusted to reflect what is happening in today's environment. If the oil companies need to pay more taxes then that is the way it has to be. They are making excessive amounts of profits even after the allowances that they are receiving. It they want the chance to reap billions more in profits they need to give concessions to get the permits to accomplish those extra profits.

I support the development of nuclear energy facilities in the United States. There are enough controls and safety factors that can decrease the risk factors. We need the source of energy and can place these facilities in areas where there will not be any chance of earth quakes or tsunami problems.

In addition, I will move forward on the reduction of the trade deficit that is adding to the deficit every year. The United States needs to start placing a tariff on goods shipped into the United States from China and other countries. Our annual trade deficit is causing the national debt to increase every year.

I will propose legislation that the United States abolishes the NAFTA with Mexico. We need to keep our jobs in America in the United States and let Mexico take care of their own needs. The policy of out sourcing jobs to foreign countries needs to be stopped. One way to stop the flow of jobs will be to place a payroll tax upon every corporation that is out sourcing jobs to a foreign country. This payroll tax will be paid monthly by the companies that are out sourcing the jobs and will be equal to the amount of wages paid to employees in the United States. This will return the work force back to the United States. It will generate payroll taxes on the foreign employment until the jobs are returned to America. Once the jobs are returned it will lower the unemployment and create income for Americans. When Americans are working and paying income taxes it will reduce the annual deficit.

Second, I am going to propose legislation that will deal with what the citizens of the United States require with regard to securing our borders. There is no excuse for the government not taking the proper steps to secure the Untied States.

I will promote legislation that will allow the United States to proceed with a policy that is committed to securing our borders at all costs. There are laws in place to accomplish this we just need a dedicated President to mandate there enforcement. We do not know how many terrorists have already entered into the United States because of this lack of enforcement of the laws. It has to be stopped.

I will promote the following plans to create jobs in the United States. The people have watched since President Clinton and the Democrats passed the North Atlantic Free Trade Agreement (NAFTA) in January 1994. During the last few years the United States has seen the number of jobs being sent to foreign countries increase every year. Now, with the unemployment reported by the government in the 9.4% range we are wondering why there are not any jobs available in the United States. Even though the government is reporting the unemployment rate at 9.4% every unemployed American knows that the real rate of unemployment is closer to 18% to 20%. The government conveniently does not factor in all the workers that have had to take meaningless part time jobs to buy groceries for their families.

What can America do that will create more meaningful jobs for our people? There are many different things that will all contribute to the number of employed Americans. We are going to try and break down the different items that will help Americans recover and find jobs. It is past the time to start "Taking Back America".

We will start with the easiest project that will create thousands of jobs in the shortest time frame. The United States needs to complete building the remaining 1300 miles of border fence between the United States and Mexico. This project will create jobs that will require a variety of different skills that the employees will be able to utilize when the project is completed. The United States could build the "Americas Highway" and rest stations along the border fence to make it practical to monitor and enforce our laws concerning the illegal entry into the United States. This will create jobs in the engineering field to design the fence. This fence will be designed for construction in sections and all of the sections will be exactly the same. This will make the construction much easier and the fence will look uniform for the entire distance. Then there will be the actual construction of the fence which will create thousands of jobs since it can be completed in sections instead of one long project. This will put many different crews on the project. This could also create a competition between the crews with prize money to the crew that completed their section in the shortest time and under budget. This will create jobs in the manufacturing of the components of the fence. It will create jobs in the transportation of the materials to the job sites. It will create jobs to support the crews that are doing the construction including lodging, meals, laundry services, convenience stores and many others. The building of the "Americas Highway" will require many different crews since it too can be completed in sections. This will require the manufacture of materials, transportation of materials, large equipment, earth moving equipment, surveyors and basically the same type of support personnel and services that are required to complete the border fence. Then we could have the rest stations placed about 50 miles apart so that the border patrol would have access to everything that a convenience store provides on a daily basis. These rest stations would also be used as tributes to the Presidents of the United States. Each rest area would contain information about one of the Presidents and would contain a statue of the President that was featured at the rest station. The United States is on the 44th president that would enable the "America Highway" to honor all of the prior presidents of the United States.

Going back into history we can see that these kinds of projects can be very successful. When President Hoover started the Hoover Dam Project on the Arizona and Nevada border it provided thousands of jobs for several years. The end result was that the city of Las Vegas was born and the dam provides electricity for millions of Americans. It was an engineering project that no one in their right mind would have tackled except that the United States needed the jobs.

Then there was the waste land known as South Dakota that did not have one thing to draw people to their state so an enterprising individual decided to carve Mount Rushmore into the side of the mountain. Now,

South Dakota is a great tourist attraction and the state has been doing very well since.

There is no reason that this project to create "Americas Highway" will not end in having the same results since it will be an attraction that will honor every president that has been in office in the history of the United States. Americans would be glad to have the opportunity to work on the project and it will create jobs immediately.

The rules for the projects would be very simple. First, no one will be hired to work on the projects unless they are able to prove that they are an American citizen. That also means that green cards will not be allowed on the projects. Second, the unemployed will be offered the opportunity to work on the projects before other employees are hired. Third, if an unemployed refuses to work on the projects, they will lose their unemployment benefits unless they are physically unable to work. Fourth, the contractors that are hired for the projects will not be union companies. These are great projects to start "Taking Back America".

The problem that the American citizens are facing is that the government does not want the border secured. When we elect representatives that are concerned about America we will be able to move forward on this type of projects. Vote for representatives that are going to support securing the border. We can not afford any more illegals entering the United States.

The projects of completing the border fence and "Americas Highway" will do more for America than our politicians are willing to admit. All the politicians can see is the cost of the fence, "Americas Highway" and the rest stations.

The politicians are not willing to look at the facts concerning the number of illegals that are entering into the United States every year and what these illegals are costing the local, state and federal governments.

The Conservative estimates of the annual costs of illegals in the United States of America are a staggering $350 to $400 billion per year. It seems like a good investment to spend what ever it costs to

stop this drain on the economy of the United States. Has anyone seen anything reported by the main stream media concerning the number of terrorists that have entered the United States through our unprotected southern borders?

I would love to be the first American to travel the length of the new "Americas Highway" and visit all of the 45 rest stations that are created. I am hoping that the 45th president the American people elect will support the securing of the southern border. It would be a wonderful way to see what the presidents have contributed to the history of the greatest country on earth. We need to get started on these projects immediately.

Jobs can be created in the United States immediately for thousands of senior citizens and the youth of America. We can mandate that all employers are required to E verify to make sure that all of their employees are citizens of the United States. When the illegals are eliminated from the fast food and restaurant jobs it will create several million jobs for the Americans. This should be a solution so simple that even a cave man can understand. There was the case of the Chipotle restaurants in Minnesota a few weeks ago. There were approximately 500 illegals working in these restaurants in Minnesota alone. When the illegals were fired all they would say is that they will go down the street and get a job at another restaurant. They all have their illegal identification documents and the other companies will hire them since they have experience.

The United States needs to start deporting all the illegals that are in the United States as they are fired from the jobs. Instead these individuals seem to just continue to live in America and enjoy the benefits of our wonderful country. If each of these employees is earning $1,000 per month in pay, they are likely to be earning $2,000 per month in tips if they are experienced. That means that most of these employees are not going to be declaring the tips and paying taxes on the money they earn.

These are estimates about 1.5 million illegals that are working in the fast food and restaurant operations. Each of these is taking a job from an American that would be able to do the same job. The feeling by the supporters of the illegals is that they only do the jobs that Americans will not do. That is an absolute propaganda play by the main stream media and the ACLU. Americans have done every type of work imaginable and will continue to do what ever it takes to put food on their table. We need to stop the dependency upon the government entitlement programs. By the way, Social Security for our senior citizens is not an entitlement program. Most Americans have worked the majority of their life and paid into the Social Security fund.

Another solution to the jobs market would be to eliminate all double dipping by the employees at all levels of the government. When an employee holds down a job after retiring from a government agency or the military of the United States and then becomes an employee of the government it takes away from the people that need the jobs. When the double dipping employees are fired they should not be eligible to receive unemployment. If these employees wanted to keep on working they should have remained on the previous job and not taken the retirement benefits. The double dipping is causing thousands of highly skilled Americans from becoming employed. Since the fired double dipping employees are not eligible for unemployment it will reduce the unemployment rate in the United States. These are permanent jobs for the benefit of all Americans.

Other projects that will create jobs in a short period of time will be in the development of the natural resources of the United States. The exploration for oil and gas reserves will create thousands of jobs in the oil industry. In addition, there will be jobs in the support industries as well. Just think about building a refinery in Alaska where the Alaska Wildlife Refuge Area (ANWR) is located. It would create permanent jobs and instead of using a pipeline to ship crude they could refine it and ship the finished products. This will provide jobs in the transportation industry, housing industry, service industry, supply industry and many more. This program will provide a permanent job solution that will benefit all the citizens of the United States. There are many other side benefits from the exploration of the ANWR in addition to the jobs that are created. The oil that is produced from this project will reduce the amount of crude oil that is imported from other countries. The net effect of reducing the amount of crude that is imported is that it also reduces the deficit spending that the United States is incurring every year. Now that the United States is also in a limited war with Libya there is going to be more pressure on the drilling for natural resources on land within the United States. When you can create thousands of jobs and reduce our balance of payments it sure seems like a great way to start "Taking Back America".

Then we can take the same approach to the exploration for natural gas and shale oil reserves in the Williston Bay Area of the United States. These exploration projects will create thousands of jobs in the Rocky Mountain Region of the United States. We can not afford to develop our own resources since the United States is virtually broke.

Just think about building a natural gas processing facility and refinery in the Williston Bay Region. It would create permanent jobs and instead of using a pipeline to ship the shale and gas they could refine it and ship the finished products. This will provide the same type of jobs that developing the ANWR is going to produce. The products that are produced from these projects will reduce the amount of crude oil that is imported from other countries. The net effect of reducing the amount of crude that is imported is that is also reduces the deficit spending that the United States is incurring every year.

Then there is the most critical area of job creation. That would be to stop the flow of illegals into the United States and deport approximately 12 million that are taking jobs from the American people. Only about 2% of the illegals are working in agriculture in contrast to what the main stream media would like the Americans to believe. When we deport the illegals our job solution in the United States is going to improve dramatically. One of the benefits of deporting the 12 million illegals would be that they would not be able to send $25 to $40 billion in cash to Mexico every year. That would keep the money in the United States to stimulate our economy. About the only complaint would come from Wal-Mart since the majority of their customers are low income families from Mexico.

The situation of the illegals holding down 12 million jobs is not only hurting the unemployment numbers it is killing the United States economy as well. Take the 12 million illegals making an average wage of $20,000 per year. That means that $240 billion is taken away from the United States citizens and provided to the illegals. This is about as stupid as the politicians can become. The politicians need to understand that they were elected by the people to do a job for the people of the United States of America. Stop the bleeding heart attitude for the illegals and start thinking about the American citizens. When the $240 billion is earned by the American taxpayers it is going to reduce the annual deficit of the United States. The revenue to the government from just the collection of Social Security and Medicare from these employees amounts to about 15.4% of the wages or $36.96 billion. Since a very large number of the illegals are working under the table, the United States government is not going to be able to receive those funds. It only makes sense to remove the illegals and employ the citizens of the United States.

What is the ulterior motive of the President and Democrats in not wanting to deport the illegals? Could it be that 67% of the Hispanics voted Democratic in 2008 and they want to maintain their voting base? Then I read an article a few days ago that there are 4 states that allow drivers licenses to be issued to illegals. How are the voting booths going to determine if they are illegal or not?

We have not touched upon the need to create incentives for the small businesses to create more jobs. They have historically been the reason that unemployment was low. The government needs to create some programs that will benefit the small business owners to justify the hiring of new employees. The prime reason that small businesses do not expand is that they can not afford the added costs involved with employees. The added cost of each employee to a small business is approximately 12% to 14% of the amount of wages that are paid to the employee. To keep it simple, if you pay an employee $10,000 the business has an added expense of $1,200 to $1,400 per employee. The small businesses will increase the number of employees when the government gives them a credit for the amount in excess of the actual wages for a period of two years. This will let the employee become more proficient and produce the extra products for the business to offset the added costs.

The government also needs to implement a payroll tax tariff on the large companies that are outsourcing jobs to foreign countries. This tariff would make the amount of wages paid to employees in the United States about the same as the wages that they are paying in the foreign countries. The tax would be paid directly to the Treasury of the United States on a monthly basis just like withholding on American employees. The funds generated by this tariff could be used to supplement the unemployment funds. The tariff would be calculated on the difference between the foreign wages and the wage scale in the United States. If the job pays $10.00 per hour in the United States and $4.00 in the foreign country then the tax would be $6.00 per hour or 150% of the foreign wages paid. Big business is going to start whining and you will hear it all across the country. That is just too bad and I don't think that the unemployed are going to do anything but laugh at the big businesses that are outsourcing their jobs.

The banks and mortgage firms could be required to hire a few thousand more employees so that they can start to straighten out the loan document mess that they have created.

I am sure that I have not covered all the possibilities for the creation of jobs in the United States. This is just a few of the possibilities that are available to create more jobs in the United States. To make these suggestions work it is going to take the President and Congress to acquire some courage. They have been ignoring the problem for way too many years. The representatives need to start thinking about solving the jobs problem now. It has been going on for way too long and it is time to start "Taking Back America".

We need to elect politicians that understand the size of the federal budget must be reduced. The country can not continue to support such waste and duplication in the different departments of the government. Elect the next President and members of Congress that will tackle the problem and reduce the size of government. As your President, I will promise to reduce the size of government. There should be legislations that make it illegal for any government department or employee to be represented by unions. The government should be capable of running fair enough employee programs without union representation.

I will support the candidates the United States needs to elect that will enact laws that restrict the flow of products into the country from foreign manufacturers such as China. We need to balance the trade with other countries. One way will be to place tariffs on the goods coming into the United States. This will reduce the flow of products from other countries and raise the cost of their products to a level that they are competitive with the same type of products that can be manufactured in the United States. This will reduce our deficit and bring manufacturing back to the United States.

I will direct the 113th Congress of the United States to pass legislation that will establish qualification requirements for all federal elected officials. There is just too much corruption in our federal government. We have representatives that have not paid their taxes and broken ethics laws. We need to return respectability to the members of the Congress. These very special 535 members have to be elected with clean records and knowledge about the Constitution of the United States. These members are making decisions that affect every American and we must make sure that they are qualified to make these decisions.

The people of the United States must demand the very best from these representatives.

I will direct the 113th Congress to prepare legislation that will correct the corporate tax laws of the United States. I will recommend that the income used in the corporation's annual report be taxed at the rate of 35%. These major corporations are presenting outlandish earnings reports to their shareholders for the purpose of increasing the price of their shares. Americans want to see the federal deficit reduced and the best and fairest way is to make the corporations pay their fair share. Since the corporations are including in their annual reports income from foreign countries they should pay the taxes on the income. When the taxes are paid the bonuses will go down since there will be less retained earnings. The major corporations are sitting on trillions of dollars and they should be paying their fair share. No exceptions and cut out the tax credits for corporations that are reporting annual earnings in excess of one billion dollars. Tax losses will only be allowed to be carried forward. If the management of these corporations does not perform they should not be allowed to recover income taxes that they paid in prior years.

I will work with the 113th Congress of the United States to prevent the government from providing funds for another bail out or stimulus package. The American citizens have watched as these programs have failed miserably. If any other major company in the United States is mismanaged let them fail. That is why there are bankruptcy laws. The government needs to get out of private business. Our government is a total wreck and is having a difficult time functioning. How does the government expect to know how to run a private business? Take a look at the United States fiscal policy from the past administration. The Obama administration has not had a budget passed on time for the years 2011 and 2012. I am going to propose budgets that will reduce the spending by our government. By increasing the employment situation we will also increase the amount of funds that the government receives. Cutting spending and improving income is the road to a balanced federal budget. Then we will work on the debt.

I will present a program to the 113th Congress of the United States that will require the Department of Education to return the educational system back to the state and local level. There is too much duplication of efforts and it is impossible to mandate policies that will be effective for every part of the country. The states and local governments know what is needed in their school districts better than the federal government. Take all union representation out of the school systems. If a teacher or administrator is not performing at a satisfactory level the school board should have the power to fire them for undesirable performance. All collective bargaining for teachers and school systems should be prohibited. All they are doing is driving up the cost of education for every American.

I will work with the main stream media with regard to some of the articles that are produced. They are totally biased towards any opinion that is favorable to the unions and the Democratic Party. They are promoting articles that are designed to scare the general public. It is not going to work since the American voters are getting much smarter. This type of rhetoric is geared to the minorities and Hispanic populations to make sure they continue to vote Democratic. This is not the way the political system was designed to work. Every piece of news should be presented with an unbiased opinion. No exceptions. Forget about attacking the candidates and stick to the real issues that are being presented.

I will work with the Congress to press legislation that will insist upon an audit of the Federal Reserve System. It was established in secrecy and has remained that way for 110 years. It is past time that they show some transparency and face a compete audit. That also means disclosing who exactly are receiving the Federal Reserve's profits and who are the real owners of the shares in the Federal Reserve? The Federal Reserve is establishing policies that are affecting all the citizens of the United States and we are entitled to know the answers. The need for transparency has never been greater than it is in today's weak economy.

I will present a program to the 113th Congress of the United States and hope that they will have the courage to do what they were elected for. The budget deficit is a disgrace to every American. The government could reduce the amount of money provided to each department of the government by 10% and it would save the taxpayers $351.8 billion per year. Why is that such a difficult decision to make? Every department should be able to manage on 90% of what they are asking for. Besides if the truth were known every department probably has enough hedge funds built into their budget requests that will more than offset the 10% reduction. If they can not operate on the reduction the departments need to be restructured to be more efficient and cost effective. The problem we have is that the politicians do not have the courage to do what is necessary. The politicians seem to forget that they work for the people of this great nation. It is past time to start "Taking Back America".

I will present a program to the Congress to pass legislation that will mandate disclosure to the citizens about what type of investments are being made within the government pension funds and who controls them. When the audit is performed it could possibly provide a huge stink due to the involvement of some of the too big to fail banks and investment bankers. Disclose of everything to the citizens of the United States. It is our right to know how the government is investing. Then the people will know just how much corruption has been perpetrated by the 535 members of the Congress of the United States and the government.

I will work with the candidates for election that the citizens of the United States need to elect the next group of politicians that want the job because it is an honor to serve the people of our country. The following will never be passed into law due to the fact that the old timers and dead weight in the Congress are holding on for dear life. They know just what kind of a gravy train they are riding and will not get off. There should be term limits placed on every member of the Congress. The Senate should be limited to two terms of six years. The members of the House of Representatives should be limited to 6 terms of 2 years. That will mean 12 years of service for all of the members if they do their jobs and get re-elected for each term. The retirement benefits should be prorated by the number of year's service. For each 6 years of service the member will receive 50% of their benefits. Anything less than 6 years will not receive any benefits. The honor and respect of the job should be enough incentive to serve the United States. Think about it, there are only 535 of these honor positions and the politicians will spend millions to be elected to one of them. Why do they need all the benefits that they are receiving?

I will work with the Congress to pass legislation that will phase out the Fannie Mae and Freddie Mac from the federal government. The mortgage business does not belong under the control of the government. The policy that Fannie Mae and Freddie Mac are too big to fail is inaccurate and promoted by the Democrats and the main stream media. The government under President Carter started the whole process by insisting that every American should be able to own their own home. That policy mandated that the lending institutions provide money for mortgages and that Fannie Mae and Freddie Mac would guarantee them through the federal government. Start the phase out immediately and quit guaranteeing any more loans by the government. Make the lenders revert to the real practice of making a loan on the merits of the prospective home owner. There needs to be requirements of a 20% down payment, a history of responsible credit, an appraisal that has not been inflated, a reasonable amount of back up funds in the case of an emergency and a proven track record of earnings in the form of income tax returns as well as current pay stubs. The American citizens need to understand that it is not the government's responsibility to insure every American can have a home of their own. It is the homeowner's responsibility to earn the right to own a home and then be responsible in making the payments on time. It should be the banks responsibility to provide a loan at the terms favorable to both parties and not sell the loan to another mortgage company to be packaged and guaranteed by the government. The housing market will recover when responsible policies are put into place so that every purchaser of a home will get a clear title and a reasonable interest rate. The housing market can not be artificially supported by the Fannie Mae and Freddie Mac guarantees any longer. The tax payers of the United States are not going to stand still for anymore waste. Getting the government out of the mortgage business will be one of my priorities.

The reports released on March 8, 2011 indicate that over 23% of the homes that have a mortgage are underwater. That was caused by the irresponsible policies that were enacted by the Democrats. President Bush tried to stop the fiasco and warned the Democrats that there should be restraints placed on the program or we would have the real estate explosion. Unfortunately, it became a reality since the Democrats would not listen.

I will support legislation that will put God back into the United States of America like our founding founders determined when they wrote the Constitution of the United States. The Pledge Allegiance is American and should not be banned from our school systems.

As your candidate for President I hope that the people of the United States will study the policies that I am going to try and accomplish and how I am proposing to accomplish them. I do not want people to vote for me because I am white or a woman. I want the votes to be about what I intend to do for the United States of America and all of the citizens. By the same token I would hope that the people will not vote for any candidate because of the color of their skin. The black voters of America voted for Obama by a 95 to 5 margin. Americans need to vote for the candidate and the issues that are going to be addressed by the candidate and how they are going to accomplish their mission? The American voters need to look at the issues and proposed solutions and not the rhetoric that is spread by the main stream media and political unions. The United States needs to return to the policy of government by the people and for the people. There just can not be any other way.

GOD BLESS AMERICA.

America is going to hold an enormous celebration in November 2012 when the Obama administration has been defeated at the polls. We made headway in the mid-terms. Now, since the Democrats are still not listening to what the people want, we should be able to continue the process of regaining the Senate and remaining in control of the House of Representatives. I hope American will elect a Republican to the office of President of the United States. Then the country can start "Taking Back America" for the next four years. All Americans need to vote for the candidate that will support the people instead of the government.

CHAPTER SIXTEEN:

STOP OBAMA'S RE-ELECTION

The American Citizens Political Action Committee needs to impress upon every voting citizen of the United States that we can not let this President be re-elected. The United States can not survive four extra years of this incompetent President. With Obama's policies the United States will be an additional $6 trillion in debt. The policies that Obama has presented to the People are nothing more than spending and more spending so that Obama can try to appease his supporters and the unions. This insane practice has got to stop. At the current rate of Obama's policies the United States would be trying to justify to the world a national deficit of over $20 trillion. We are already broke and Obama just wants to keep on spending. The rhetoric that Obama has presented in his coming out campaign is nothing more that the same old garbage, just different promises that will again go ignored if Obama was re-elected. America needs to wake up to this fake snake oil salesman. How are we going to educate the poor and dependent citizens about the lies that have been presented by Obama? The United States can not afford to have 95% of the blacks and 67% of the Hispanics to continue voting for Obama because he is black and wants to make sure that more and more people become dependent upon his entitlements. It is past time for the American citizens to start "Taking Back America".

Obama re-election launches with email, website

By LIZ SIDOTI, AP National Political Writer – Monday April 4, 2011

WASHINGTON – President Barack Obama formally launched his re-election campaign Monday, urging grass-roots supporters central to his first White House run to mobilize again to protect the change he's brought over the past two years.

The official start of his second White House bid, in the midst of three wars, a budget fight with Congress, and sluggish economic recovery, comes 20 months before the November 2012 election.

"We've always known that lasting change wouldn't come quickly or easily. It never does," the Democrat said in an e-mail announcing his candidacy to more than 13 million supporters. "But as my administration and folks across the country fight to protect the progress we've made — and make more — we also need to begin mobilizing for 2012, long before the time comes for me to begin campaigning in earnest."

He told them he was filing the necessary paperwork with the Federal Election Commission, and directed them to his new campaign website where a launch video featured clips from supporters talking about their continued backing of the Democrat.

"I don't agree with Obama on everything but I respect him and I trust him," Ed from North Carolina says, delivering what's certain to become a key part of the president's pitch as he tries to re-energize liberal backers who have criticized some of his policies and independent voters who have fled from him in his first term.

Between now and the election, the incumbent Democrat will work to convince a fickle America that he has delivered change, made the right moves and earned the chance to continue the job. He will have to defend policies that have proven divisive, chief among them his sweeping health care overhaul and his efforts to boost the slow-to-rebound economy.
Obama announced his bid just as the White House is in a budget standoff with Congress that could lead to a government shutdown, weeks after the commander in chief directed U.S. military operations to a third major

warfront, Libya, and days after the post-recession economy showed more signs of a rebound with a report that the still high unemployment rate had fallen to 8.8 percent.

Republicans were quick to criticize the news.

The Republican National Committee circulated a research document that accused Obama of failing to lead on the budget and entitlement spending. And former Minnesota Gov. Tim Pawlenty, a Republican competing for the chance to take on the Democrat next fall, released his own web video in which he says: "How can America win the future, when we're losing the present? In order for America to take a new direction, it's going to take a new president."

Widely expected, Obama's campaign launch was planned to coincide with the second fundraising quarter of the year. Filing paperwork will allow the president to begin raising money in earnest for what allies say could be a record-breaking haul of more than $1 billion for his campaign. That begins this month; he's slated to visit major money venues of Chicago, San Francisco and Los Angeles in the coming weeks.

The campaign is based in Chicago, and many of the same people from his first bid remain involved, including former campaign manager David Plouffe, who now is in the White House, and chief political strategist David Axelrod.

Managing the campaign this time is Jim Messina, who played a senior role in the first bid and in the White House. Messina has spent the past few months touring the country to lay the groundwork with donors in hopes of building a massive fundraising network featuring both large and small contributions. He's asked some 400 donors — called bundlers — to bring in at least $350,000 this year; the re-election website is geared toward raising money from grass-roots backers. Obama raised $750 million for his 2008 campaign.

Obama faces no primary challenger.

On the other side, the race for the GOP presidential nomination is just getting under way; more than a dozen Republicans are considering seeking the chance to challenge Obama in the next election. Only a few have taken the initial steps toward a candidacy; Pawlenty is among them. Several more are expected go forward to this month, including former Massachusetts Gov. Mitt Romney, who ran in 2008 and lost the GOP nomination.

It's a wide open race with no clear front-runner.

Nevertheless, Obama said he's not taking anything for granted.

"We're doing this now because the politics we believe in does not start with expensive TV ads or extravaganzas, but with you — with people organizing block-by-block, talking to neighbors, co-workers, and friends. And that kind of campaign takes time to build," he said in the note to supporters.

"So even though I'm focused on the job you elected me to do, and the race may not reach full speed for a year or more, the work of laying the foundation for our campaign must start today," Obama added. He directed them to the new red, white and blue website for what he said was "a campaign that's farther-reaching, more focused, and more innovative than anything we've built before."
The website features Obama's new campaign logo — 2012 with the rising sun in the background, a version of his 2008 campaign logo — and announces that the campaign is kicking off.

"We're opening up offices, unpacking boxes, and starting a conversation with supporters like you to help shape our path to victory, and this is where you say you're in," it says, urging people to organize and donate.

The video is a montage of testimonials from a demographically diverse group of backers who intend to stay involved in this campaign.

"It needs to reflect the changes that we've seen in the last two-and-a-half years," says Katherine from Colorado. "Then we had an underdog senator. Nobody thought that he had a chance. And now he's the president."

Gladys from Nevada adds: "We're not leaving it up to chance" and "It's an election that we have to win."

Here are the comments from average American citizens and what they think about President Obama and his early entry into the 2012 presidential race for re-election. In some cases the comments are extreme but for the most part they are right on. They have not been altered in any way except for spelling and grammar. I hope you enjoy the comments and can get a clearer picture of what is happening with the President of the United States of America.

The American people are just too complacent! When will we get pissed off enough and have the balls to get up from the computers and TVs and really do something about what's happening to our lives. Our country was not built by a bunch of "do nothings" and our fore-fathers would have never put up with this abuse! It's a country for the people and by the people and only the people can do something about fixing things or we can just lay back and continue to get walked all over.

Considering many of our politicians appear to be mentally incompetent, the next presidential election should prove interesting. Who will run for office, from either the Democrats or the Republicans that anyone in their right mind will have confidence in? Campaign promises are nothing but dust in the wind, and the means to achieve an end. How many millions of dollars will go to support the undeserving? When people show you who they really are, believe them the first time.

Why doesn't Obama just put the money he will waste into Social Security so we can give to those who have paid in for years can get a raise? I guess Obama thinks they were stupid enough to elect me once, they will do it again, but who knows what the hell he is thinking? Obama flip flops on so many of the issues that Americans really do not know what is going on in Obama's mind. What ever suits the crowd he is speaking to?

Would be nice if Obama's supposedly 1 billion dollar campaign money would go towards the deficit the President's administration has created. Democrats complain about the rich but look at all this money within their party...poor hypocrites! Will Obama disclose just where this $1 billion has been donated by? I doubt it. Obama only wants the Republican Party to disclose where the campaign funds come from.

Obama raised an eye-catching $750 million for his 2008 campaign. When the Republicans raise a million dollars the main stream media reports that the system is broken and that they are buying the election. When a Democrat raises a billion dollars its eye catching and they are rock stars. The double standard is pathetic and the main stream media needs to start reporting correctly on the issues.

2008, 2009, 2010 Obama said that he would make jobs his main priority, on December 24 2010 Obama said I will now PIVOT and make jobs my top priority, again on January 25 2011 Obama said I will now make Jobs my number one priority. What part do Americans not understand? Jobs for Americans have not been a big concern to Obama.

This article is a joke. Obama has never stopped campaigning. He was campaigning while he was voting 'present' as a Senator, and it has snowballed since. Only now he's been using taxpayer dollars on that fuel guzzler called Air Force One to travel from city to city, state to state on a daily/weekly basis for photo ops. Obama's never in the White House unless it's for a party that we're also paying for. He has never been a leader, wrote or read a bill, he just has more photo ops for signing very expensive unread bills (sometimes other states, like the Stimulus signing in Colorado... still trying to figure out that one). Expensive, bribe-laden bills written by sleazebags like Pelosi and Reid. Someone needs to give him his own reality TV show and get him away from the citizens of the United States. He'd be super happy and so would we.

Viewed on a current bumper sticker: "If Al Qaeda wants to change America as we know it today they better hurry up Obama is beating them to it."

If you want to destroy America, then vote for this idiot. If you love America, you'll everything you can to keep him out of office. The only change Obama knows comes in the form of a diaper.

So, all of what's going on and Obama is going to concentrate on another Presidential run? That alone is a good reason not to vote for him.

I can't believe this man, the audacity of neglect and despair. Where's the hope and change Obama? All you're interested in is giving speeches and not have to deal with the federal deficit. Stop being silly and say you're not running for president. Snooki could run and beat you with little sweat.

If George W. Bush had doubled the national debt, which had taken more than two centuries to accumulate, in one year, would you have approved?

If George W. Bush had then proposed to double the debt again within 10 years, would you have approved?

If George W. Bush had criticized a state law that he admitted he never even read, would you think that he is just an ignorant hot head?

If George W. Bush joined the country of Mexico and sued a state in the United States to force that state to continue to allow illegal immigration, would you question his patriotism and wonder which side he was on?

If George Bush had pronounced the Marine Corps like Marine Corpse would you think him an idiot?

If George W. Bush had put 87,000 workers out of work by arbitrarily placing a moratorium on offshore oil drilling on companies that have one of the best safety records of any industry because one company had an accident would you have agreed?

If George W. Bush had used a forged document as the basis of the moratorium that would render 87000 American workers unemployed would you support him?

If George W. Bush had been the first President to need a Teleprompter installed to be able to get through a press conference would you have laughed and said this is more proof of how inept he is on his own and is really controlled by dumber men behind the scenes?
If George W. Bush had spent hundreds of thousands of dollars to take Laura Bush to a play in New York City would you have approved?

If George W. Bush had reduced your retirement plan's holdings of General Motors stock by 90% and given the unions a majority stake in General Motors would you have approved?

If George W. Bush had made a joke at the expense of the Special Olympics, would you have approved?

If George W. Bush had given Gordon Brown a set of inexpensive and incorrectly formatted DVDs, when Gordon Brown had given him a thoughtful and historically significant gift, would you have approved?

If George W. Bush had given the Queen of England an iPod containing videos of his speeches, would you have thought this embarrassingly narcissistic and tacky?

Glad his supporters can afford him. Maybe some just like Pelosi and Company. The First Family is really inspiring jet setting around and fighting wars and kicking balls at the same time. Maybe some work for the government or a union member with government contracts, maybe well to do, with lots of wealthy liberal family and friends? At the moment, some people just can't afford all these hard-left experimental, partisan policies, bills and speeches that amount to more debt, government control and higher prices.

What is really sad is that despite all he has done to destroy this country and the anti American Czars he has forced in circumventing congress, there are millions of black and Hispanic voters who still support him. They want to say thank you for the entitlement programs. Keep them coming and we will continue to keep voting for you.

Obama probably thinks that he has let enough ILLEGAL invaders in to vote Him back in. Obama even makes Jimmy Carter look good. Don't give Obama a chance to totally destroy what is left of the United States. It is our Country!

I feel so much better now. I thought for sure Obama would resign before now, he is such a strong leader, a man of conviction, able to make tough decisions, he needs a little more time for the hope and change to kick in, meanwhile, disguised as a real American President, Barry (community organizer, world traveler) has not completely destroyed America, but is close…thanks to brain dead voters, he has a chance to complete his goal

He shouldn't even bother to run again. He's already "RUN" this country into the ground. We'll be lucky if there is a country left that even remotely resembles the America our founding fathers put in place.

What else can I say…he's spent the last 2 1/2 years golfing and vacationing, breaking to occasionally throw Tomahawks at a country that did nothing to us, and somehow he thinks he's done something???
Like I said…ROFLMFAO…he's going to be lucky not to be impeached for declaring war on Lybian, re-election is out of the question! That he even thinks differently should give some of you folks and idea as to how big a narcissist he is!

Of course he will run again! Mrs. Obama hasn't seen enough of the world yet! File papers? Why bother. He didn't even have to qualify last time. Perhaps someone should REQUIRE a birth certificate to see if he even qualifies to be President of the United States. Beside Obama is not a "Naturally Born Citizen" which disqualifies him.

He officially started his 2012 campaign? I didn't know he'd stopped his 2008 campaign yet. It kind of all just runs together as a big blur.

How long will Obama blame Bush? Is it about time for him to step up and accept responsibility for the increasing number of jobless, homeless and those in poverty? Is it time he changes his motto from yes we can to yes we will? Obama has failed; his movement is not a movement, just another man with no direction.

"Launching his re-election bid", you are kidding right? He's been on the campaign trail for quite sometime. He's doing the same thing Clinton did, pretending he's a moderate. This administration has taken a bad situation and compounded it immeasurably possibly beyond repair. The radical left occupying the capitol must be expelled in 2012. Our Constitution depends on it.

He doesn't deserve reelection. In my opinion, he's got a lot of nerve to even ask for something he's done nothing to deserve. Where are the jobs? Where is the end to wars? All things he promised but has not delivered on. Now he wants four more years to achieve what he said he'd do in four? Sorry, Obama, you won't get my vote.

Obama is out of his mind! What is it called when some one does so many bad things and in there mind they think they are right? This is Obama I also wonder how many idiots in this country will vote for him again. Hopefully not 95% of the black voters and 67% of the Hispanic voters!

This is the most anti-American you can have as a leader. If you want the United States to fail keep him. Some people just don't understand that not everyone is or wants to be your friend. Most of the world wants your money not your way of life. Why is the United States with Obama leading the way just dumb enough to keep giving it away?

Simply put, another term with this current President will spell the end of America. At the rate he is going, I am actually hoping we can just get past the next 21 months without the wheels falling completely off. Obama and his perverted vision of the future of America must be stopped.

Support a good candidate by what ever means you are able. Put up a sign in your yard, write letters, talk to your friends, attend rallies... Do not assume other people will do the right thing. If we want the right thing done it is up to us to do it. And by all means VOTE and give someone else a ride if you can.

Boy! You can see Obama has his staff working on this site today! My god! What does he have to do to make people see the truth about him! How blind can you people be? He is a LIER, he is TWO FACED and he is a WAR MONGER! Obama has spent more than all the past Presidents COMBINED! He refuses to show America his BIRTH CERTIFICATE! His SCHOOL RECORDS! He SEALED those records the SECOND DAY IN OFFICE! He is an example of BI POLAR ON ACID! If Obama gives a speech, he will not ANSWER QUESTIANS! Because the questions are not on his teleprompter! People still even after just these few small things listed and hundreds of more lies, more things taken away from there rights, his secrets with Libya... God you can go on for hours! Some people! You CANT FIX STUPID! And we all have to live with STUPID PEOPLE!

I would not vote for Obama if he were the last human standing. What a waste of money even trying to get re-elected. I can't believe he would even face the American people with his pack of lies again. HE HAS NO SHAME. SCARY!

Obama signed executive order of no lobbyists in your administration and then hired lobbyists the next day. Our troops are still in Iraq, take that to the bank. You re-authorized the Patriot Act. You Won the Nobel Peace Prize the same day the USA bombed the Moon and now we are in three WARS instead of two. We've had no budget and increased spending. The facts on the ground say we are worse off than when you took office. No matter what you promise this time around......I won't believe you.

Obama should not be too sure that his own party will want him to run again. The Democrats could save a lot of face by just saying no. The problem is that the Democrats do not have anyone that wants to run since they know they will probably lose. It would be nice if the Democrats had Harry Reid run for President with Pelosi as his running mate. That might get rid of both of them.

I wonder what Obama is going to do in the States that passed the requirement that he show his true birth certificate, in order to be placed on the Ballot? Bet he sues instead of showing it. This would show that he does not have one and I don't want to hear about the one they put on then internet. Most want the one signed by a doctor. Produce it or hit the road.

They also would like to see your college application, supposedly indicating you claimed to a citizen of another country to be admitted. Cough them up or hit the pavement.

Any of his 'change' better? Other than being reported 'over' by the media which is Democrat controlled, did we see an 'end' to Iraq? I mean the guy proves he can start wars with Libya illegally without any congress or American approval or concern for our economy or jobs? He claims to have 'created' lots of jobs. How are all you unemployed people doing? More cities have become ghost towns. Great job growth, eh? Obama's 'change' says 'let old people die' I suppose old people are anxious to vote to die for Obama for no reason?

Obama please do America a big favor and run. That way we are sure it won't be you elected. We don't like the change you said you were giving us. You have done nothing but spend us in debt. .Bail out the unions lie to us any chance you can. .Let illegals run the streets with no worry of being arrested. Never tighten up the borders. Don't uphold the laws of the land. But chose what laws you want to uphold. Illegals should be deported not running the streets with no worries of being arrested. You have no idea what Americans want or need unless you are union. So Obama come January 2013 you and Michelle and the kids and your mother in law can get the hell out of the White House as you are fired. You have no clue what the hell you are doing. Go back to Chicago where you belong and go down in history as worse than carter and I never thought that would ever happen.

All he's done since 2008 is speech, campaign, spend, spend again, spend more and disrespect America. Do you want 4 more years of that?

Obama should announce on the Web that he is being impeached for his unilateral, unconstitutional decision to involve the U.S. military in Libya.

Tim Kaine cannot state that Obama will be challenged. As chairman, he has to put keep up the charade that the Democratic Party has support for Obama. I cannot imagine that some Democrat won't

challenge him in 2012. The Democrats know that Obama is a cancer almost as much as the Republicans do.

The Socialist, don't want him, the Democrats that are left, don't want him and the Republicans wouldn't give him a class of water, if he was on fire. The Latinos know he's fake, most Blacks now Know he's a, Mac-Daddy. The U.S. Muslims, might be, his best voters. Kenya might want him to be," KING ALI'BABA", for their country, with his Muslim roots.

This jerk has been campaigning since he ran for the Senate. He can't seem to stop. He thinks all the underhanded, behind closed doors passages of bill that he favored will miraculously disappear from our memories, like the 'Death Panel' regulation he slipped into Medicare on December 11 and rescinded on January 6 because to many media outlets and citizens learned about it and that would "create havoc in his re-election campaign" - his words, not mine. Let's just keep remembering all of his dishonesties and talking about them so he can't gain any ground at the polls.

"He told them he was filing the necessary paperwork with the Federal Election Commission."

Will he file a birth certificate this time? Or will he spend another $1.2 million to hide it?

I say this with all due consideration and honesty, and I am NOT a Republican. Obama is the worst President in the nation's history. Worse even than Jimmy Carter, or Woodrow Wilson. He cares NOT for the nation or the world, but his view of what he feels it should be. He cares less about our freedoms than any President ever has, and more freedoms have been lost in his first term than in ALL of the terms of the nation's Presidents in total. He has spent more of our money than ALL OF THE PRESIDENTS OF THE UNITED STATES COMBINED - and that is an actual FACT. His ideology is without question ANTI-AMERICAN and most certainly RACIST, in a 'reverse - racism' manner. He is an amateur, and a liar.

We will be lucky if ANY President can ever dig us out of the mess Obama and his Chicago thugs have created. He has all but destroyed the nation. To HELL with him.

"Obama plans to stay focused on his day job." STAY focused? The American people would like Obama to GET focused on his day job - something he hasn't even begun yet! He keeps mouthing that the economy is his first priority - but NOT with his actions!

"Obama set to launch re-election bid". Obama has been running for re-election for the last three years on our tax dollars. Only the Associated Press could come up with such tripe! Just more fair and unbiased reporting by the main stream media! It can be expected for the months that are remaining until November 2012.

I sincerely hope the American people have had enough of Barrack Hussein Obama, I have. Anymore change from him and you can kiss America good bye.

About The Author:

I was born in Grundy Center, Iowa on October 21, 1937 and raised in Cedar Falls, Iowa until I enlisted in the United States Air Force. I have served my country for 8 years, 1 month and 6 days and have two honorable discharges to show for it. I am currently raising my 9 year old son as a single parent. I have been the Committee Chairman of the American Citizens Political Action Committee since it was founded. It really disturbs me that the governments at all levels are more concerned about keeping their voting support than they are about the welfare of all the citizens of this great country. I was involved in the stock brokerage business for about 20 years and was an accountant for about 25 years. In addition, for about 10 years I have attempted to help start-up companies to have a method of raising capital. As with all start-up companies some of them made it and the majority of them did not. I try to use common sense. I have also written the following books: "A Beautiful America" "America Can Recover" "Bashing Sarah Palin" "Proud To Be American" "Taking Back America" and "My American Dream". For more information on my views and photos visit my websites:

www.thomasmeinders.com
www.americancitizenspac.com